LEGAL INSTITUTIONS TODAY and TOMORROW

THE CENTENNIAL CONFERENCE VOLUME
OF THE COLUMBIA LAW SCHOOL

LEGAL INSTITUTIONS

TODAY and TOMORROW

Edited by MONRAD G. PAULSEN

1959

COLUMBIA UNIVERSITY PRESS, NEW YORK

Contents

Foreword

There was a sort of historical propriety in holding the opening session of the Columbia Law School's Centennial celebration at the House of The Association of the Bar of the City of New York; for our founder, Theodore William Dwight, was also one of the founders of the Bar Association. The cordial relations between our Faculty and the Bar have persisted from that time. Before 1858, the unorganized Bar was our rival in training for the profession. It was then still an open question whether the study of law was an appropriate academic enterprise. Today, no matter what disagreements may exist about legal education, no one seriously proposes that the study of law take place outside university-affiliated law schools.

It was not until the turn of the century, however, that the advantages of academic instruction in law were generally admitted. Lawyers, as everyone knows, are hard people to convince.

In our own case, although the great James Bryce publicly sang our praises in the early 1870s and went so far as to suggest it would profit English students to make the transatlantic journey to study at Columbia, the burden of proof for a specialized course in law lay on us. I suspect it was not until the Bar was well manned by our graduates that the verdict was finally in our favor.

Columbia Law School has had a proud past. It stands at the threshold of even greater achievement. During the Centennial Conference, ground for our new building was broken. We are confident that we shall continue to have a student body of high caliber. The maintenance of a Faculty of the first rank is assured.

But Columbia is deeply concerned with present and future developments in the law. We look ahead so that we may study the vital forces at work in the present, so that we may plan for change. The papers collected in this Centennial volume reflect some of our preoccupations. The alacrity with which the invitations to participate in the Conference were accepted is a mark of the great importance the speakers and commentators attached to the occasion. The excellence of the prepared papers and the comments made the Conference more than a celebration of an anniversary: they are contributions of a scholarship which is well aware of the needs of our day. For the men and women of the Bar, as well as for interested laymen, they will be a source of stimulation, enjoyment, and intellectual growth.

WILLIAM C. WARREN
Dean of the Faculty of Law
Columbia University

Kent Hall
October, 1959

Introduction

The Conference marking the Centennial of the Columbia Law School, held in New York City on November 6, 7, and 8, 1958, brought together thirty leading judges, law teachers, practicing lawyers, and legislators to discuss the future of American legal institutions. At the Conference sessions, each topic was summarized by the principal speaker, after which prepared remarks were delivered by commentators who were among the special guests of the Conference. This volume is composed of the main papers of the Conference and the commentaries. The Conference program is included at the end of the volume.

The papers concern themselves with the operation of legal institutions rather than with developments in specific areas of the law, although the address of Professor Jessup on the "Future of International Lawmaking" is in some measure an exception. Each of our legal institutions has functions appropriate to it which that agency can perform more effectively than any other. Every paper and comment is in some way related to this basic proposition.

We have engaged in too little reflection upon the capacities and limitations of our lawmaking institutions. Yet it is only by understanding these capacities and limitations that we can judge which tasks are best performed by this or that institution. Each institution possesses a manner of working which at once enhances and confines its usefulness. It is as vicious to try a case by the legislative process as it is unwise to legislate drastically by using the courts. Institutions, designed properly for efficient work, are indispensable to the rule of law.

Although each paper, of course, treats its subject in a special manner, recurring themes can be identified. We live in a time of great legislative activity. Therefore, it is not surprising that Justice Breitel, in writing of the role of the courts in lawmaking, is very much concerned with the responses of judges to statutes and with the question of the legislature's fitness to undertake the task of "the complete management of the general law." Mr. Seymour's paper on the "Bar as Lawmaker," while telling of the activity of lawyers' organizations on behalf of court reform and improvement in the law, gives evidence that the principal means of realizing reform and improvements is legislative action.

The integrity of the legislative process has been an American concern for the hundred years the Columbia Law School has existed and more. The most casual examination of state constitutions will reveal the efforts of the constitution makers to prevent the hasty passage of bills which are little understood and, therefore, may be the product of those who serve special interests. Problems of legislative integrity are still with us. Granting that the legislature operates in a context of politics, Professor Newman raises questions about the proper role of lawyers who serve their clients by representing them in legislative matters. The rise in importance of the investigating committee has presented new problems of morality both for the legislature and for the committee witness.

Only by making proper distinctions can the true unity of a subject be perceived. Justice Breitel asserts that all statutes cannot be treated alike. Different kinds of enactments require different responses by judges. Furthermore, Justice Breitel takes the bold position that even statutes of the same general sort may receive different treatment, depending upon the realities of legislative history which lie behind the passage of the law. No single set of interpretive canons can embrace the variety of the legislative product.

In a similar way, Mr. Gardner's paper on the "Administrative Process" denies that all-encompassing generalizations are possible in his field. He writes, "Each agency, arising from a particular practical context, is different from the others, and no procrustean code can be applicable to all."

Legal institutions are operated by men and obviously, while the rule of law protects against the most arbitrary official action, legal processes most adequately fulfill human purposes when they are carried out by able and honest persons. The organized bar has long been concerned with improvement in the selection of judges. Mr. Seymour speaks of this concern together with the lawyers' interest in improving the quality found in their own ranks. The bar has actively supported higher standards in legal education and the practice of law. Mr. Gardner underscores the need for first-rank personnel in administrative agencies. Mr. Justice Douglas agrees, saying, "One chief task ahead is to re-create the conditions that make a career with government an exciting life." The need for talent is, indeed, generally felt by all the institutions of the law.

The times set new problems or call forth special modes of old ones for legal institutions. Equally molded by change are the fields of substantive law. The law is altered not only by man's discovery of the world about him but also by his invention of new organs of government. Science in the space age has made new demands on the international lawyer. Professor Jessup makes an estimate of some of these. His paper suggests, for example, that such technical developments as an inexpensive process for taking the salt out of sea water might provide the basis for revolutionary international cooperation. Furthermore, the evolution of newly created international agencies into entities which have rights and duties separate from those of all other levels of government has startling implications for international law.

Legal institutions and substantive law presuppose the rule of law itself. In England, two wars within a generation accompanied by profound social and economic changes have presented a much sharper challenge to the institutions of law than in the United States. The progress of American law—law taken so largely from England—may perhaps be forecast by the English experience. Lord Denning addresses himself to the challenges which four decades of change have presented to law in Great Britain. Some of the problems there have been overcome. His paper encourages us to believe that those unresolved will, in due time, yield to the rule of law.

Mr. Justice Douglas's address is not only a comment on all the discussions of the Conference, but also an independent statement by one who has participated in the legal system as lawyer, teacher, administrator, and judge. Law and its institutions exist to serve men, and men are served, in part, by providing them with freedom. Mr. Justice Douglas's paper speaks of legal institutions in terms of their contributions to the achievement of human liberty.

At the present time, the Supreme Court of the United States is being most heavily criticized. It is under such steady fire that we are tempted to despair of its future. The temptation must disappear in the light of Mr. Justice Douglas's defense of judicial checks on legislative and executive action and the faith in the Court's vigor expressed in the addresses which Mr. Justice Reed and Dean Warren delivered at the Centennial Dinner. Mr. Justice Reed gives the work of the Justices a firm place in the growing law of the future. Dean Warren, by looking to our history, points out that the Court has rarely lived a quiet life and that, in spite of this fact, its prestige has grown over the years.

The Conference sought to penetrate the future. In spite of the variety of approaches and themes, a fundamental similarity among the papers is apparent. As each scholar reflected upon the future for his subject, he underscored the most vital problems of the present. Thus, the papers are not mere images in a crystal ball but true mirrors of the most pressing concerns of our day.

Apart from the valuable survey of American legal institutions in 1958 and their prospects, made through the scholarly contributions of the participants, the Conference itself was a delightful occasion. Several hundred alumni and friends of the School were in attendance at the seven Conference sessions and the Centennial Dinner. The first session started at 8 P.M. Thursday, November 6, 1958, at the House of The Association of the Bar of the City of New York. The session was preceded by dinner at the Bar Association given by the School in honor of the Conference participants. The next day the locale of the Conference was moved to Morningside Heights, and three daytime sessions were held at the Horace Mann Auditorium. After a luncheon in the Rotunda of Low Memorial Library, President Grayson Kirk presided at groundbreaking ceremonies for the new law school building on the site at 117th Street and Amsterdam Avenue. At the close of the fourth session, a reception for all members of the Conference and their families was given by Dean Warren and the Faculty of Law in the library of Kent Hall. That evening many of the guests enjoyed a theater party, attending Eugene O'Neill's *A Touch of the Poet,* then playing on Broadway. On Saturday, the three final sessions were once more shifted, to the House of The Association of the Bar of the City of New York. After the final paper, the Law School Centennial Dinner was given at the Hotel Sheraton-East. Lord Denning, as well as Dean Warren and Mr. Justice Reed, addressed the dinner guests. Lord Denning made an eloquent, informal address which was not intended for publication. In it he set forth the lawyer's task of attending to law with justice, impartiality, and mercy. He concluded with the inquiry of the prophet Micah, "What doth the Lord require of thee but to do justly and to love mercy and to walk humbly with thy God?"

At each session of the Conference a moderator presided: Judge Harold R. Medina '12, Arthur A. Schwartz '26, Walter Gellhorn '31, A. Donald MacKinnon '22, Adolf A. Berle, Jr., Elliott E.

Cheatham, and Carrol M. Shanks '25. (Biographical sketches of the moderators, as well as of the Conference participants, are included at the close of the text.)

To Dean William C. Warren and the faculty of the Law School belong the credit for setting in motion the plans for a Centennial observance. The general planning of the Conference was executed by the Centennial Committee, composed of Professors Monrad G. Paulsen, Chairman, Noel T. Dowling, Julius Goebel, Jr., Herbert Wechsler, and William F. Young, Jr., in consultation with Dean Warren. The Conference could not have been held without the generous cooperation of the Law School administrative officers and staff, especially Dean Ellis L. Phillips, Dean John S. Bainbridge, Mr. H. Gilbert Nicol, Miss Rosalind Rosenthal, and Miss Carolyn Wood. The editor is particularly grateful to Miss Rosenthal and Miss Wood, who devoted many hours to the task of preparing this volume for publication.

MONRAD G. PAULSEN
Professor of Law, Columbia University

New York
June, 1959

LEGAL INSTITUTIONS TODAY and TOMORROW

The Courts and Lawmaking

BY CHARLES D. BREITEL

JUSTICE OF THE APPELLATE DIVISION OF THE SUPREME COURT OF THE
STATE OF NEW YORK

Mid-twentieth-century courts are embattled. In the commercial field there is flight to arbitration. In fields of law directly involved with governmental regulation there is wholesale displacement by the administrative agency. In the busy and mushroomed area of tort law there is acute calendar congestion, typified by years of delay, and accompanied by the commercialization of professional standards. In a high-cost society the expense of litigation has become intolerably irksome. There is angry impatience with litigation procedure. Crossing the entire terrain of law there is the massive outcropping of statute law—law enacted by legislatures rather than developed internally by the courts under the precedent system in the tradition of the common law.

All of these conditions raise questions about the role and effectiveness of the courts. Each merits serious consideration. But the one to which consideration will now be given is the effect of the tremendous, unprecedented growth of statute law on the judicial process. This, more than the other conditions, raises profound conceptual distinctions, which must be apprehended if the judicial process is to be understood.[1] Moreover, intertwined with such understanding are fundamental questions about the place of the courts in a democratic political system—courts which developed

[1] See Stone, *The Common Law in the United States*, 50 HARV. L. REV. 4, 12-16 (1936); Pound, *Common Law and Legislation*, 21 HARV. L. REV. 383 (1908).

under the common law and which bear the marks and habits of the common law precedent jurisprudence.

There are those who believe that the role of the courts has been, or should be, reduced to that of mere appliers of law. They say the common law has matured, and is closed. Any changes in law should be achieved by legislative action. Legislatures are the proper and popular instruments for determining and expressing policy. Statutes provide clear and simple sources for finding and knowing the law. There is no room for judicial creativeness.

Others believe that the courts' role in lawmaking has not declined, but has actually increased with the growth of statute law. Statutes simply provide a new source of principles and rules, much as custom and usage did before. The growth of statute law has provided just that many more sources of law to be handled in the courts. Statutes also present problems of construction and application, peculiar to themselves, which require judicial creativeness in order to make them effective. Courts, in applying statutes, must elaborate by way of subordinate generalization, just as much as they do with common law principles and rules. If statute law is to be viable, the courts must supplement statutes with their own unique lawmaking function.[2]

Obviously, because statutes consist of language, they require construction. Because statutes, although general in statement, are designed to govern particular transactions, there must be application. It is in this process that the different approaches—close application or creative elaboration—whether overt or disguised, or even unconscious, influence the result.

The unresolved conflict between the opposing approaches stems from the false assumption that all statutes are alike. All statutes are not alike, and, in fact, are not treated similarly. Yet judicial standards of construction and rationale of interpretation purport to apply a single approach to all statutes. What is re-

[2]See Freund, *Interpretation of Statutes*, 65 U. PA. L. REV. 207 (1917).

quired is an acknowledged pluralistic treatment.[3] The close application approach is appropriate to one kind of statute, and the creative elaboration approach to another kind of statute. There are intermediate variations suitable to statutes of intermediate kinds. Confusing the conflict is an anachronistic and sometimes contradictory system of canons for the construction and application of statutes. This is aggravated by an absence in the courts of realistic standards reflecting what is known by them about the legislative process, but is not expressed, and what is done by the courts about legislation, but is not admitted.

The role of the courts in lawmaking—what it is and what it should be—in the light of the extensive statutory development, with more to come, requires inquiry into the lawmaking process.

Basic to the analysis which will follow is a brief review of three things with which lawmaking is involved. The first relates to what is meant by a working statement or proposition of law; the second is the nature of the judicial process; the third, the nature of the legislative process.

LAW AS GENERAL STATEMENTS

A proposition of law may be stated in a statute, or it may be stated in a judicial opinion as derived from case precedents by a process of deduction, with more or less reasoned elaboration. In either event, it is a generalization.

So a statute may provide that operating a motor vehicle on the highways at a speed which endangers others is an offense. It therefore states a proposition of law. It contains a generalization which will apply to instances to be subsumed under it. The significant thing is that the statutory proposition may be more or less general.[4] It may provide that speed in excess of 50 miles per hour shall be

[3]Frank, *Words and Music: Some Remarks on Statutory Interpretation*, 47 COLUM. L. REV. 1259, 1265-67 (1947).

[4]See, *e.g.*, People v. Firth, 3 N.Y.2d 472, 146 N.E.2d 949, 168 N.Y.S.2d 949 (1957).

presumptively excessive; or, it may be even more particular, and provide that speed in excess of 50 miles per hour shall be conclusivly excessive, without the flexibility of the presumption.

A similar analysis can be applied to decisional rules of law evolved through the precedent system by the courts without the benefit of legislation. It is a decisional generalization that one who intentionally injures another without excuse or justification will be liable in damages. As a self-contained statement this proposition of law would be useless. What is excuse? What kind of injuries are cognizable in law? Each of these questions opens up a whole world for exploration and delineation. Moreover, continued innovation is required to adapt the principles to ever-changing conditions. Is trade competition justification? But then is any kind of competition—ruthless, deceitful, or by combination with others—fair, and, therefore, justification? What should be the effect of our constantly changing notions as to what constitutes fairness in competition? These questions are just as broad as, but hardly broader than, those raised, say, by an antitrust statute.

As is readily evident, the scope for creative adaptation, for whoever must make the application—court, administrative agency, or other governmental official—varies directly with the degree of generalization. The burden of elaboration will be greater if the proposition of law is more general; while the burden will be smaller if the proposition is less general.

In the case of a statute, a court, for example, will have a larger responsibility in applying a rule of reason in a speed statute or an antitrust law, than it would have in applying a statute making illegal the sale of liquor without a license or one providing prescribed minimum wages for employed workers. That responsibility, of course, is reflected in the necessity for establishing subordinate rules with which the more general rule is to be understood and applied.

THE JUDICIAL PROCESS

In the judicial process, courts decide cases, and that is all they do.[5] In doing so, they apply principles and rules. If the principles and rules are not at hand, they must devise them. Cases are particular things, involving particular parties and particular issues. This contractual transaction has broken down. This duty to avoid harm to this person has been breached. This marriage has been disrupted. This director has selfishly appropriated this corporate opportunity.

The procedure is correspondingly particularized. Proof or argument is taken with respect to particular issues. Under our adversary system the proof or argument is tendered by the interested parties, the ones most affected by the outcome. The scope of relevance is therefore narrow, confined as it is to the particular case, though the inquiry may be great in depth.

The judges are detached, disinterested, and independent. But their judgment must be rationally supported or supportable. They must justify or be able to justify the rightness of their decision. This they must do on the basis of the law given or deducible from the decisional precedent system or from the statute.

Moreover, courts must decide the cases presented to them; they have no choice to abstain for any reason. Their unsureness, the difficulty of the case, or the absence of clearly applicable law is no excuse. At the same time judges are personally not answerable in any official way to anyone for their decisions.

Characteristically, in the Anglo-American system of jurisprudence, a body of law, derived from precedents in particular cases, is utilized. The precedents imply or express generalizations of principle to be applied to particular fact situations. Their ultimate origins may be found in ancient days—in ancient customs and usages, or even in ancient statutes. The origin of other precedents

[5]See Pound, *supra* note 1, at 403-04.

is more visibly recent, suggested by newer conditions in society, and applying new or modified older principles in response to the newer conditions. But, always, the precedents are supposedly framed in an open-ended deductive system, with the initial and most general principles resting on a traditional court-devised and applied system of justice.[6] The system of precedents is represented as being consistent. A court is obliged to harmonize its decision with a consistent system of precedents. This makes for interesting difficulties.

And then the courts apply the statutes enacted by legislatures to govern conduct in the social order. These, too, provide principles and rules, and where they differ from decisional principles and rules, they, rather than the decisional principles and rules, are to be applied to the particular case before the court.

In general, courts are bound to follow precedents, under the doctrine of stare decisis. This means that elements of certainty and stability are available in decisional law. It also has the effect of pooling the experience and wisdom of many men and even generations of men. On the other hand, courts are, under the common law system, permitted to innovate upon and change decisional law in order to bring the precedent system into line with current conditions. The impact of each of these doctrines has varied from legal generation to legal generation. Sometimes, one or the other doctrine has greater impact in one field of law and less in another. These doctrines, formally opposed to each other, also make for interesting difficulties.

THE LEGISLATIVE PROCESS

The legislative process presents a quite different face. While the legislature is engaged in enacting general law, it does much more. It partakes in political debate, the appointment function, fiscal matters, broad investigations for a variety of purposes, and

[6]Stone, *supra* note 1.

in many direct political activities. In short, it is a political engine, and the supreme instrument for the making and expression of public policy.[7] General private lawmaking, as distinguished from its activity in public and governmental law, occupies neither first rank in the concern of the legislature, nor more than the smaller part of its time. The legislator is not only occupied with his labors in the legislature; he is also required to apply himself continuously to the constituency which elected him. The legislator is not detached or disinterested; he is an advocate for the policies he espouses. He is subject to frequent periodic election. He wins and loses elections because of his involvement on issues. In consequence, he sustains losses and gains in his personal status because of the outcome of issues on which he takes a position. He is responsible for and judged by his official record.

Even when engaged in lawmaking the legislature does not purport to decide cases, but lays down general principles and rules to be applied, for the most part, to future cases determined by others. Because the legislature only purports to generalize, the scope of relevance is wide, and the scope of inquiry almost unlimited. Every aspect of the social, economic, and political panorama may be explored in ascertaining what should be done. While there are contending adversaries with respect to proposed legislation, the adversary system does not control the procedure. Anyone interested is entitled to make his views known and exert political or other persuasive pressure to accomplish his purpose.

The legislature is not bound to act at all when confronted with a problem. It may enact a law or decline to do so. There is no time limit, except in emergencies, and then for practical reasons only, when the legislature must act. It may consider and reconsider, put over and put over again, until it is quite ready to legislate, if ever.

Legislatures may keep a record of all their proceedings or only certain parts. These records may or may not be available to others.

[7]Pound, *supra* note 1, at 406.

Notably, the legislature does not have to support its action by reasoned elaboration according to a deductive system. Of course, there may be political defense of action taken, or there may be silence. On the other hand, legislatures are free to obtain official assistance through the use of extensive staffs, and from various committees of the houses, and from commissions which are set up outside the legislature.

A COMPARISON OF THE LEGISLATIVE AND JUDICIAL PROCESSES

It is elementary, as we have seen, that the legislative process is a political process. Because it is dependent politically, it expresses, more or less, the general will and popular needs. But because of that very dependence and direct political involvement, it is subject to undue pressures, either of a rash majority of the hour, or of a determined and strategically effective minority.

Courts and judges, on the other hand, being relatively independent and benefited by long tenure, are more detached. But by the same token, contact may be lost. Judicial freedom of action is not absolute; the discipline imposed by a deductive system demanding rational consistency makes for control of and continuity in judicial action.

Statutes, because their language is fixed by the legislature, have rigidity. The language is not changeable except by the legislature by way of amendment. Sometimes such amendment is easy; other times it is difficult. It is seldom practicable to make minute adjustments to the fine shadings suggested by particular cases.

Common law is more flexible. Particular language is less likely to become fixed. There is leeway in the choice of principles. Fine adjustments based on fine shadings suggested by particular cases are constantly made. The doctrine of stare decisis, however, by requiring adherence to precedent, sometimes prevents such fine adjustment, and more, sometimes prevents greater adjustment to changed conditions. When the last happens, it is the legislature rather than the courts that is readier to make the necessary changes in the law.

The most significant distinction between the two processes is that courts act in the particular, while the legislature acts in the general. The court has the concrete case with its particular facts and circumstances. The case is real, and there is a persistent demand to produce a result serving the ends of law, however defined. While every decision by a court projects a generalization for the future, it is neither so binding nor so inclusive as one contained in a statute. The statute lays down a principle which must be applied in cases and circumstances not yet in being. Obviously, while it is difficult enough to determine the rule for transactions which have arisen, it is all the more difficult to do the same for transactions that have yet to occur.[8] Hence, a legislature must speculate more perilously as to how future cases will arise and what contingencies they will involve.

Because perfect generalization for the future is impossible, no generalization is complete. Aware of this impossibility, legislatures often do no more than purport to lay down the most general statements of law, intending that the courts and other law-applying agencies shall creatively adapt the general principle to specific cases.[9] Thus, every time a statute uses a rule of reason, or a standard of fairness without specification, there is conscious and deliberate delegation of this responsibility to the courts. Illustratively, the antitrust statutes have been retained, consciously, for several decades now, in such general form that the burden of elaboration remains a judicial one.[10]

On the other hand, when the path seems clearer, the legislature does not hesitate to detail the directions to be followed. The motor

[8]Corry, *The Use of Legislative History in the Interpretation of Statutes,* 32 Can. B. Rev. 624, 625-26 (1954).

[9]See *id.* at 625, 627-28.

[10]United States v. Associated Press, 52 F. Supp. 362, 370 (S.D.N.Y. 1943) (L. Hand, J.), *aff'd,* 326 U.S. 1 (1945).

vehicle statutes or the minimum wage laws are fair examples of this, as are most occupational licensing statutes. Then again, there are whole branches of the law, such as conflict of laws, torts, and the like, where the legislature rarely or never treads. When it does, it makes quite clear that it does not intend to preempt the field but only to make a limited correction or change. Beyond the legislated change, it intends that the judicial process continue to develop principles and rules case by case, and from particular to particular. This occurs, most often, where the emphasis is on experimentation and evolutionary development, or just because the permutations of the problems, as in conflict of laws, are too difficult to submit to advance general classification.

Offsetting its natural advantage in handling particular cases, the judicial process is confined by the narrow scope of its inquiry, arising as it does in relation to the particular case.[11] When the broad reaches of the social and economic scene must be probed to adapt the law to social needs, the legislative process, with virtually uninhibited inquiry, is a rich and efficient instrument. This, added to political responsiveness, makes the legislative process unmatched as the primary source of new and changing policy.

There are interesting and paradoxical crosscurrents. Sometimes courts do not do what should be done in the area where they are most expert and should be adept. Then, the legislature comes to the assistance of the courts, and, in quite an ancillary manner, removes the block to the sluggish stream of precedent law. Examples are statutes abolishing the effect of the seal on instruments,[12] or providing that relief for mistake should not be denied merely because the mistake was one of law.[13] Sometimes, too, the legislature fails to do what it should in its own proper field, and then the courts come to the assistance of the legislature. Examples

---

[11]See Cardozo, *A Ministry of Justice*, 35 HARV. L. REV. 113 (1921).

[12]*E.g.*, N.Y. CIV. PRAC. ACT §342; *Study Made in Relation to the Seal and Consideration*, 1936 N.Y. LAW REVISION COMM'N REP. 287-373.

[13]*E.g.*, N.Y. CIV. PRAC. ACT. §112-f.

may be found in emergency legislation, hastily drawn and passed, as in wartime or in periods of grave economic distress. Further examples may be found where legislation is drawn without sufficient reference to existing law. The new legislation may be contradictory of or inconsistent with existing law, and, yet, there is evidently no intention to change or repeal the existing law.

These, then, are the broad settings in which the legislative and judicial processes work. There are unique values which each has in exercising its general lawmaking function; and there are some inherent infirmities.

THE SIGNIFICANCE OF LEGISLATIVE INACTION

Because of the common law background for our law we have two broad sources of law: decisional rules established by case precedents, and statutory rules enacted by the legislature. Although statutes have grown great in number and coverage, for the most part they represent an addition to the common law rather than the displacement of common law rules. This is not to say that there has not been significant displacement; but examined in the large, most statutory law is additive.

In so far as common law has not been displaced by statute, the courts continue to perform their traditional function of shaping its principles to changing conditions with little or no legislative assistance. With respect to statute law, the judicial function, circumscribed by the language of the statute, is that of adaptation and application. This, in turn, is related to the degree of generality of the propositions contained in the statute and the degree to which policy has been actually determined by the legislature.

With two such divergent sources of law, a critical problem arises in determining whether the failure of the legislature to effect a change in law represents a policy that there shall be no change, rather than that any change shall be effected by the courts. The question may be raised where there has been little or no statutory activity, and it may be raised where there has been some legislative activity in the past.

As earlier observed, legislatures are not bound to enact laws when confronted with a problematic situation. Nevertheless, the legislature is exercising a power, albeit negative, when it decides that a particular proposal shall not be adopted, and even when it fails to consider a proposal. But it is not always clear that there has been a negative exercise of power; for inaction may, but need not, be an expression of legislative will.

The difficulty lies in discovering the reasons for legislative inaction, and, therefore, its significance for the judicial process. The inaction may mean no more than that the legislature has not considered the problem. It may mean that the legislature has decided that there shall be no change in the law. It may mean that it has concluded that the principles and rules should be evolved by the courts. Our legislatures are steeped too in the common law tradition. Consequently they can expect and rely on the judicial process to innovate.

Or the legislature may not have acted for a variety of narrow political reasons not relatable to public policy, the popular will, or public needs. This, of course, raises the gravest institutional problem, if the courts are to avoid encroachment on the legislative province.

In short, legislative inaction, total or partial, in a troubled area, may indicate a rejection of proposals; or it may indicate a warrant to the courts to exercise the traditional common law responsibility of piecing out, case by case, the necessary legal innovations. Unfortunately there is no rule of thumb to distinguish these contradictory indications; the only course is exam-ination of legislative purpose by investigation of surrounding circumstances and the available legislative history.

The so-called "hospital immunity rule" provides an interesting example of legislative inaction. For many years, in many jurisdictions, the rule obtained that hospitals were not liable for injuries sustained by patients caused by careless professional work of physicians, nurses, and certain subprofessional technicians. The theory was that the hospital, whether it employed or compensated the professional persons, was merely providing their services in the same way that it provided the convenience of its physical facilities. The further theory was that the hospital had no control or supervision over professional conduct or those who acted under what was described as independent professional direction. A corollary development was the fantastic and troublesome distinction between professional acts and administrative acts. For administrative acts, even if performed by professional persons, the hospital could be liable.

For many years, also, it had been increasingly evident that the rules were outdated, inconsistent with the general development of tort law, and productive of serious injustice. Moreover, to avoid unjust impacts, many "hard cases" were making "bad law." All sorts of verbalistic distinctions were being resorted to by the courts, with the result that everyone was at a disadvantage in determining what would or should be the outcome in any particular case. The courts in many states, including those of New York, waited for the legislatures to act. They did not.

It was a nice question whether the failure of the legislatures to act was because there was an affirmative view that the liability of hospitals should not be enlarged; or whether the problems and their factual varieties were too complex to submit to statutory draftsmanship, at least, within reasonable limits; or whether the door to legislative relief was being kept shut by the efforts of organized medical and insurance groups; or whether there were other reasons which could not be discerned. Finally, in some states,[14] the courts broke through the barrier. New York was among

[14]Ray v. Tucson Medical Center, 72 Ariz. 22, 230 P.2d 220 (1951); Silva v. Providence Hosp., 14 Cal. 2d 762, 97 P.2d 798 (1939); Wheat v. Idaho Falls Latter Day Saints Hosp., 78 Idaho 60, 297 P.2d 1041 (1956); Haynes v. Presby-

them.[15] There followed in some states complete, in others piece-meal, overturn of the rule. It was done in the best common law tradition, the problems being solved on a case-by-case basis. There has been no ensuing legislative action to undo this "judicial legislation," which one might expect if the legislature, by its inaction, had intended that there should be no change in the hospital rule.

There is good argument to be made for the thesis that the legislative inactivity in the hospital field meant that the courts either were to undertake the necessary revision, or were free to do so. At least in New York, there is no dearth of legislation affecting hospitals, so that it is not a situation where the legislature had no contacts with the field and no experience. A supporting reason may be found in the complexities that the question of hospital liability introduces.

Involved in hospital liability are varied and even peculiar relationships. This is so as compared with other employer-employee relationships, where the doctrine of *respondeat superior* applies, namely, that the master is liable for the wrongs committed by the servant in the course of and in pursuance of the employment. Is the staff doctor compensated by the patient or some outside agency? Is he regularly "employed," or only intermittently, or only on a case basis? Is there any supervision over his work or his time? Is he selected for the case by the hospital, the patient, or the patient's general practitioner, or by someone else? Although on the hospital staff for some purposes, and maybe even compensated, was the physician who attended the patient in the hospital also the patient's physician before the hospitalization began, who simply continued to care for his patient? In short, is the phy-

---

terian Hosp. Ass'n, 241 Iowa 1269, 45 N.W.2d 151 (1950); Noel v. Menninger Foundation, 175 Kan. 751, 267 P.2d 934 (1954); Mississippi Baptist Hosp. v. Holmes, 214 Miss. 906, 55 So.2d 142 (1952); Avellone v. St. John's Hosp., 165 Ohio St. 467, 135 N.E.2d 410 (1956).

15Bing v. Thunig, 2 N.Y.2d 656, 143 N.E.2d 3, 163 N.Y.S.2d 3 (1957); Berg v. New York Soc'y for Relief of Ruptured and Crippled, 1 N.Y.2d 499, 136 N.E.2d 523, 154 N.Y.S.2d 455 (1956).

sician, in the particular case, to be regarded as an independent contractor for whose acts the hospital should not be liable; or is he the agent of another physician; or is he in some private relation with the patient, with all of which the hospital has little or no concern and, therefore, should have no responsibility? Or is the physician, in fact, or should he be regarded as, the employee of the hospital, even though as a professional, he performs his professional responsibilities completely free from detailed or general direction from the hospital?

The permutations of facts can be carried further, and then repeated for nurses, laboratory assistants, anesthetists, and so on, and so on. The evident difficulty of attempting advance legislative generalization or ordering in this complex is staggering. Perhaps, the legislatures, or those who advise them, saw it just that way. Or, maybe, it was total lack of interest, the preoccupations of the legislatures being with matters of greater governmental and political importance.

Obviously, quite critical to the role of the courts is the resolution of the questions discussed above. These questions bear heavily on evaluating an approach which would have courts recede to being merely appliers of law, leaving all creative lawmaking, save the most minute adaptation, to the legislature to accomplish. To answer the questions requires examination of the legislative history, evaluation of the political process, assessment of the difficulties in obtaining legislation, and a historical analysis of the legal development of hospital law. In making the evaluation, distinction must be made between what legislatures in fact do; what, in fact, they are capable of doing; and what some would ideally posit as the legislative responsibility for and responsiveness to the need for a dynamic lawmaking process.

THE SIGNIFICANCE OF LEGISLATIVE ACTION

Where the legislature does act, indisputably, the role of the courts in lawmaking is influenced. But how, is not a matter for categorical determination resting on some single universal principle.

At least three aspects of statutes influence the lawmaking role of the courts. Statutes may be more or less general. They may be more or less expressive of a determinate public policy. They may reflect more or less technical quality in their draftsmanship and conceptual development.

THE GENERALITY OF STATUTES. There are some statutes so general in their statement of principle that they, indeed, do little more than provide starting points for judicial elaboration, and, therefore, entail considerable judicial lawmaking, if the purpose of the legislature is to be fulfilled.[16] A classic example would be a statute making any combination illegal if it is in restraint of trade. Such a proposition, treated as a self-contained statement, is meaningless and useless; or it is utterly destructive, if applied with one word—one meaning literalism.

Does such a general statute cover any and every combination, for any combination to some degree eliminates a competitor and, therefore, can be said to restrain trade? Does it cover interlocking stockownership? Does it cover conscious, simultaneous, conforming action? Does it require an actual intention to restrain trade, or is it sufficient if that be its effect? When earlier statutes were amended to include effect as a criterion, the degree of effect or dominance of the market became a serious problem in applying the law.

Through all the years since there have been antitrust statutes, it has been clear that the legislature intended the courts to improvise and elaborate upon the very general principle laid down. None has questioned the conscious reliance by the legislature on the courts to perform this creative function.

On the other hand, there are statutes so particularized that the mandate to the courts is clear and narrow; there is consequently

16Frankfurter, *Some Reflections on the Reading of Statutes*, 47 COLUM. L. REV. 527, 528 (1947); Frank, *supra* note 3, at 1266.

little room for judicial elaboration. The particularization may even
direct the court how, within limits, it must find the facts. The last
is accomplished by statutory directions as to presumptions, allowable inferences, and upon whom, between the parties, the burden
of proof rests.

A statute makes the possession of a firearm, capable of being
concealed on the person, a crime, unless the possession is first
licensed. This seems reasonably particular, but that is not the
end. Finding of the firearm in an automobile in which the defendant is present, the statute provides, sustains a presumption
that the defendant is in possession. And the statute further
provides that if, at the time, there is more than one occupant,
the presumption is that each is in possesion of the firearm.
Such particularization certainly reduces the area for judicial legal
innovation, and the contrast with a broadly stated statute, like
the antitrust laws, is readily evident.

But even such a particularized statute does not eliminate the
necessity for some judicial elaboration. Suppose, as has happened,[17] an automobile driver and his vehicle have been taken
to a police station on reasonable suspicion that the vehicle had
been stolen. The vehicle remains for two hours in the police
station yard while its driver is being questioned. It turns out
that it has not been stolen, but then a police officer finds a
firearm on the floor of the automobile. Its doors had been un-
locked and it had not been attended. Does the presumption apply,
and must the driver, if charged with the offense, come forward
with proof that the firearm is not his, or that it was not in his
possession or control, or that he knows nothing about it? And
what could he show about the two-hour interval while he was
detained inside the police station?

The answers to the questions are not difficult, but they are
not found within the language of the statute. For obvious reasons,

[17]See *e.g.*, People v. Spillman, 309 N.Y. 295, 130 N.E.2d 625 (1955); People
v. Crenshaw, 202 Misc. 179, 117 N.Y.S.2d 202 (Bx. County Ct. 1951).

the legislature could not foresee all eventualities, nor would it wish to draft a statute which would cover all foreseeable eventualities. Inevitably, then, even with a statute that is less rather than more general, there must be judicial elaboration.

STATUTES AS PUBLIC POLICY. There is another aspect to statutes which bears on the lawmaking role of the courts. In some instances the legislature avowedly lays down lines of public policy to be followed strictly. At other times there is no such clear direction. Instead, the legislature intends that the courts should elaborate further, even on lines of public policy, in the same way that the courts are expected to innovate in implementing the purpose of the statute. The distinction, of course, is not always clear. At all times it is an intangible, and the variation in degree is unlimited.

Some statutes, such as those that strike out in new fields, provide new principles where there has been no law in any specifically allocable sense. Or new policy may be made in older fields. In either event, there may be deliberate, conscious, and motivated declaration of policy, or the legislature may be acting in aid of the common law system, making threshold changes which it expects the courts to develop.

A statute provides for taxation and payment of disability and sickness benefits to the employed worker for physical conditions not arising in connection with his employment. Here a broad new public policy is involved, and the legislature has spoken as the prime and authentic voice of public policy. While some elaboration may be necessary, as with all statutes, the policy lines are determined and largely untrammeled by overflow from other fields of law. The job of the courts is to understand the policy and apply it as closely as possible. The leeway for judicial policy innovation is quite narrow. This remains so, however involved may be the task of fitting technically the new statutory scheme into the general body of the law, for, inevitably, the legislature has drawn on the vocabulary and concepts of the general law.

In contrast, there are statutes where there is leeway for judicial policy innovation. This is most likely to occur in areas where there have been many other precedent statutes or a rich development of decisional law. This time the reference to the courts contemplates policy implementation, or, at least, freedom in the courts to elaborate on policy. Broad adaptation rather than close application will be the primary responsibility of the courts.

The New York legislature enacted a statute abolishing the effect of the seal on private documents.[18] The statute was not a response to a political demand but to a conceptual evolution in judicial and professional thinking.[19] The statute, taken as a self-contained statement, was meaningless. What is a seal? What has been the effect that was ordered nullified? What did the statute mean in saying that the seal's effect was abolished? Did the statute mean only that there is no longer conclusive evidence of consideration in sealed contractual instruments and that undisclosed principals might be held liable? Did the statute eliminate the longer statute of limitations for sealed instruments? Did it do so if the statute of limitations relating to sealed instruments had not also been repealed? Such a statute, instead of being a detailed direction to the courts, was truly a warrant, so intended, for judicial elaboration. The courts were free to develop the answers to the questions from decisional precedents and in cases subsequent to the statute. The legislative guidance was intentionally minimal.

On the other hand, in an old field a new statute may announce a public policy departure which the courts are to follow closely. A statute changing the incidence of liability, for example, in the case of hotels or carriers for loss or injury sustained by patrons or passengers might well illustrate a determinate public policy man-

[18]N.Y. Civ. Prac. Act §342.
[19]Cammack v. J. B. Slattery & Bro., Inc., 241 N.Y. 39, 45-46, 148 N.E. 781, 782 (1925); see note 10 *supra*.

dated on the courts. The fitting of the statute into the body of law will remain a grave judicial responsibility, but the warrant for judicial policy elaboration will be sharply constricted.

But then again there are statutes addressed to technical and professional problems in the law in which neither the public nor the legislature takes any direct or involved interest. Codifications, practice statutes, and even statutes developing or modifying refinements in property and commercial law may be of that character. In such cases, the legislative enactment does not purport to impose any special policy determinations on the courts. The judicial role remains largely as it was before the enactment, broad or narrow, depending upon the antecedent development and the generality of the legal proposition involved.

It has been said, truly, that with respect to most general private lawmaking, the function of the legislature is not so much that of making law or policy, but of exercising a limited veto on proposals drafted and developed from without. The veto may be expressive of public policy, and always is to some degree. But the principal purpose is to screen legislation, merely to make sure that nothing affecting a political interest passes, by inadvertence, through the neutral channel provided for noncontroversial legislation. If a broad interest is found, then the legislation will receive the committee attention, floor consideration, and debate it warrants.

In summary, in the one kind of statute, namely, that affected by a conscious and deliberate public interest, the legislative evaluation may be purposive, considered, and motivated. In the other kind of statute, where there is no significant political interest, the legislative evaluation may be minimal. The extent of legislative evaluation will, of course, determine the extent of permissible judicial elaboration.

THE QUALITY OF STATUTES. There is, also, the inescapable, additional fact that statutes vary in the quality of their draftsmanship and supporting conceptual analysis. This is not unlike the variations in quality in the work of judges and courts when participating in the innovation and development of decisional law.

None would contend that the products of all judges and courts of equal rank are equally good. The differentiation affects the authority of the product. In decisional law, the recurring formula consists of reference to particuar well-considered or exhaustive expositions by courts, or to the authoritative standing of particular judges. Indeed, even the assistance rendered by able counsel, and notable briefs submitted by counsel, are properly accorded recognition as contributory to the judicial result, and, therfore, as basis for placing higher authoritative valuation on the result.

So it is, too, with statutes. Some bear internal evidence of keen analysis, foresight, and skill in the use of language and legal concept. Others reveal the very opposite, or something intermediate. Notably, some show hasty draftsmanship, perhaps caused by the pressure of urgent conditions. Apart from the face of the statute, the antecedent legislative history will spell out sharply the consideration and skill brought to bear in the creation of the concept and language of the statute. This will be shown by the presence or absence of studies, commentaries, and reports, and by their scope and depth. In this very connection, the various uniform statutes, such as the negotiable instruments law and the sales act, are outstanding examples.

Courts and lawyers are aware of this. Sometimes there is express reference to these relevant circumstances. The conclusion naturally follows that for the better-made, better-considered statute there is, correspondingly, a reduced function of elaboration for the courts, while the contrary is true for the stautute that is not.

In short, then, the lawmaking role of the courts is not determined primarily by whether stated principles or rules of law are statutory or decisional in origin. Looming largest as a factor is the degree of generality of the proposition contained in the statute. Next, the courts are controlled directly to the degree that the legislative action represents considered and determined policy. Last, courts are inevitably influenced by the quality of the statute, and therefore, whether it represents deliberate, skillful, and complete legislative expression of the purpose to be achieved.

THE JUDICIAL APPROACH TO STATUTES

Turning to the actual practice of the courts in handling legislation, the process is described as one of construction or interpretation.[20] Thus stated the problem seems to be one simply of determining the meaning of language.

This approach suggests an analogy to the problems in construction of a private written instrument. Meanings may be found literally or, that is, by the strict reading of words. This implies that the actual intent or purpose is irrelevant; one will be held to the language used. It is a sort of Portia standard of interpretation, good for printed lease forms, insurance policies, and the fine print on the back of railroad tickets and baggage checks. Or, conversely, the meaning will be rendered liberally, as we would like done with beneficial contracts between parties of equal bargaining power, represented by equally good lawyers. Then the intent with which the language has been used, and its purpose, will be sought. Under modern rules, such inquiry inevitably leads to the surrounding circumstances, and if the parol evidence barrier is passed, even to the history out of which the document comes into being. This documentary approach has influenced statutory construction. Yet one might well question why the narrow technique, grounded in the policy of holding men to the written records of their bargains, should delimit the search for the intent and purpose of legislative law, concededly the paramount source of law.

[20]Modern rules for the interpretation of statutes trace to Heydon's Case, 3 Co. Rep. 7a, 76 Eng. Rep. 637 (Ex. 1584).

Without diverting into a historical essay, the clues to the reason are apparent everywhere. The common law courts, and the lawyers, imbued with the tradition and convinced of the superiority of the precedent system of law, treated statutes as, it has been said, "an alien intruder in the house of the common law."[21] The maxim that statutes in derogation of the common law should be strictly construed epitomizes the view.[22] It has been many years since that maxim was supposedly done to death, and since it was criticized by Holmes and Stone; but, not infrequently, it still reappears in the opinions of the best of courts. Even statutes specifically addressed to the maxim, may fail to eradicate it.

Apart from the old maxim, the courts have a full arsenal of canons of construction which are supposed to guide to the meaning and purpose of statutory language.[23] Some canons employ a rule of strict construction. This means, as it does with private documents, that the literal language will be applied—even if it means ignoring intent and purpose.

Penal statutes, for example, are to be strictly construed.[24] Indeed, this principle as to penal statutes stubbornly persists despite statutory efforts to destroy it. Remedial statutes, on the other hand, are to be liberally construed, meaning that here intent and purpose will be accorded generous recognition and effectiveness. Nevertheless, this is not universally true. It does not apply in practice, for instance, to arbitration statutes.

Language in a statute which is clear and unambiguous will be applied, the canons tell us, in accordance with its doubt-free meaning (as if ever there is such language, when the very meaning of the statute has been placed in serious issue).[25] Of course,

[21]Stone, *supra* note 1, at 15.
[22]The maxim can be traced in the United States to the opinion of Ellsworth, C.J., in Brown v. Barry, 3 U.S. (3 Dall.) 365, 367 (1797). See Fordham & Leach, *Interpretation of Statutes in Derogation of the Common Law*, 3 VAND. L. REV. 438, 440-41 (1950).
[23]See *e.g.*, 1 McKINNEY'S CONSOL. LAWS OF N.Y. ANN. (1942).
[24]3 SUTHERLAND, STATUTORY CONSTRUCTION §5604 (3d ed. 1943).
[25]2 *id.* §4702.

this simply means that to the court—usually only to a majority of the court—its view of the statute's meaning is supported by the literal language in question.

Statutes, of course, are to be construed as a whole, and thus inconsistent parts reconciled, as in some great Hegelian synthesis. Recently, in New York, that rule was applied in construing certain provisions in the 1925 Civil Practice Act.[26] The particular provisions had derived from the old Code of Civil Procedure, which was established just over a hundred years ago. The Civil Practice Act contains almost 1,600 sections, has been amended innumerable times in the last three decades, and is itself little more than a partial recodification and reorganization of the Code of Civil Procedure. Actually, specific legislative history was available, but it was ignored. Reading the massive codification as a whole was much like taking the dictionary or Corpus Juris Secundum as a whole.

One could go on at greater length about the many canons and their contradictory import, and even about the nice Latin maxims which may be used as subordinate canons. But enough has been said to illustrate their character and their language-tied concept. Moreover, the literature of the law is rich in criticism of the canons, and repetition is hardly required.

Some think the canons are all but totally useless.[27] Such an extreme view need not be taken. In proper context, after intent and purpose have been explored, they may be meaningful.[28] To some extent they embody logical rules to be applied within a system. Then they become a check on one's reasoning, very much like a syllogism. Like a syllogism, too, they do not advance but may serve to verify an approach to a disputed question.

Despite the persistent use of the canons, the courts have not remained bogged down with them. In ever-increasing degree,

[26]Levine v. Bornstein, 4 N.Y.2d 241, 149 N.E.2d 883, 173 N.Y.S.2d 599 (1958).
[27]E.g., Fordham & Leach, *supra* note 22.
[28]Frankfurter, *supra* note 16, at 544-45.

courts have looked to surrounding economic and social data in construing statutes and making them intelligently purposive. While this is an enriching development and an excellent direction, the new has not displaced the old but has only been added to the old. For obvious reasons, many of the canons and the use of legislative history to uncover legislative intent and purpose, constitute divergent, and even contradictory, approaches.

The use of legislative history in construing statutes provides its own problems too. It involves the complicated business of evaluating the data and the particular sources of data yielded by legislative history—ranging from commission and committee reports to newspaper handouts by a private or legislative sponsor of legislation. No set of standards or rules has been attained or agreed upon in the courts to guide in the use of materials in legislative history. Most vexing, of course, is the problem of the inferences to be drawn from the partial activity or total inaction of the legislature in any given field. The courts have little control over the legislative facts which base such inferences. Yet they do have the responsibility for making the inferences, and, therefore, of knowing all there is to know about the legislative facts upon which the inferences are to be based.

An overly simple and insufficiently informed approach to legislative inaction readily becomes a barefaced question-begging process. Just as often as not the same judicial result can be sustained variously—for instance, on the argument that, since the legislature has not acted, the courts should move to relieve the legal condition, or that, since the legislature has not acted, it is quite clear that it is satisfied with the existing condition. The process is not unlike that in biblical exegesis; either side to the argument can support its position by well-chosen antagonistic principles. And in a statutory case, the contending parties usually do just that.

Short of a thorough inquiry into legislative history and purpose, the legislature's intention cannot be discovered, because inferences cannot be safely drawn as to whether the legislature intended that no new law be made. Even after inquiry it is often difficult enough to draw a satisfactory inference.

In summary, the courts are still prone to treat statutes as interlopers, but much less often than in the past. Canons of construction are used, although they are rarely of significant value in uncovering the intent and purpose of statutes. Even more to the point, the canons are born of an analogy between statutes and private documents, and the analogy is an utterly false one. In looking to surrounding circumstances, the courts are doing an effective and realistic job, and can do an even better one if only they surmount the barrier of "the clear and unambiguous language of the statute," another questionable borrowing from the law applicable to private documents. To the extent that legislative history is used, there is an absence of adequate techniques, standards, and critical understanding of the legislative process. In so far as inferences to be drawn from the activity or inaction of the legislature are concerned, there is utter confusion and there are baldly contradictory results, even when there is not ill-disguised question-begging.

LEGISLATIVE PRIMACY

Both as a starting point and as a concluding guide the institutional status of the legislature as the ultimate and paramount source of law must be unreservedly accepted. Although with the passing of years it has come closer to being true, this is not universally accepted in the courts, if the deed be distinguished from the word.

Legislative primacy means total acceptance of the position that statutes are entitled to a construction in accord with legislative purpose.[29] It means reduction of the canons of construction to tests of validity after the fact of construction. It means that

[29]See Llewellyn, *Remarks on the Theory of Appellate Decision*, 3 VAND. L. REV. 395, 400 (1950).

construction must first be effected with full commitment to legislative intent and purpose, in so far as it is determinable, from text, context, and legislative history. It involves rejection of the view that the legislative will is to be followed only where the mandate is literally and inescapably clear. It involves, too, a recognition of the fundamental difference between construing a legislative mandate and construing a private document. In the case of documents, extrinsic matter is excluded, generally, in order to avoid fraud, perjury and inaccuracy. No similar reason exists for limiting aid in the construction of statutes or with respect to the interpretation of legislative history, save, perhaps, in some special situations.

The suggestion that legislative intent and purpose be followed provokes the plaint that intent and purpose are frequently not discernible, or, cynically, that in fact there is no legislative intent.[30] This represents a failure to recognize that there are levels of legislative intent and purpose, just as there are levels of generalization in the stating of propositions of law.

Of course, there is no legislative intention specifically with respect to every statute, and every part of every statute. In the enactment of statutes there is delegation, too, with respect to sponsorship and draftsmanship, just as there is delegation to the courts to implement statutes. The legislature expects that statutes will be drafted by others, not only by its arms, such as committees and commissions, but also by agencies and individuals outside the legislature. In such situations the intent, purpose, and draftsmanship of others is adopted as its own by the legislature. On this theory there is no statute without a legislative intent or purpose. It is a glib superficiality to suggest otherwise.

To legislative primacy there are fundamental and constitutional limitations. There are, of course, the positive constitu-

---

[30]Curtis, *A Better Theory of Legal Interpretation*, 3 VAND. L. REV. 407, 410 (1950); Freund, *supra* note 2, at 231; MacDonald, *The Position of Statutory Construction in Present Day Law Practice*, 3 VAND. L. REV. 369, 371-76 (1950).

tional prohibitions on the exercise of legislative power. This has led, in our system, to the doctrine and practice of judicial review. Beyond that, however, there is still a further limitation. Construing statutes cannot become an exploration of the unexpressed legislative psyche.[31] People to whom the law is addressed must, within reasonable limits, be able to read it and understand it. Consequently, there must be a recognizable minimum of disclosure of meaning by the language of the statute; otherwise, the intent, even if provable extrinsically, must be denied. This is, however, a low threshold to be surmounted. While this qualification permits some judicial encroachment on the legislative province, that is unavoidable.[32]

The many difficult problems in judicial review are not our present concern. Nor should the power to strike down legislation as unconstitutional be confused with the judicial construction of legislation not involving constitutional validity. Although the two blend and overlap at various significant points, judicial review involves distinct and larger political and historical factors.

A material difference in consequence between judicial review and general statutory construction is that in judicial review, if the legislative act is struck down, there is no way, short of constitutional amendment, for the legislature to overturn the judicial determination. But in general statutory construction, every time the court errs in construing legislative purpose or intent, and, perforce, this will occur with some frequency, the legislature is free to correct the error by further legislative action.

Concededly, legislative primacy in the making of law does not, however, in the slightest reduce the judicial burden of statutory adaptation and application in the several ways discussed. It is because of the burden, shifting as it must between the need for

[31]United States v. Public Utilities Comm'n, 345 U.S. 295, 319 (1953) (concurring opinion by Jackson, J.); see Frankfurter, *Foreword to a Symposium on Statutory Construction*, 3 VAND. L. REV. 365 (1950).

[32]See Frankfurter, *supra* note 16, at 544-45.

greater or less creativeness, that the role of the courts in lawmaking persists, despite extensive statutory growth.

A REALISTIC APPROACH

This discussion rests on the view that, realistically, statutes are not fungible, and are not so treated by the courts. It depends upon the view that no single principle, equally applicable to all statutes, is available in the management of statutes by the courts. Rather there is, and should be, a pluralistic approach depending upon the generality of statutes, the indicated extent of public policy legislatively determined in them, and their qualitative completeness. This suggests varying or multiple standards to match these factors as presented in different statutes.

Foremost in the determination of the judicial role in statutory construction is the level of generalization. This involves immediately an examination of the statutory text and the context of circumstances in which it was drafted. The results may define, preliminarily, the breadth or narrowness of the judicial obligation to elaborate creatively upon the statute in remedying the mischief it was designed to correct.

But it is the rare statute, general or not, that will make its intent and purpose clear from a mere reading. Moreover, whenever the intent and purpose of a statute is seriously in dispute, inquiry into legislative history is inescapable. It is in this framework that the test of "clear and unambiguous language," serving to bar further inquiry, is a hapless one.

THE DATA IN LEGISLATIVE HISTORY. Legislative history opens an unchartered area. Perhaps this explains the reluctance to resort to it. Indeed, in England, the door to it is closed shut,[33] as it is in some of the dominions. The available data in legislative history is of widely different value,[34] but our courts are only at the

[33]Davies, *The Interpretation of Statutes in the Light of Their Policies by the English Courts*, 35 COLUM. L. REV. 519, 531 (1935); Corry, *supra* note 8.
[34]Cohen, *Towards Realism in Legisprudence*, 59 YALE L.J. 886 (1950).

threshold of establishing standards for use in interpreting and evaluating such data. There is no common agreement in our courts on the extent to which such data should be used. There is marked difference, for instance, between the federal courts and those of the states. In the federal courts, there has been greater recourse to legislative history. This is partly due to better legislative records in the national congress, although it does not account entirely for the difference.

Despite the many difficulties in using legislative history, however, its examination should be uninhibited.[35] No data which may cast light on the intent and purpose of a statute should be excluded. Of course, the data must be evaluated. It must be evaluated in a hard, critical fashion.

As has been noted many times, debate in the legislature is only rarely a good index to the legislative purpose.[36] Debate may express only the view of the more vocal protagonists and antagonists of particular legislation. Or it may even be designed to create a legislative history without actually expressing the view of those who enacted the legislation.[37] Statements of sponsors of legislation, whether the sponsors be members of the legislature or not, can create precisely the same difficulties of evaluation as those of debate in the legislature. Particularly the statements of sponsors outside the legislature are filled with seeds of peril. Such statements may have all sorts of devious purposes. They may mislead as often as they provide sound reflections of the statute's meaning or purpose.[38]

On the other hand, when one turns to reports of committees and commissions, if available, they are likely and rich sources of

[35]See Landis, *A Note on "Statutory Interpretation"*, 43 HARV. L. REV. 886 (1930). *But see* Radin, *Statutory Interpretation*, 43 HARV. L. REV. 836 (1930).

[36]See *e.g.*, United States v. Trans-Missouri Freight Ass'n, 166 U.S. 290, 318 (1897).

[37]Cohen, *supra* note 34, at 892; Corry, *supra* note 8.

[38]Curtis, *supra* note 30, at 411-12.

information.[39] But they must be examined carefully for actual reliability. They must be equally carefully examined for relative disinterestedness or for special, self-interested motivation. They are especially valuable, because, regardless of motivation, experience shows that they are most likely to have been the persuasive factors which elicited enactment of the bill into law.

The Chief Executive takes part in the legislative process, despite the rubric about the separation of powers in the American system. He takes part in the beginning by the making of recommendations which have considerable weight. He takes part in the end by the exercise of the power to approve or veto legislation already passed by the legislature. In consequence, the recommendations and memoranda of the Chief Executive in respect to particular legislation have great significance. But even here a caveat is necessary. The memoranda which accompany the Chief Executive's approval of legislation follow legislative action. Strictly speaking, then, such memoranda show the Executive's intent and indicate how the Executive construed the legislature's purpose and intent.

Memoranda and recommendations by executive departments may also have varying value, to be discovered only after careful analysis. These may have been created before or after the passage of the legislation. If the memoranda were prepared before passage and actually circulated in the legislature they are entitled to high significance in construing the legislative purpose. Like a committee report, they may have been one of the larger factors considered by those who voted the bill. On the other hand, if the memoranda were prepared after passage, for the use of the Executive, or for public distribution, it may be another matter. This distinction is pointed up by the fact that there may be a variance

[39]Fisher v. State Retirement Sys., 279 App. Div. 315, 110 N.Y.S.2d 16 (3d Dep't 1952), aff'd, 304 N.Y. 899, 110 N.E.2d 733 (1953); Interchemical Corp. v. Mirabelli, 269 App. Div. 224, 227, 54 N.Y.S.2d 522, 525 (1st Dep't 1945); In the Matter of Estate of Moroney, 203 Misc. 557, 118 N.Y.S.2d 349 (Surr. Ct. 1952).

between memoranda prepared before and those prepared after legislative passage. The variance may be for good and legitimate reason but nevertheless emphasizing the shifting value of such data.

Private reports and studies in connection with proposed legislation are significant if, in fact, they were considered in the enactment of the legislation. This stems from the view suggested earlier that there are different levels of legislative intention. Legislatures are free, and exercise the freedom, to delegate the responsibility for the development and drafting of legislation. If such reports and studies will be of assistance to the courts in determining the legislative intent and purpose, thus conceived, then they should be used. Of course, the fact is they are used.

Bearing closely on legislative intent and purpose is the antecedent history.[40] An evil to be corrected may have been uncovered in the courts and discussed in opinions. The evil and its correction may have been the subject of studies and commentaries in the professional literature. The ultimate legislation, when it is proposed, obviously is the product of this history. The key to the statutory meaning will be found in this antecedent history.

Inescapably, as the legislative history of the statutes is examined, the need for another kind of evaluation arises. The history may show careful, considered, and skillful application to the problem at hand. Or it may show the very contrary. It may show haste, inadequate study, and inadequate consideration of the ramifying effects of the proposed legislation. It is evident that a court cannot accord the same value to a statute that is ill prepared as compared with one that is well prepared. This does not mean inquiry into the wisdom of the legislation; that is exclusively within the legislative province. This does not mean that the statute can be nullified. It does mean that the statute will

---

[40] SUTHERLAND, *op. cit. supra* note 25, §5002; Frankfurter, *supra* note 16, at 537.

require more careful judicial elaboration to accomplish whatever intent and purpose can be discerned, whether that intent and purpose is favorably viewed by the court or not.

Inquiry into legislative history is likely to uncover a variety of political pressures which influence the course of legislation. This refers to determined and strategic manipulation in legislative halls. Such activities are not necessarily representative of any public interest or any general will. There are even "sleepers," namely, provisions so deftly concealed in a morass of language that those who vote on them are designedly kept unaware of their presence or purport. When these are facts they will be found. Having been found they will not be completely ignored, despite resort to fictions concerning the legislative process. It is only the indulging of a fiction to pretend that courts are not affected by such knowledge. As between a court being influenced by a factor and pretending that it is not, and being influenced by a factor, admitting it, and being bound to evaluate it rationally, the choice should be with the latter. While this may shock some in the stating, the fact is that the books contain many instances in which the courts have done just that. With the expanded use of legislation, it is inevitable that this approach will become more widespread and explicit. A statute which would reveal such a seamy side may not be nullified, but, obviously, the handling of its intent and purpose would be narrower than if its history had been different.

It is useless to be dogmatic about the fiction of legislative completeness and conformity with the popular will. The democratic process is neither preserved nor protected by pretending that there are no pressure groups, no political coercions or intimidations, no blunders, or that legislation is the oracular expression of the will of the majority. Of course, the game must be played according to the rules. So statutes are law and must be applied, but the legislative purpose will be found on a basis of realistic analysis, and not by convenient selection among contradictory canons to suit the particular case.[41] For the judicial responsibility in shaping the law can not be so mechanical a thing that it will not take cognizance of the inherent values of legal events, statutory or decisional.

LEGISLATIVE DIFFICULTY IN ENACTING LAW. A realistic approach to the management of legislation in the courts will not be complete if it ignores the fact of legislative difficulties in enacting laws and amendments. In fact, these difficulties, too, are recognized by the courts. The degree of lawmaking responsibility assumed by the courts is influenced by an evaluation of particular difficulty. This is not unlike the problem discussed earlier of legislative inaction, which must be interpreted to determine whether the inaction means that there should be no change, or that the courts should make it.

In some areas of the law, and at certain times, there are recognized political and practical difficulties in obtaining legislative action. Everyone is aware of this. The awareness is acute when one thinks of civil rights legislation, antilynching legislation in the Congress, or divorce legislation in New York and other states. Inescapably, these facts will affect the course of judicial handling of existing statutes and judicial innovation in nonstatutory fields.

The involved and sometimes very peculiar doctrines in the field of matrimonial law are explained on this basis. The doctrine of divisible divorce can only be understood against a background of legislative inaction in a field of statutory law. Full faith and credit will be given to an out-of-state divorce, but the duty of the former husband to support the former wife will continue because of a preexisting separation judgment. Parties may be divorced and the guilty party forbidden by law in the home

41See Llewellyn, *supra* note 29, at 401-08.

state to remarry; but an out-of-state remarriage will be recognized even in the home state.

For political reasons emergency rent control legislation, in New York, can only be amended significantly in odd-numbered years. In intervening even-numbered years, when legislative elections are held, only the most noncontroversial amendments will be passed. Unfortunately, transactions do not wait on years determined by political considerations; decision is required and the situation is that of emergency by legislative determination. There are many other instances that can be called to mind to illustrate judicial response to legislative difficulty in enacting law.

It may be suggested that this denies the democratic process as signified in a representative legislature. It would, but only if we assume that legislatures are fluid, completely reacting institutions, with no barriers of time or prior political concern, and that legislatures expect of the courts no more than application of law given to them by statute. All of these assumptions are false. And it is no disservice to the democratic process to give it understanding. It is a disservice to falsify its operation in fictions no one believes.

It is interesting to compare the slowness and difficulty of constitutional amendment with the problem just discussed. Courts are expected to handle constitutional language with breadth and flexibility. They are not bound by so strict a doctrine of stare decisis or as narrow a reading as might be the case in connection with general statutory construction.

The fact is that constitutions, too, may be amended. In some instances obtaining a statutory amendment may be no less difficult or slow than obtaining a constitutional amendment. Yet it would shock most, if courts, in interpreting a constitution, took a relatively literal and narrow approach, and suggested that, if any changes were to be made in construction beyond what was actually in the minds of the original draftsmen, then they should be accomplished by constitutional amendment. The answer is, of course, that we have long recognized that the ultimate purpose of a written constitutional system would be frustrated if constitutions were so handled.

Our statutes, of course, should not receive the same standard of interpretation as a constitution. Nevertheless, the comparison reveals that in the handling of enacted language a realistic evaluation of the fluidity of amendment must be considered.

CONCLUSION

The analysis just concluded would not permit the courts to arrogate control of the lawmaking process. If the analysis is correct, the false logic is with those who believe it possible to premise a viable legal system on a completely statutory system of generalization. It is but another version of the fallacy of the code makers of the last century. Indeed, the experience of the Civil Codes on the European Continent offers further confirmation. The necessity for judicial elaboration of the most formal codes is now accepted. Inevitably, too, the practice of judicial elaboration in the Code countries has resulted in something very much like a supplement precedent system to the Civil Codes.

At the root of the problem is the difficulty of meaning in language; the fact that all propositions of law must be stated at greater or lesser levels of generalization; and that generalizations are, perforce, imperfect. If legislative purpose is to be achieved, and if legislative action is to be fitted, as intended by the legislature, into the body of the law, adjustments, creative innovations, and dynamic synthesis are required of the courts. If more is not to be expected of legislatures than they can possibly carry, without diverting them from their other heavy and grave responsibilities, the courts have an obligation to see that the common law system does not become closed and static, changing only as the legislature may direct.

Of course, none of this means that the courts are to do other than take primary direction from the legislature, when such direction is given. And such direction may include a delegation to execute lawmaking functions of wide or narrow degree. It is folly to assume that in general, or that in most particulars, the legislature purports to provide complete direction. On the contrary, the legislative tradition in this country assumes and depends upon a dynamic and modernized common law system of law. Not to be confused with this, as has been said before, is the arrogation by the courts of the determination or redetermination of policy where the legislature has expressed itself on policy. Such arrogation is always annoying, and it becomes viciously destructive when it is perpetrated in the guise of judicial review of the constitutional validity of statutes.

Some may say, and some already have, that all this would be nonsense if only the legislative process were improved. Is not the goal, they ask, precisely such improvement? On this view, all lawmaking would be in the province of the legislature. The part of the courts would be to act only in the minimal degree that any application of law requires, or when the legislature has explicity delegated a larger function as is frequently done with administrative agencies. There are several answers to this position.

In the first place, the quintessence of the legislative process in a democratic culture is its political character and motivation. The complete management of the general law is incompatible with the political concerns and preoccupations of the legislature. Put another way, with the present institutional structure—and that institutional structure is likely to exist for a long time— complete legislative management of the general law is a practical impossibility.

Moreover, inherent values of an adjudicated process which is concerned with the particular transaction are not to be lightly disregarded, or discarded if it were possible to do so, which it is not. Generalizations in law are designed to provide certainty, stability, and, therefore, predictability. By the same token, they cause much injustice in the particular. Indeed, there are those who would seek a completely individualized intuitive process of adjudication, in order to achieve justice in the individual case. Most of us would not accept such a system. A soundly based adjudicative process, however, may provide just the leeway for the individual case and the micrometric movement that is desired in any legal system. It is for these reasons, among others, that the judicial process may not retire to the mere application of law given by others.

On any view, so long as the legislative process does not, in fact, undertake the complete management of general law, the judicial role in lawmaking is correspondingly enlarged. If greater management were assumed in the legislative process, there would be corresponding withdrawal by the courts. Indeed, the twentieth-century development of statutory law has deeply affected the role of judicial lawmaking as compared with the last century, and the periods before that. Nevertheless, the judicial function in lawmaking persists. This is because the legislative growth, deliberately, has never attempted to embrace all areas of law, or even to make statutory law so complete that there is no need for judicial creative elaboration.

To the extent that there is statutory development, judicial standards and techniques must accommodate to advanced legislative activity. To the extent that there is legislative abstention, the judicial function remains basically unchanged. But in both areas there is need for realistic appraisal of the legislative process and the casting aside of fictions and outdated standards of interpretation derived in large measure from the law of private documents. Supremacy is to be accorded to the legislative process. This is not done, however, by treating statutes with long-legged tongs, but by embracing the legislative process as a source of law and policy.

An analogy may be drawn from past experience to support a realistic appraisal of the factors which influence, and should influence, judicial handling of statutes. The analogy concerns the first recognition of social and economic data as relevant to a legal evolution in the courts.

There never was a day when courts were not influenced by the social and economic facts of life, or what they were believed to be. But there was a time when it was regarded as a corruption of the pure deductive system of the law to introduce such factors. So they were not mentioned, and their influence was not admitted or even recognized. As a consequence, the inquiry into social and economic data was never systematic, conscious, or deliberate; it was incomplete and ignored by adversary counsel. Even Harlan Fiske Stone, when he was still dean of the Columbia Law School, was criticized as radical and worse, because he contended that the course of constitutional interpretation was influenced by economic predispositions. With the leadership of such jurists as Holmes, Brandeis, Pound, Cardozo, and Stone, the relevance of economic and social data has now become a commonplace. Although it has added to the burdens and difficulties of the courts, the process of evaluation is exposed and openly used to serve the ends of the law.

If the analysis is correct, then the task of the courts is difficult. The task is made the greater by the duty to make broad inquiry into legislative purpose and history. It is also made the greater by the dangers present in the interpretation of legislative history. But the task is hardly made more difficult than it was by the burdens and dangers created by the acknowledgment that law is influenced by social and economic factors. When that acknowledgment was yet new, shocking, and radical, it seemed to many that all the stability, certainty, and discipline of a self-contained logical system was being driven from the courts. Thenceforth, all judges would be politicians, and justice would vanish. It has not so eventuated. By the scourging of the myriad fictions which concealed the truth, our lawmaking institutions are the better.

Comment

BY HENRY MELVIN HART, JR.
CHARLES STEBBINS FAIRCHILD PROFESSOR OF LAW
HARVARD UNIVERSITY LAW SCHOOL

THE NATURE OF THE PROBLEM

In commenting on Justice Breitel's paper, I shall begin by taking issue with certain statements in Professor Newman's on the legislative process in order to highlight the problem. Professor Newman first concedes that "Statutes are not ideal laws." But then he goes on to say that "nonetheless, there seems to be agreement that legislatures are better entrusted with lawmaking than are courts and agencies." Now, if I had to say "True" or "False" to that statement (in the fashion required by an outrageous form of examination sometimes given in law schools), I should say "False," and I believe that Justice Breitel would do so too. But the basic fallacy of the statement, I venture to think, lies rather in the way in which it poses the question than in the sort of answer it demands. Courts and legislatures and agencies are not engaged, as the statement and its context seem to imply, in a contest for "preeminence" in lawmaking, as if that were an undifferentiated field of activity. In some types of lawmaking, legislatures are not only "preeminent" but without any competition whatever. Administrative agencies are well adapted to carry out other kinds of lawmaking tasks which neither courts nor legislatures can do. Courts, too, have their distinctive contributions to make, which are our particular concern tonight. The relationship, in other words, is much more significantly one of collaboration than of competition. The crucial problem is to come to a better understanding of what each institution is good for so that the collaboration can be more effective. Justice Breitel's paper is valuable because it recognizes that this *is* the problem, and because, by drawing some discriminating and highly useful distinctions, it adds materially to the understanding of the problem which is so greatly needed.

THE POTENTIAL CONTRIBUTION OF THE COURTS

The courts can make their distinctive contribution as lawmakers only when they are acting as agencies for the settlement of controversies—either of controversies between individuals or of controversies between an individual and the government. This fact marks the outer limits of the potential area of competition between courts and other lawmaking institutions. The first factor which will determine the future of the courts as lawmakers is the extent to which we choose to keep on using them for the purpose of settling controversies. Resisting the temptation to elaborate the point, I assume that the phenomenon of controversy will survive, and that the courts will continue to have a major share of the responsibility for dealing with it.

So long as this is true and cases keep coming to the courts, we will continue to have the problem which Justice Breitel states with accuracy: To what extent should we try to use the courts as "mere appliers of law" which has been worked out in both general principle and detail in previously enacted statutes or administrative regulations? To what extent, instead, should we continue to depend upon them for "creative innovations, and dynamic synthesis"?

On this issue my only quarrel with Justice Breitel, if I have one at all, is that he has written too judiciously. I would state some of his propositions more strongly.

At bottom, I suggest, the question is this: Do we or do we not want the general body of our law at the end of the next half century to rest upon a coherent and intelligible fabric of principle? Do we or do we not want it to have the qualities of understandability, of acceptability, and of susceptibility to being reasoned about which only a body of law that is founded on such a fabric of principle can have? If this is what we want, then we will have to depend heavily upon the courts to give it to us. No other agency of lawmaking is equipped to do the job without the assistance of the courts.

The basic reason why this is so is that there is no substitute for the intensive analysis and the creative exposition of principles and policies at the point at which general propositions come into contact with concrete situations, so that they can be tested there. The courts are the only institution of solid authority in our society engaged in making decisions at this point.[42] In addition to this, the courts are the only institution which is manned by personnel with the training that is requisite, and which operates by the procedure that is appropriate, for the authoritative exposition of principle.

If one were to pursue this theme, four lines of inquiry—four major tasks of the courts—would invite discussion.

There is, first of all, the task of developing the fundamental body of constitutional principle which is necessary for the guidance of both official and private conduct and for the sound interpretation of enactments and decisional doctrines.

There is, secondly, the task of keeping the underlying body of the unwritten general law alive and growing, and not only rationally consistent within itself but rationally related to the purposes

---

[42]Administrative agencies engaged in adjudication may be thought to be an exception to this statement. But each agency deals only with a specialized segment of the law. Nor, for the most part, have administrative judges shown themselves to be adept or persuasive expositors of principle. Perhaps for this reason, their expositions do not enjoy a prestige with the public comparable to that of the courts.

which the social order exists to serve. Basic to the successful performance of this task is the development of an adequate conception of stare decisis and its limitations so as to free the legislature from avoidable pressure to replace the unwritten law with law which is cast in the more rigid and often less desirable form of an enactment.

Thirdly, there is the task of working over the statutes which come from the legislature, as well as the regulations which come from administrative agencies, and giving them an interpretive analysis and gloss which will bring them to life and endow them with as much coherence and reason as they are capable of expressing.

Finally, there is the closely related but much neglected task of taking the isolated enactments of the legislature and weaving them into the general fabric of the law as well as they can be made to fit. This is not simply a job of confining the reach of a statute when that is appropriate. As Justice Breitel makes clear, it is a job also of the perceptive use of policies embodied in statutes as bases for development of the general law.

Effective collaboration between legislatures and courts requires, on the one hand, that legislatures leave room in their enactments for the exercise by the courts of their distinctive function of reasoned elaboration of the law. It requires, on the other hand, that courts have a conception of their function which is adequate to enable them to make good use of the room which the legislatures leaves them.

THE APPROPRIATE CONTRIBUTION OF THE LEGISLATURE

The legislature makes its principal contribution to the development of the law through the introduction and improvement of techniques of legal control which are beyond the power of judicial innovation. Examples of these are the various forms of administered regulation, licensing and the like, as well as the great variety of government services. One's estimate of the shape of the law in the future must depend largely upon a judgment as to the extent to which legislatures are likely to continue to resort to these forms of legal control in displacement of the traditional common law technique of general directions enforceable after the event by a right of action in court.

In addition to this function of innovation of techniques of control, the legislature can and does perform an important function of review, and on occasion of correction, of the grounds of decision developed by the courts. But this is a secondary, backstopping job. It is a far cry from the job of originator or manager of the whole body of legal doctrine to be applied by the courts. The legislature as an institution, as Justice Breitel says, is wholly unfitted for the task of "complete management of the general law.[43] The quickest way to satisfy oneself about this is simply to look at the hard realities of the ordinary legislature's agenda. Add up all the work that a legislature has to do that no other agency can do. Add to this all the tasks of governmental housekeeping that the average legislature, wisely or unwisely, is unwilling to delegate to other agencies. Then see how much time is left for even occasional correction of decisional doctrine let alone for systematic manage-

[43]In speaking of the task of "complete management of the general law," I mean, as I understand Justice Breitel to mean, responsibility for continuous oversight and revision of the whole body of legal doctrine administered by the courts, especially substantive doctrine. To say that the legislature is unfitted for this task is not at all to disagree with Professor Wechsler in his insistence that the legislature must assume responsibility for developing and perfecting "the framework of decision" in the legal system—that is, the working structure of powers, both official and private, pursuant to which all the various questions of social living are decided. The job of institutional architecture—completing the outline of powers sketched in the Constitution—the legislature must do for the simple reason that no other agency can do it. Yet this fact poses difficulties of great magnitude—difficulties which lie close to the heart of the questions to which this Conference is addressed. As Justice Breitel points out, and as Professor Newman emphasizes even more strongly, the legislature is essentially a political institution. Can such an institution acquire the insight and summon the spirit of long-range statesmanship which is necessary to the creation and maintenance of a fruitful and viable system of powers? Certainly Professor Wechsler is right in saying that the legislature, if it is to meet this responsibility, must depend heavily upon "patient and disinterested effort by the bar and the judiciary and the schools."

ment of the whole body of the law. In much current discussion, and in many judicial opinions, responsibilities are attributed to the legislature which rest on fantastic assumptions about its capacity to handle its business—assumptions which a few moments' attention to its actual agenda ought to be enough to dispel.

In terms of efficient social engineering, moreover, we make an ill use of the legislature when we ask it even to try to assume a primary responsibility for all the questions of interstitial and subordinate policy making which come before the courts. The legislature has no automatic or instinctive wisdom in these matters. It is most significantly an instrument of negotiation and compromise of highly charged political issues which cannot be brought to acceptable settlement through the everyday processes of administration and adjudication. For the performance of this function it is superbly and uniquely equipped. It is not so equipped in relation to the questions of policy presented in the ordinary run of civil litigation. In relation to such questions, its effort ought to be limited to occasional review—as a tribunal of second resort—of the policies developed by the courts through the characteristic judicial process of discerning the implications in reason of the settled principles of law and the necessities of the social order.

THE FALLACY OF LEGISLATING BY NOT LEGISLATING

This leads me to my one serious disagreement with Justice Breitel—in relation to his discussion of "The Significance of Legislative Inaction."

This problem he rightly describes as "critical." It is the problem, he says, of "determining whether the failure of the legislature to effect a change in law represents a policy that there shall be no change, rather than that any change shall be effected by the courts." He goes on to say:

As earlier observed, legislatures are not bound to enact laws when confronted with a problematic situation. Nevertheless, the legislature *is* exercising a power, albeit negative, when it decides that a particular proposal shall not be adopted, *and even when it fails to consider a proposal.* But it is not always clear that there has been a negative exercise of power; *for inaction may, but need not, be an expression of legislative will.* (Italics added.)

Now I hasten to make clear that Justice Breitel is not alone on his side of our disagreement. He has, or at one time or another has had, with him most of the recent Justices of the Supreme Court of the United States. He also has on his side hosts of other judges of both federal and state courts, as well as occasional commentators, who have been similarly bemused by this anomalous idea that a legislature can legislate by not legislating. In spite of this great array of authority, it needs to be said loudly and clearly, in the same way that the small boy said that the emperor had no clothes on, that this is a fallacy. The Constitution of the United States and each of the state constitutions prescribe the ways in which bills shall become law. Failing to enact a bill is not one of these ways, even when a bill has been introduced and voted down. A fortiori, the failure to act is not an authorized way of making law when no bill on the subject was ever introduced in the first place.

There are profoundly important reasons why no wise constitution maker would deliberately entrust a legislature with the power to do something by doing nothing, and these are also the reasons why courts should refrain from according the legislature such a power extraconstitutionally. A legislature is a deliberative body. It is an instrument for arriving at a consensus, not an instrument for recording a consensus previously arrived at, as if by some mysterious emanation from the electorate. To arrive at a consensus, the legislature follows an elaborate procedure of investigation and consideration eventuating in the approval of particular form of words as law. For the courts to treat the legislature as making law by any other means is to treat this procedure and this agreement upon a particular form of words as mere froufrou—without any real function. But it is not froufrou. This is borne out, among other ways, when an effort is made to interpret the legislature's silence, without benefit of any form of words. The possible reasons for the legislature's failure to act, and hence the possible interpretations of the silence, are always numerous and sometimes innumerable. No wonder that Justice Breitel says it is difficult to find out whether "there has been a negative exercise of power." Often it is not merely difficult; it is impossible.

What we have here is a manifestation in exaggerated form of the contemporary cult of the legislature. We are asked to think of the legislature as omnipotent and omnicompetent—aware like the Almighty of every leaf that falls and able to prevent it from falling if it wishes to do so, so that if the leaf does fall it must be because the legislature has so directed, even though the legislature has failed to comply with the constitutional requirements for the enactment of bills, and by the same token has failed to apply its collective mind to the problem.

When the courts accord significance to the inaction of the legislature, what they are really doing, I suggest, is avoiding responsibility. They do so by shifting the responsibility to an institution which has already evaded it, or at least refrained from assuming it. This is one reason why the practice is not good. It diffuses the responsibility for lawmaking instead of centering it.

The practice is also bad for another reason—which brings me back to my main thesis, and to Justice Breitel's as well. What, in the end, is crucial here is one's judgment about the distinctive value in the growth of the law of the judicial process of reasoned development of principle. If we value this process of growth as highly as I have urged that we ought, then we should always be reluctant to conclude that the legislature, in relation to any matter, has tried to paralyze the process. We should welcome a doctrine which says that the legislature can do this, if it can do it at all, not by silence but only by unmistakable words. Only by adherence to such a doctrine can the resources of the judicial process for the infusion of reason into the law be fully utilized.

Comment

BY ROGER J. TRAYNOR
ASSOCIATE JUSTICE, SUPREME COURT OF CALIFORNIA

We have come a long way from the time when courts were on guard to keep statutes in their place, in the shadow of the stone tablets of precedent. For a good many years now legislatures have been erecting some formidable stone tablets of their own, inscribed in language richly current if not always clear and crisp. Justice Breitel recognizes not merely that the legislatures are now dominant in the formulation of laws, but that they must be, in a world undergoing change too rapidly to await the slow elaboration of new hand-tooled precedents or the painful deciphering of modern meanings from the fading language of the old. In most of their affairs when regulation seems necessary, men now look to the next legislative session, not to the day of judgment. In street wisdom, it is easier to legislate than to litigate. This commonplace connotes a flexibility of legislative action frequently synonymous with sensitivity to community needs though sometimes no more than a capitulation to special interests. A legislature can run up a law on short notice, and when it has finished all the seams it can run up another and another. It is engaged in mass production; it produces piecework of its own volition or on order. The great tapestry of Holmes's princess, the seamless web of the law, becomes ever more legendary.

Whatever our admiration for ancient arts, few of us would turn the clock back to live out what museums preserve. The law of contracts was once well served by delightful causeries of learned judges that clarified the meaning of obligation. Such causeries, however, proved inadequate to provide an expansion and diversification of words to correspond with that of business enterprise. Thus it fell to the legislators to spell out whole statutes such as insurance codes and the uniform laws dealing with negotiable instruments, sales, bills of lading, warehouse receipts, stock transfers, conditional sales, trust receipts, written obligations, fiduciaries, partnerships, and limited partnership. Such statutes can take a birds-eye view of the total problem, instead of that of an owl on a segment. They can encompass wide generalizations from experience that a judge is precluded from making in his decision on a particular case. Legislatures can break sharply with the past, if need be, as judges ordinarily cannot. They avoid the wasteful cost in time and money of piecemeal litigation that all too frequently culminates in a crazy quilt of rules defying intelligent restatement or coherent application. Most of all they can take the initiative in timely solution of urgent problems, in contrast with the inertia incumbent upon judges until random litigation brings a problem in incomplete form to them, often too soon or too late for over-all solution. What passes before them on the reviewing stand is not a well-programmed orderly parade, but fragments from a circus on the loose, collared by anxious barkers for a motley procession across the line of vision that defies the viewing judges to guess at all that has escaped notice and to foresee what may still appear. Understandably, they are wont to shirk the difficulties of working out program notes for the future from such a scene. Their professional training, moreover, fosters reactions to present impressions that hark back to the past; they search for resemblance between what goes on and what has gone before. And because the usual judge is no less lethargic than other human beings, he is predisposed to accept a specious analogy and to freeze it into the law. It is not thereafter easily defrosted, as some of us well know who have had to deal with icebergs that have developed beyond reasonable proportions.

There is now general agreement that we have moved out of the Ice Age. It is no longer enough for lawyers to have a respectable training in precedents and a respectful preoccupation with the past. There are no adequate precedents for much of the law that must be formulated today to regulate multiminded, multihanded human beings. The main preoccupation of such law must be with the future. Its main formulation belongs appropriately to legislators, who are freer than judges to write on a clean slate, in terms of policy transcending case or controversy, and to erase and rewrite in response to community needs.

Some fear that the proliferation of statutes and administrative regulations will subject the judge to an impossible burden of review. Others fear instead that it will lead to his rapid technological depreciation. A judge unaccustomed to public sympathy must nonetheless be disconcerted if he receives it for the wrong reasons. He knows these two concerns on his behalf to be mistaken as well as contradictory. As he plods his way from one controversy to another, he is inured to overemployment. He fears no unemployment, for he knows that *plus ça change, plus c'est la même chose* in action. Television has not superseded radio, nor radio the phonograph, nor any of them the live musicians. Instead all have flourished and the miracles of technical reproduction have but quickened our awareness of how inimitable is the live performance. The endless statutes and regulations should in time, by the very impersonality of their numbers that yet reflects the involvement of their drafters, engender a new appreciation of the irreplaceable humanity in the individual judicial opinion that yet reflects the detachment of its author.

When Warner Gardner finds it impossible to make a still-life definition of the administrative process he knows so well, he nonetheless sharpens our perception of the *fait accompli* of this now massive fourth power of government by illustrating the variety and suppleness of its operations and then emphasizing that on the whole the administrators are discreetly aware of the omni-presence of judicial review, however limited its scope. When Justice Breitel finds it impossible to make a categorical definition of the statutory process, he nevertheless succeeds in clarifying it by emphasizing the startling range in its methods and in the quality of its products which, whether works of art or inventions of the devil, reflect on the whole indifference to judicial review, however wide its scope.

Likewise one may find it impossible to speak categorically of the judicial process as felt influence or unseen power or simply as wilderness crying in a judicial voice. Here too, however, one can summon illustrations of its infinite variety that yet reflect the general awareness of the judges that however others hasten forth they must make their own haste slowly. Their task will become the more important as it increasingly involves not only decision on actual cases but decision on the selection of cases for review. Certainly no rude priority is accorded to common law cases over those arising out of statutes. Moreover, the distinction between so-called "private law" and so-called "public law" becomes in-creasingly blurred in a crowded society that is continually dimin-ishing the boundaries of private lives as it expands the boundaries of public interest.

It is true, as Justice Breitel has noted, that whole subjects of the law are still largely unclaimed by legislatures. Although they are free to make such appropriation, that possibility cannot justify judicial abdication of present responsibility for their develop-ment. A generation ago Mr. Justice Cardozo reflected from experi-ence that the judicial process had recurringly to be creative. For recurringly it happened that a judge failed to find the amiable *ratio decidendi* supposedly awaiting discovery among the reeds of precedent to swaddle a foundling case becomingly and set its cries at rest. Since he could not let it cry forever, he must needs swaddle it with some inventive covering suitable for the occasion and durable enough to serve the future. Every basic precedent was thus once made up out of whole cloth woven by a judge.

There is now wide agreement that a judge can and should participate creatively in the development of the common law. Yet each time he does so, he must reckon with the ancient suspicion that creativeness is a disturbing excess of skill, at odds with circumspection, darkly menacing the stability of the law. Actually, the creative decision is circumspect in the extreme, for it reflects the most careful consideration of all the arguments for a conventional solution and all the circumstances that now render such a solution so unrealistic as to doom its serviceability for future cases. Although the judge's predilections may play a part in setting the initial direction he takes toward the creative solution, there is little danger of their determining the solution itself, however much it bears the stamp of his individual workmanship. Our great creative judges have been men of outstanding skill, adept at discounting their own predilections and careful to discount them with conscientious severity. The disinterestedness of the creative decision is further assured by the judge's arduous articulation of the reasons that compel the formulation of an original solution and by the full disclosure in his opinion of all aspects of the problem and of the data pertinent to its solution. Thereafter the opinion must pass muster with scholars and practitioners on the alert to note any misunderstanding of the problem, any error in reasoning, any irrelevance in data, any oversight of relevant data, any premature cartography beyond the problem at hand. Every opinion is thus subject to approval.

The real concern is not the remote possibility of too many creative opinions but their continuing scarcity. The growth of the law, far from being unduly accelerated by judicial boldness, is unduly hampered by a judicial lethargy that masks itself as judicial dignity with the tacit approval of an equally lethargic bar. The legal training that should quicken imaginative use of the rich grammar of the law in opinions and also in briefs induces a disquieting number of sanctimonious copies of old forms of speech that bear little relation to present-day life. We have a plethora of copycats. Whatever progress we are making, as in rules of civil procedure, is woefully inadequate to meet the need for a modernized law. Massive anachronisms endure in its substance, their venerability discouraging judges from voicing the rude possibility that they may have reached retirement age.

What of the vaunted stability in this enshrinement of precedents? In practice, distinctions of all manner are appended to the shrine. No one knows what fiction is to be taken straight; no one can be sure what constitutes the present object of veneration. Law offices, wise in the ways of our unstable idol worship, meditate well their emphases and understatements in the presentation of a case and sometimes present it with substantial omissions. A judge learns from experience to be wary of giving full faith and credit to any presentation, however plausible, however polished. He must educate himself as best he can to the possibilities that may be lurking in the wings. Even with the advantage of detachment, however, he cannot hope to ferret them all out, for they are legion. He too must select, on another plane from that of the advocates, the issues that appear to him salient and the data that appear significant. In a morass of uncertainty lie a variety of precedents, and the judge makes selection upon selection before reaching his decision. It is no ready text to come by and there is no well-edited chapter to which it can be added. The precedents are writ in type that moves like water and they are not holy writ.

For the most part the precedents serve well enough to guide men in their legal affairs. When they invite litigation, however, their stability is already in question, perhaps because they have been rendered ambiguous by conflicting interpretations, or have grown archaic, or have been challenged at last as they should have been earlier for their original nonsense. Why then should we not welcome their frank renunciation when it is reasonably clear that there has been no reliance on them[44] or that they have cast enough shadows behind them to render any further reliance on them unjustifiable? Those who plead reliance do not necessarily practice it. Thus counsel for a client that had sold liability insurance to a state agency pleaded the sovereign immunity doctrine; on questioning, however, he conceded that the agency had insured itself in awareness of the growing limitations on the doctrine as set forth in a case decided in 1898.[45]

The plea of reliance would perpetuate archaic precedents. We have not begun to make use as we should of the sensible solution approved nearly a generation ago in *Great Northern Ry.* v. *Sunburst Oil & Refining Co.*[46] The court simultaneously protected those who might have relied on such a precedent and gave warning that it would no longer control future cases. One who has invoked this solution to no avail may be permitted to lament that it has met with such resistance.[47]

The alternative is to live uneasily with an unfortunate precedent by wearing it thin with distinctions that at last compel a cavalier pronouncement, heedless of the court's failure to make a frank overruling, that it must be deemed to have revealed itself as overruled by its manifest erosion. It must be cold comfort to bewildered counsel to ruminate that the precedent on which he relied was never expressly overruled because it so patently needed to be.

[44]See CARDOZO, THE GROWTH OF THE LAW 122 (1924); SCHAEFER, PRECEDENT AND POLICY 12-13 (1955).

[45]Guidi v. State, 41 Cal. 2d 623, 262 P.2d 3 (1953).

[46]287 U.S. 358 (1932).

[47]Sutter Basin Corp. v. Brown, 40 Cal. 2d 235, 249, 253 P.2d 649, 656 (1953); Boyd v. Oser, 23 Cal. 2d 613, 623, 145 P.2d 312, 317 (1944); *cf.* County of Los Angeles v. Faus, 48 Cal. 2d 672, 680-81, 312 P.2d 680, 685-86 (1957); People v. Ryan, 152 Cal. 364, 369, 92 Pac. 853, 855 (1907); People v. Maughs, 149 Cal. 253, 263, 86 Pac. 187, 191 (1906).

Still, if all is not at attention in the courts, neither is all at ease. They have significantly expanded the concept of obligation. They are recognizing a much-needed right to privacy. They are recognizing a right to recovery for prenatal injuries and intentionally inflicted mental suffering.[48] They are recognizing the right of one member of the family to recover against another.[49] They are recognizing liability once precluded by charitable or governmental immunities. The now general acceptance of the manufacturer's liability to third persons for negligence has stimulated inquiry into appropriate bases for possible strict liability for injuries resulting from defective products.[50] The courts are moving closer to open preoccupation with compensation for personal injuries, which is bound in turn to augment the scope of insurance.

Obviously, however, they cannot undertake the comprehensive studies, or act upon them, for rational solution of such overwhelming problems as arise from the daily destruction on the highways. They cannot even begin to cope with the resulting litigation. There is grave question that adversary presentation and jury findings reconstruct the circumstances of an injury accurately enough to assess liability justly and to award appropriate damages.[51] There is such extraordinary inconsistency in the determinations as to cast doubt upon the rationality of expressing liability in terms of fault. A Columbia University study has demonstrated that liability turns on many things besides fault, notably on ability to pay, usually tantamount to insurance, and on insurance company practices as to settlement.[52] In all likeli-

[48]State Rubbish Collectors Ass'n v. Siliznoff, 38 Cal. 2d 330, 240 P.2d 282 (1952).

[49]Emery v. Emery, 45 Cal. 2d 421, 289 P.2d 218 (1955).

[50]Gordon v. Aztec Brewing Co., 33 Cal. 2d 514, 523, 203 P.2d 522, 528 (1949) (concurring opinion); Escola v. Coca Cola Bottling Co., 24 Cal. 2d 453, 461, 150 P.2d 436, 440 (1944) (concurring opinion).

[51]See Traynor, *Fact Skepticism and the Judicial Process,* 106 U. PA. L. REV. 635, 640 (1958).

[52]COLUMBIA UNIVERSITY COUNCIL FOR RESEARCH IN THE SOCIAL SCIENCES, REPORT BY THE COMMITTEE TO STUDY COMPENSATION FOR AUTOMOBILE ACCIDENTS 92 (1932).

hood the reforms that such studies suggest will sooner or later materialize in legislation, where they most appropriately belong. The courts will then no longer spend most of their time on the highways; they will be freer to consider the large problems that have preceded and succeeded the comparatively recent advent of the automobile.

Prophecy is more difficult in areas such as the criminal law, whose development has rested with the courts since time immemorial. Had the world always known what we know now, had the learned judges of other days enjoyed the advantage of later learning, had more of them been courageous and imaginative as well as merely learned, had customary beliefs not always constituted a phalanx against new ideas, we might have had a rational development of criminal law. Instead, its development has been warped by successive irrationalities that have matched the potions and bloodletting of medicine. The persistent inadequacy of our senseless hodgepodge of precedents is the more shocking in comparison with such undertakings as the Model Penal Code of the American Law Institute now evolving under the leadership of Professor Wechsler of the Columbia Law School. One hesitates to plead for reforms in the name of common sense, however, for we belong to a profession that prides itself on not throwing chaos lightly to the winds.

Nowhere do its excesses of caution persist more tenaciously than in the law of evidence. Warily it resists the seductive reason of such proposals as the Model Code of Evidence and the Uniform Rules. It is still possible to say, as Professors Morgan and Maguire said some twenty years ago, that "there is scarcely a segment of the subject which does not call for re-examination and revision."[53] We can ill afford such passive resistance. Were we to keep accounts as business must, we would soon realize how

[53]Morgan & Maguire, *Looking Backward and Forward at Evidence*, 50 HARV. L. REV. 909, 922 (1937).

seriously our obsolescent methods impede our productivity and impair the quality of our products. The legislatures are quite properly uninterested in undertaking reforms that are so plainly a responsibility for bench and bar. Unfortunately bench and bar have shirked that responsibility with assiduous care.

Justice Breitel has noted that the legislature also properly keeps its distance in those areas of the law whose problems are so complicated and whose development is therefore so unpredictable as to defy formulation of rules in advance. When, as in conflict of laws, new cases not only fail to portend future directions but also fail to respond to the facile theories of the past, the need is all the greater for judicial imagination in decision bold enough to reject already unrealistic rules, yet cautious enough not to make formulations that reach too zealously into the future. More, it must also be skillful enough to strengthen emphasis not only on the freedom of the forum in choice of law but also on its corresponding responsibility for the local law it thus makes. Such responsibility calls for perception in distinguishing between real and spurious conflicts at the outset. It precludes a provincial point of view, for the responsible decision proceeds from reflection as to which jurisdiction has the dominant interests and a consideration of these interests against others in the light of local policy.

Though the main responsibility for rational development of conflict of laws rests with the courts, it is for the legislatures to modernize existing statutes, in such fields as the administration of decedents' estates, where provincial preoccupation with local interests makes administration needlessly slow and cumbersome and costly. Increasingly they must envisage uniform laws where states are at odds not on basic policy but on such mechanics of regulation as notice to creditors and creditors' priorities.[54]

The relatively undeveloped field of conflict of laws serves to dramatize not only what large creative jobs the courts must under-

[54]See People v. One 1953 Ford Victoria, 48 Cal. 2d 595, 311 P.2d 480 (1957).

take but also what comprehensive statutory revision falls to legislatures. Such creativeness and such revision is needed in every
field of the law to keep pace with the epochal changes in our once
self-contained little world. The task of the judges will continue to
be the lonely one of detached adjustment of controversies. These
are becoming so complex that we should be concerned less to mul-
tiply judges than to minimize sources of controversy. We tend to
think that legislators can minimize controversy if they are so
minded by producing model laws. Justice Breitel rightly reminds
us that they are now so heavily engaged in investigation and lawmaking on so many fronts that we cannot expect them to close
ranks for the single-minded task of making repairs and renewals
in the common law. What they can do is to follow the example of
such states as New York and California and set up law revision
commissions, secure enough to withstand the prevailing winds of
pressure groups, that would make timely use of the abundant wast-
ing assets of scholarly studies in a continuous formulation of statutes that would command respect for their careful drafting without
claiming a sanctity for their printed words that would discourage
periodic reexamination of their fitness for survival.

There are those who would entice us with the proposition
that we can solve our problems by reducing the number of our
laws. Theirs is a siren song to lure us from the arduous labor that
the times call upon us to perform. We cannot revert to a primitive
simplicity in our laws when our mode of living becomes ever
more complex. However much a law revision commission can
expedite the liquidation of obsolete or superfluous statutes, it must
be prepared to formulate new and better ones.

The day is fast coming when no state can afford to be without
such a commission. The complexities hastening that day are
bound to hasten also the wholehearted recognition, advocated by
Mr. Justice Stone in 1936, of statutes as sources of law, "starting points for judicial lawmaking comparable to judicial deci-

cisions."[55] Sporadic recognition there has been and it is growing, as Justice Schaefer of the Illinois Supreme Court recently noted, citing such illustrations as judicial development of the law based upon the Married Women's Acts but transcending their literal terms.[56] Nevertheless courts have not begun to utilize all the latent energy in statutes to generate new law. Clues to the possibilities appear in the analogies the courts have already made from statutes. They have long been invoking in negligence cases the standards of conduct set forth in penal statutes as a test for civil liability. There is of course great variety of invocation. Thus in a single case the judges stated their separate views that the statutory standard for criminal liability was the appropriate one for civil liability, that violation of the penal statute created a rebuttable presumption of negligence, and finally that such violation was merely evidence of negligence.[57]

However bumbling, such invocation of statutes exemplifies their kinship with precedents and tolls the weakness of the lingering pedantry that sees them only as alien successors or usurpers. Statutes, like precedents, may be radioactive, their emanations expanding with the times. Such may be the penal statutes specifying liability with reference to a particular area or class. Suppose, for example, a penal statute regulates conduct only on the public highways, in a jurisdiction where all crimes are statutory. The court could not properly extend the area of crime by applying the statute to conduct on private roads. If the statute sets forth an appropriate standard of reasonable conduct for all roads, however, the court should be free to invoke it in a civil case involving negligence on a private road even though there has been no criminal violation.[58]

[55]Stone, *The Common Law in the United States*, 50 HARV. L. REV. 4, 12 (1936).
[56]Schaefer, PRECEDENT AND POLICY 18-19 (1955).
[57]Satterlee v. Orange Glen School Dist., 29 Cal. 2d 581, 177 P.2d 279 (1947).
[58]*Cf.* Clinkscales v. Carver, 22 Cal. 2d 72, 136 P.2d 777 (1943).

The court should also be free to make broad use of the standards in penal statutes preoccupied with the protection of a particular class. It is literal in the extreme to regard that preoccupation as indicative of indifference to the protection of any others. Yet the rule persists that a plaintiff cannot base a cause of action for negligence on the violation of a penal statute unless he is a member of the class the statute was designed to protect. Thus one who is not an employee is precluded from invoking a statute designed solely to protect employees even though he is injured by the very conduct proscribed. It is logic run riot that a statute requiring the barricading of an open well or elevator shaft for the protection of employees cannot, by virtue of its particularity, be invoked for the protection of any others.

We have been slow not only in drawing pertinent analogies from statutes but also in expanding the connotations of their own terms to keep pace with the incessant inventiveness of our economy. We forget that legislatures are neither omnipresent nor omniscient. Whatever their alertness to the times, the currency of their statutes begins to depreciate the moment they are enacted. Even if they were in perpetual session they could not possibly enact all the postscripts to yesterday's regulations that the events of each day would suggest. And if some machine could conceivably be devised to tabulate such postscripts they would be self-defeating, for their very numbers would defy intelligent application. To say as we did earlier that we are bound to have more laws is not to advocate that they should roll off a ticker tape.

If in many fields it is impossible to prophesy forthcoming events and idle to tabulate actual ones, we must expect our statutory laws to become increasingly pliable to creative judicial elaboration. Nevertheless, in Justice Breitel's apt words, "the legislative tradition in this country assumes and depends on a dynamic and modernized common law system of law." In some fields more than in others the courts have been responsive to this tradition.

One might note by way of illustration how the California courts have interpreted an 1872 statute authorizing service of process on foreign corporations doing business in the state. Since 1872 there has been great diminution in the protection from suit afforded foreign corporations by the due process clause. The mutations in that clause have had their effect on the state court's interpretation of the phrase "doing business in the state." They have reasoned that at the time of its adoption it afforded not so much a test for immunity as a test for jurisdiction, consonant with the tenor then of the due process clause. The elastic contours of that clause make it unlikely that any test for jurisdiction geared to its then current tenor was more than illustrative of service of process in accord with the jurisdictional concepts of that period. As those concepts have expanded, the courts have found that the literal wording of the 1872 test correspondingly expanded in meaning.[59] One could find other illustrations of the leeway afforded to courts by a changing Constitution for the interpretation of statutes closely tied thereto.

Many a statute, however, stands outside the radiations of the flexible Constitution and is contained in terms that have no radiations of their own into the common law. The task of the courts is then not creative utilization of the statute as a source or supplement of the common law but merely a rendition of its meaning that conforms to the legislative purpose. Yet even here, as Justice Breitel reminds us, there are large problems of interpretation. Certainly the court is not at liberty to seek hidden meanings not suggested by the statute or the available extrinsic aids. Speculation cuts brush with the question: what purpose did the legislature express as it strung its words into a statute?

An insistence upon judicial regard for the words of a statute does not imply that they are like words in a dictionary to be read with no ranging of the mind. They are no longer at rest in their alphabetical bins. Released, combined in phrases that imperfectly communicate the thoughts of one

[59] Henry R. Jahn & Son v. Superior Court, 49 Cal. 2d 855, 323 P.2d 437 (1958).

man to another, they challenge men to give them more than passive reading, to consider well their context, to ponder what may be their consequences.[60]

Judges have found more than once that absolute phrases are
subject to qualifications implicit in the context of the whole
statute. Judge Edgerton has invoked the classic illustration of
the Bologna ordinance against bloodletting in the streets, which
did not make criminals of surgeons.[61] The United States Supreme
Court has interpreted a statute, forbidding encouragement to
aliens to migrate to this country to perform services of any kind,
as not applicable to the employment of a clergyman by a church.[62]
Our own court in California has made a comparable interpretation of a phrase specifically requiring dismissal of an action
not brought to trial within five years.[63] Certain express exceptions
in the statute afforded a basis for implied exceptions in the
seemingly absolute phrase, when the statute was read as a whole
in the light of its legislative purpose "to prevent *avoidable* delay
for too long a period."[64] Hence, the statute did not compel
dismissal when it was impossible, impracticable, or futile to
bring the action to trial.

There are times when words thus tested prove themselves so
at odds with a clear legislative purpose as to pose a dilemma
for the judge. He knows that there is an irreducible minimum
of error in statutes because they deal with multifarious and
frequently complicated problems. He hesitates to undertake
correction of even the most obvious legislative oversight, knowing
that theoretically the legislature has within its power the correction
of its own lapses. Yet he also knows how cumbersome the legislative process is, how massive the machinery that must be set

[60]People v. Knowles, 35 Cal. 2d 175, 182, 217 P.2d 1, 5 (1950).
[61]Ross v. Hartman, 139 F.2d 14, 16 (1943).
[62]Church of the Holy Trinity v. United States, 143 U.S. 457 (1892). *Compare*
Caminetti v. United States, 242 U.S. 470 (1917) (reliance on literal words) *with*
Mortensen v. United States, 322 U.S. 369 (1944) (reaction against such reliance).
[63]CAL. CODE CIV. PROC. § 583.
[64]Rose v. Knapp, 38 Cal. 2d 114, 117, 237 P.2d 981, 983 (1951).

in motion for even the smallest correction, how problematic that it will be set in motion at all, how confusion then may be worse confounded.

What a court does is determined in the main by the nature of the statute. It may be so general in scope as to invite judicial elaboration. It may evince such careful draftsmanship in the main as to render its errors egregious enough to be judicially recognized as such, inconsistent with the legislative purpose. Thus a revenue act that set forth the basis for determining uncompensated loss from damage to nonbusiness property failed to specify that depreciation should enter into the computation. The taxpayer claimed that since he was not allowed depreciation under another section he need not compute it in determining his loss. He therefore claimed a deduction of $1,635 based on original cost although his actual loss was only $35. In rejecting his claim the court found that the missing specification was implied by the apparent legislative purpose in the statute read as a whole and declared that the reason of the law in such cases should prevail over its letter.[65]

The experienced draftsmen of tax laws find it impossible to foresee all the problems that will test the endurance of their words. They did not foresee the intriguing question whether the United States is a resident of the United States, which arose under a revenue act taxing interest received by foreign corporations from such residents. What to do when a foreign corporation received interest from the United States? Mr. Justice Sutherland decided that this country resided in itself. He found a spirit willing to take up residence though the flesh was weak, if indeed not entirely missing. The ingenuity of the solution compels admiration, whatever misgivings it may engender as to our self-containment.[66]

[65]Helvering v. Owens, 305 U.S. 468 (1939); see Traynor, *Tax Decisions of The Supreme Court,* 1939 PROCEEDINGS OF THE NATIONAL ASSOCIATION 27, 55-57.
[66]Helvering v. Stockholms Enskilda Bank, 293 U.S. 84, 92 (1934).

So the courts now and again prevent erratic omissions or wayward words from defeating legislative purpose, even though they thereby disregard such conventional canons as the one that tax statutes are to be strictly construed against the government. We may well ask why they should not disregard such a canon altogether when it so handily serves the tricks and devices of taxpayers who would avoid their tax liabilities at the expense of their fellows.[67] The image persists of a Gargantuan government pitted against a little taxpayer carrying a burden too big for his frail bones. Actually, of course, there are millions of taxpayers sharing the burden of payment for the services they have come to expect of their government. Whenever one of them is successful at tax avoidance the burden on all the others, most of whom are quite little, becomes so much the greater. If we accept the legislative purpose of distributing the tax burden justly, that purpose should prevail over a pedantic strict construction against the government that in effect militates against other taxpayers.

We might well look askance at all canons of interpretation that deflect attention from the legislative purpose. The more courts intone these ancient saws, the less realistic is their concern apt to be with the meaning of the statute they are asked to interpret. They should be particularly on guard against repetitive invocations in areas such as criminal law, already obscured with archaic classifications of offenses. In California the Penal Code specifically places the courts on guard with the injunction that "its provisions are to be construed according to the fair import of their terms with a view to effect its objects and promote justice."[68] The courts are thus encouraged to abandon clichés in determining the legislative purpose.

This freedom has enabled them to reflect critically on the recur-

[67]See Latilla v. Inland Revenue, [1943] 1 All E.R. 265; Howard de Walden v. Inland Revenue Commissioners, [1942] 1 K.B. 389, 397 (C.A. 1941); discussed in Friedmann, *Statute Law and Its Interpretation in The Modern State*, 26 CAN. B. REV. 1277, 1282, 1298 (1948).

[68]CAL. PENAL CODE § 4.

ring problem of when *mens rea* is an essential element of a crime whose statutory definition does not specify it although general provisions in the Penal Code[69] appear to require it without exception. Our court has resolved this problem in the case of bigamy[70] and the felonious possession of narcotics[71] by making wrongful intent an essential element of the crime. We have resolved the problem in manslaughter[72] by making criminal negligence an element. Again, to insure its constitutionality, we have read into a statute compelling the forfeiture of any automobile used to transport narcotics a requirement that the possessor of the automobile have knowledge of what he is transporting.[73] In contrast, we have interpreted as primarily regulatory rather than penal, and therefore as requiring no interpolation of *mens rea*, the so-called "public welfare offenses" carrying light penalties and involving no moral obloquy. Thus a druggist who innocently sold an adulterated drug that caused a death was guilty of violating a statute prohibiting such sales; but since his offense lacked the essential *mens rea* it was not an "unlawful act" within the definition of involuntary manslaughter.[74]

The court's broad use of its authorization to interpret the fair import of statutory language in the interest of justice had necessarily to be creative in interpreting incompletely coordinated provisions with due consideration for the public interest in both crime prevention and protection of the innocent. It is important to add that any court undertaking such interpretation should articulate with particular care the reasons that led to its choice of alternatives.

We come upon an intriguing but quite different problem when we consider what should be the fair import of legislative silence in the wake of statutory interpretation embodied in the occasional

[69]CAL. PENAL CODE §§ 20, 26.
[70]People v. Vogel, 46 Cal. 2d 798, 299 P.2d 850 (1956).
[71]People v. Winston, 46 Cal. 2d 151, 293 P.2d 40 (1956).
[72]People v. Stuart, 47 Cal. 2d 167, 302 P.2d 5 (1956).
[73]People v. One 1941 Buick Sport Coupe, 28 Cal. 2d 692, 171 P.2d 719 (1946).
[74]People v. Stuart, 47 Cal. 2d 167, 302 P.2d 5 (1956).

precedent that proves increasingly unsound in the solution of subsequent cases. Barring those exceptional situations where the entrenched precedent has engendered so much reliance that its liquidation would do more harm than good, a court should be free to overrule such a precedent despite legislative inaction.

It is unrealistic to suppose that it [the legislature] can note, much less deliberate the effect of each judicial construction of statutory provisions, absorbed as it is with forging legislation for an endless number and variety of problems, under the constant pressure of considerations of urgency and expediency. The fiction that the failure of the Legislature to repudiate an erroneous construction amounts to an incorporation of that construction into the statute not only commits the Legislature to embrace something that it may not even be aware of, but bars the court from reexamining its own errors, consequences as unnecessary as they are serious.[75]

Nonetheless we can rest assured that any backwardness of the courts is sooner or later noted by the commentators. Judicial lethargy sometimes enables unworthy decisions to endure longer than they should, but at least they are in the public stocks and subject to the critical glance of any passer-by. The commentators might well begin to emulate such examples as that of the Columbia Law School, whose leadership is noted by Professor Newman, and train their critical eyes on statutes as they long have on judicial opinions.

Still we can hardly expect that there will ever be widespread heed to the subdued alarums of scholars. So we come to it that it is for the bar to participate in far larger measure than ever before in the rational development of the law by giving consistent and organized help in the transformation of scholarly projects into laws. It is not too much to expect of the education that fits lawyers for private practice that it should also make them generously responsive to the need for rational laws in the public interest.

[75]In re Halcomb, 21 Cal. 2d 126, 132, 130 P.2d 384, 388 (1942) (dissenting opinion); see also Rosemary Properties, Inc. v. McColgan, 29 Cal. 2d 677, 706-08, 177 P.2d 757, 775-76 (1947) (dissenting opinion).

A Legal Look at Congress and the State Legislatures

BY FRANK C. NEWMAN

PROFESSOR OF LAW, THE UNIVERSITY OF CALIFORNIA, BERKELEY

Of all the legal institutions in America that are being discussed in this Conference, I think the legislature fared best in 1958. When Congress adjourned, the New York *Times*, the *Christian Science Monitor*, the *U.S. News and World Report*, the *London Economist*, the Chamber of Commerce, the National Federation of Independent Business, the American Civil Liberties Union, and many other observers filed their praises. From *The Reporter* we had learned earlier that "perhaps not since the post-Civil War Reconstruction Congress . . . has power been so firmly centered on Capitol Hill as it is right now."[1]

No one would argue, I believe, that the year was a happy or an impressive one for the President; and in the Executive Branch as a whole the agencies were scarcely in their prime. Nor was it a great year for the United Nations and international legal institutions—for however we credit the performance in the Near and Far East, for example, the achievements were not splendid.

[1]Kilpatrick, *Congress, Politics, and the Recession*, May 15, 1958, p. 18. The Sept. 1958 Democratic Digest, glorying in *The Record of Congress*, noted at page 2: "Perhaps the best measure of the 85th Congress' enlightened performance was the fact that columnist David Lawrence thought the 85th was 'the worst in half a century.'" *Cf.* ADA World, Sept. 1958, p. 1-M ("'58 Session Falls Short of Sputnik"). Also see McGee, *The Vitality of State Legislatures*, 31 STATE GOV'T. 9 (1958).

Some might contend that the judges chalked up an outstanding record in 1958, because of their staunch insistence on principle in the school segregation cases. But will time prove this to have been a key year for the supremacy of law; or did we merely witness the building of further barricades for a much more crucial and bitter struggle yet to come? The Supreme Court stands unscarred from attacks by its critics, but the chances are that the attackers have only been repulsed. The judicial process as a whole can hardly be eminent in a year when calendar congestion, for instance, became a headline issue, and when thirty-six state supreme court chief justices found it advisable to reprimand their distinguished federal colleague and his eight associates.

Thus, for an admirer of the legislative process 1958 is an auspicious centennial year. Moreover, the legislative process is an auspicious topic for the Columbia Law School Centennial because on this campus, more than on any other, law teachers have borne their full responsibilities to the legislature—treating it as a legal institution that merits great attention and respect, much more so than have law schools generally. Chamberlain, Parkinson, Dowling, Beaman, Jones, and Kernochan—those are distinguished names on the roster of law men whose drafting bureaus and experimental courses have given guidance. In addition, the Kent Hall directory of offices alone can be referred to for a remarkable list of noted reformers of statute law: Smith, Warren, Powell, Hays, Wechsler, Gellhorn, Weinstein, and many others.[2]

[2]For introductory comment on Columbia's legislative achievements see MacDonald, *Dean Smith and the New York Law Revision Commission,* 53 COLUM. L. REV. 155 (1953); Wechsler, *Legal Scholarship and Criminal Law,* 9 J. LEGAL ED. 18 (1956); Surrey, *The Income Tax Project of the American Law Institute,* 31 TAXES 959 (1953) (Dean Warren); Mentschikoff, *The Uniform Commercial Code: An Experiment in Democracy in Drafting,* 36 A.B.A.J. 419 (1950) (Prof. Llewellyn); Note (Prof. Jones and the A.B.A.J. Dep't of Legislation), 42 *id.* 276 (1956); Nutting, *Chief Justice Stone and Legislation,* 43 *id.* 454 (1957); *Powell at Perpetuity Ceremony,* Colum. L.S. News, Mar. 18, 1958, p. 1. FOUNDATION FOR RESEARCH IN LEGAL HISTORY: *A History of the School of Law, Columbia University* 255 (1955) describes the Legislative Drafting Research Fund but does not, in my opinion, adequately note the distinguished record of individual professors regarding statutory reform.

When one turns from the legislative achievements of the Columbia Law School, however, to those of the American legal profession, the latter's record is less creditable than the former's. The pioneering work of the Columbia faculty has not led to impressive curricular changes in the nation's law schools,[3] and lawyers in general remain far less sensitive to the legislature as an institution than they are to courts or administrative agencies.

LEGISLATURES AND LAWYERS

As individuals, lawyers have notably marked the American legislative process, but as members of an organized profession their contribution has been minimal. As individuals they recently comprised 66 percent of the United States Senate and 56 percent of the House of Representatives; 58 percent of the legislature of New York; 32, 30, 21, and 18 percent of the legislatures of California, Illinois, Missouri, and Minnesota. Their rosters include outstanding legislative leaders of past and present. Further, like senior partners in a law firm they are typically successful in procuring the services of law-trained associates—who as draftsmen, committee counsel, and other aides have made their own contribution to the legislature, as lawyers.[4]

[3]Varying courses of study in legislation are illustrated by these books: (1) COHEN, MATERIALS ON LEGISLATION (1949); (2) HORACK, CASES ON LEGISLATION (2d ed. 1954); (3) LENHOFF, COMMENTS ON LEGISLATION (1949); (4) NEWMAN & SURREY, LEGISLATION (1955); (5) NUTTING & ELLIOT, CASES ON LEGISLATION (2d ed. 1955); (6) READ & MACDONALD, CASES ON LEGISLATION (1948). In some schools local materials are used. Cf. Kelso, New Ideas in Legislation, Practical Jurisprudence, Moot Legislature, Law Revision Committee, 10 J. LEGAL ED. 347 (1958); Duffy, Drafting Legislation at Harvard, Harv. L.S. Bull., June 1958, p. 5; Dunham, Law Revision as a Teaching Tool and Public Responsibility of a Law School, 5 CHI. L.S. REC. 4 (1956). My disagreements with many teachers are discussed briefly at p. vi of Item (4), supra; Cf. Braucher, Book Review, 10 J. LEGAL ED. 535 (1958). A basic curricular defect in nearly all schools is that while most students get some training in statutory interpretation, only a handful meet problems arising out of the drafting of statutes and legal matters relating to the process of legislatures.

[4]See Rodgers, Assistance for the State Legislature, 42 A.B.A.J. 1086 (1956); Kleps, Staffing the Office of a State Legislative Counsel, 39 id. 58 (1953); Jones, A Note on Legislative Drafting Services in the State Legislature, 36 id. 142 (1950); House Stirred Over Administrative Assistants, 16 CONG. Q. WEEKLY REP. 758

The bar association picture differs greatly. Our national, state, and local bars are active as lobbying groups, but often the members' enthusiasm seems greatest when selfish interests are being served. Their record of reform of the adjudicative process has been impressive; but their concern for other legislation in the public interest—to many observers, at least—has frequently seemed narrow and parochial.[5]

Examining the legislature as a legal institution, we find that the worst default of lawyers, as bar members, has been lack of concern for reforms of the legislative process. The Legislative Reorganization Act of 1946, for example, was a political scientists' and not a lawyers' project.[6] Even Title III of that act, dealing with lobbyists, was ignored by the bar; and one result has been a twelve-year period of lax enforcement, partly caused by the bad drafting that Part III's words reflect. Major reviews of the statute have been

---

(1958); cf. Kampelman, The Legislative Bureaucracy: Its Response to Political Change, 1953, 16 J. OF POL. 539 (1954); 5 ABA Coordinator, Jan. 1, 1957, p. 3 ("State legislators in Oregon . . . [were] offered the aid of 157 hand-picked lawyers during the 1957 session of the legislature under a public spirited 'legal assistance' program inaugurated by the Oregon State Bar.").

[5]In the 1958 Congress, though the ABA backed many bills, its support of H.R. 10 ("provides tax savings for you and other self-employed persons") seemed most intense. See Donahue letter of July 30, 1958, to some 30,000 lawyers and bar officials; ABA Washington Letters Nos. 7-85-2 and 8-85-2, July 22 and July 30, 1958; cf. 104 CONG. REC. 15771 (daily ed. Aug. 12, 1958). Generally see Fordham, The Legal Profession and American Constitutionalism, 12 RECORD OF N.Y.C.B.A. 518 (1957); HURST, THE GROWTH OF AMERICAN LAW 363 (1950); DOUGLAS, BEING AN AMERICAN 52 (1948); cf. Curtis, The Lawyers' Part in Law Reform, 42 A.B.A.J. (1956). But see Rhyne, The President's Page, 43 id. 867 (1957) ("No organization in the United States does more unselfish public service or works in more fields of endeavor than the American Bar Association.").

[6]Except, of course, Title IV (The Federal Tort Claims Act), which is hardly pertinent to legislative reorganization. Generally see 60 Stat. 812; GALLOWAY, THE LEGISLATIVE PROCESS IN CONGRESS 624, n.1 (1953); Jones, The Bar's Stake in State Legislative Reorganization, 37 A.B.A.J. 74 (1951); Braham, Reform of Pennsylvania's Legislative Procedure, 25 TEMP. L.Q. 420 (1952); Proposed Improvements of Legislative Procedures in the State of New York, 6 RECORD OF N.Y.C.B.A. 404 (1951).

undertaken by both Senate and House committees, but lawyers' views are still unstated.[7]

Even as to our own ethics we have a meager record in Washington and in the state capitals of measures regarding lawyer-lobbyists, lawyer-legislators, and lawyer-politicians.[8] Our proposals for improving election and bill-passing procedures are practically nil; and though we zealously guard legislative-judicial relations, we mostly ignore the problems that plague legislative-executive relations. One bright ray beams from the work done recently by a few bar committees on legislative investigations, but even on that topic the bar as a whole is somewhat equivocal.[9]

What of the future? As individuals and as members of bar groups are we likely to engage in more, or less, activity that affects the legislature? My guess is that the patterns are pretty well set.

[7]The Lobbying Act has been studied by the McClellan and Buchanan committees. See Lyon & Stanhagen, *Lobbying, Liberty, and the Legislative Process: An Appraisal of the Proposed Legislative Activities Disclosure Act*, 26 GEO. WASH. L. REV. 391 (1958); Kennedy, *Congressional Lobbies: A Chronic Problem Re-examined*, 45 GEO. L.J. 535 (1957); cf. NEWMAN & SURREY, LEGISLATION 59 (1955); Jones, *The Proposed Congressional Lobbying Investigation*, 35 A.B.A.J. 590 (1949). The ABA Committee on Jurisprudence and Law Reform received authority in 1950 to act on behalf of the American Bar Association "to influence the nature and form of . . . [lobbying] legislation," 75 ABA REP. 221 (1950); but the next year the chairman wrote me that "the Committee made some effort to obtain suggestions from those who might have good ideas on the subject. However, no suggestions were forthcoming." Some rather vague suggestions did come from the ABA Washington Committee in Aug. 1958. See 44 A.B.A.J. 1122 (1958); cf. Deale, *Administrative Law Chairman's Annual Report*, 25 J. OF D.C.B.A. 499 (1958); *Calif. Assembly J.*, Jan. 25, 1957, 1068-77 (lawyers' views on similar state statute).

[8]Cf. N.Y. SPECIAL LEGISLATIVE COMMITTEE ON INTEGRITY AND ETHICAL STANDARDS IN GOVERNMENT, REPORT, N.Y. Legis. Doc. No. 39, 177th sess. (1954); Zbranck & Trost, *The Texas Legislator: Hon. Solon and Mr. Economic Man*, 35 TEXAS L. REV. 113 (1956); Note, 19 TEXAS B.J. 64 (1956); Note, 98 U. PA. L. REV. 412 (1950); Note, 2 WAYNE L. REV. 237 (1956).

[9]The outstanding bar report is that prepared by Whitney North Seymour's Special ABA Committee on Individual Rights as Affected by National Security, 79 ABA REP. 123 (1954); cf. 82 id. 170 and 329 (1957); 3 N.Y.L. FORUM 210 (1957) (Watkins Case Brief); 32 CALIF. S.B.J. 117 (1957); 30 L.A.B. BULL. 163 (1955). What seems lacking now is any drive for reform legislation comparable to that which characterizes ABA and state bar activity on judicial and administrative reforms.

Except for international tensions that may affect many institutions, I see no harbingers of new relations between American lawyers and their legislatures. As individuals they will continue to contribute greatly; as bar members they will remain less effective (and will affect fewer great issues) than as members of other lobbying and constituent groups.

Should we hope for more, and work toward that end? Should we, for instance, endeavor (1) to improve the quality of the lawyers who become legislators, and (2) to expand the interests and increase the effectiveness of bar groups?

As to the first point, one often hears that "lawyers who seek legislative office are the politician type." Or, "the ablest lawyers, unfortunately, are not in the legislature." To the extent those comments imply that the quality of service by lawyer-legislators is low, changes might be made in legal education. Law schools could not, I suppose, inaugurate courses in Successful Electioneering and Good Legislating; but they could temper the faculty traditions that seem to honor—because "ablest"—the students who as precision experts, first, make the law review; and second, thus qualify themselves to draft corporate indentures and serve other specialized needs of large law firms. Yet I confess my doubt as to the wisdom of manning a legislature with only "ablest" lawyers, however we define that word. Legislatures need men of ability. But they also need men of vision, of integrity, of courage, of sensitivity—and those qualities, along with others that are comparable, are not likely ever to be measured by grades in law school.

As to the possibility of making bar associations more active legislatively, the response to the public's demand for counsel on legislative investigating reforms has been encouraging. I doubt, though, that organized lawyers are anywhere near ready to assume leadership on matters such as bill-passing procedures, money-and-politics controls, or legislative-executive relations. Our ideas are too deeply rooted in court-based traditions. Even Dean Acheson, whose recent *A Citizen Looks at Congress*[10] is a remarkable contribution to legislative literature, this year stated: "I don't think a lawyer can have full judgment unless he has had court experience. That is where the law comes from." Last year at a noble gathering in Westminster Hall, where British and American lawyers joined to honor a common tradition, of six speakers only one—Chief Justice Earl Warren—saw fit to mention our debt to legislative law. Even our folklore seems judicially biased—as, for instance, when we enshrine Lord Coke as Great Judge and not as Great Parliamentarian.[11]

LEGISLATURES AND CLIENTS

Apart from their work as legislators, as aides, and as members of bar groups, lawyers tread legislative paths in pursuit of clients' interests. For both counselor and advocate the main chore involves the legislature's main product, statutes. We have mastered, essentially, the problem of making statutes intelligible and available. Problems of interpretation still plague us, but we have learned that better draftsmanship does not alone solve the difficulties. Statutes could be better drafted, better published, and better codified; but the refinements we shall seek in future years will hardly match the reforms of past years regarding crude drafting and the failure to publish or codify.[12]

[10]ACHESON, A CITIZEN LOOKS AT CONGRESS (1957).

[11]E.g., see Nutting, *Lawyers and the Legislative Process*, 54 W. VA. L. REV. 287, 288 (1952); Akzin, *The Concept of Legislation*, 21 IOWA L. REV. 713, 727 (1936). Mr. Acheson's statement is from the Washington Post, May 2, 1958, p. A14; and Mr. Chief Justice Warren's appears in *The London Meeting: Opening Ceremony in Westminster Hall*, 43 A.B.A.J. 883, 889 (1957).

Catherine Drinker Bowen begins her book THE LION AND THE THRONE (1957) by describing a scene in "this winter of 1953, [when] Edward Coke of Norfolk counted himself fortunate in that the Queen had named him Speaker of her Commons . . . ." *Id.* at 7. The final chapters ("Part III: The Parliament Man") are introduced as follows: "Grieved, humiliated, Coke [having been dismissed on Nov. 14, 1616, as Lord Chief Justice] vanished into the countryside. *Where service to the state was concerned [however], the best of life . . . still lay ahead.*" *Id.* at 393. (Italics added.)

[12]Cf. Lloyd, *The Legislative Reporter of the New York State Bar Association*, 42 A.B.A.J. 964 (1956); *Foundation Plans Four New Research Studies*, Am. Bar

STATUTE MAKING. On behalf of clients, lawyers not only use legislation; they seek it, and they battle against it. Corporations, trade groups, individuals, governments, reformists—all have bills they sponsor or oppose; and they engage attorneys to plead their cause. In years past the arena perhaps seemed perplexing to lawyers who were not of the expert few. At present, though, we have innumerable colleagues who can handle a legislative matter adequately. Each year thousands of them are retained to help plan, draft, revise, promote, and hinder new statutes. For the future I predict, first, that more and more law offices will be made aware of the phenomenon recently analyzed by Professor Cary ("What is the point of litigating a tax case when we can have the statute amended for the same outlay of time and money?");[13] and second, that legislative practice eventually will take its place along with such other routines as tax practice, antitrust practice, and divorce practice.

Bill-passing procedures can be formidable, but so can some other procedures (e.g., corporate reorganization). A legislator's vote may be more variant than the vote of a judge or jury; but attorneys who advise, say, on proxy fights and trade union representation are hardly untrained for those variations. Within legislative halls, counsel are usually not privileged to appear at crucial occasions, such as a committee's executive session or a floor debate; but we

---

News, July 15, 1958, p. 4 ("The fourth new project is a Survey of American Statutory Law, which would explore the feasibility of preparing a digest of state statutory laws comparable to the various available case law digests.").

"Too frequently lawyers blame the difficulties of statutory interpretation on the ineptitude of the legislature." Commissioner v. Shamberg's Estate, 144 F.2d 998, 1006, n.1 (2d Cir. 1944); cf. Dickerson, Legislative Drafting: A Challenge to the Legal Profession, 40 A.B.A.J. 635 (1954); Snyder, What is Wrong With the Codes, 23 BROOKLYN L. REV. 250 (1957); Fuller, Positivism and Fidelity to Law, 71 HARV. L. REV. 630, 661 (1958); Allen, Symbolic Logic: A Razor-Edged Tool for Drafting and Interpreting Legal Documents, 66 YALE J.L. 833 (1957).

[13]Pressure Groups and the Revenue Code: A Requiem in Honor of the Departing Uniformity of the Tax Laws, 68 HARV. L. REV. 745 (1955); cf. Surrey, The Congress and the Tax Lobbyist: How Special Tax Provisions Get Enacted, 70 id. 1145 (1957); Dykstra, Legislative Favoritism Before the Courts, 27 IND. L.J. 38 (1951).

now know (1) that skilled preparation can critically affect those occasions, and (2) that law-trained and ethically bound advocates are uniquely fit to supply the requisite skills.[14]

Concerning the ethics of statute making, these items merit special mention: the art of deliberate ambiguity; the manufacture of legislative intent; the "use [of] means other than those addressed to the reason and understanding"; and the handling of campaign funds.

The art of deliberate ambiguity.—Reed Dickerson, a Columbia graduate who is now a leading practitioner and scholar on legislative drafting, has cautioned that "the draftsman should always do his utmost to make his message clear. . . . Yet it is surprising how many . . . draftsmen are intentionally cagey in setting forth what should be an unvarnished, forthright statement. A more pernicious practice would be hard to find."[15] That comment is too inclusive, I think. The legislature is not a tribunal where, when humanly possible, all disputes as to law should be anticipated. Instead, it fixes guidelines for other tribunals—administrative agencies and courts. If the draftsmen of the guidelines think that certain disputes should not be anticipated in the legislature, for the reason, perhaps, that committee doubts or floor conflict might jeopardize the basic program, I see no perniciousness in shunning the "unvarnished, forthright statement." Deliberate ambiguity is a device for delegating authority to administrators and judges. Its aims may be "good" or "bad," as are the aims generally of its proponents and opponents. Its merits, however, can always be debated and voted on; and its exploitation is thus subject to checks other than ethical.[16] Given the realities of

[14] See Menard, *Proving a Case to the Legislature*, 41 A.B.A.J. 860 (1955); Cohen, *Some Observations on Advocacy: Judicial and Legislative, id.* at 656; Kernochan, *Congressional Processes: Critical Points and Individual "Pressure,"* 37 *id.* 848 (1951); *cf.* Cohen, *The "Good Man" and the Role of Reason in Legislative Law*, 41 CORN. L.Q. 386 (1956).

[15] DICKERSON, LEGISLATIVE DRAFTING 16 (1954).

[16] For an instance where the merits of deliberate ambiguity were debated and voted on see Acheson, *A Word of Praise, The Reporter*, Sept. 5, 1957, p. 8, ("For

legislative combat, I would argue that a draftsman who is loyal to the legislators who are his "clients" need not even flag the ambiguity, for the benefit of his clients' legislative opponents.

The manufacture of legislative intent.—Charles Nutting, editor-in-charge of the *ABA Journal's* Department of Legislation, has extended his comments on "deliberate ambiguity" as follows:

> The great reliance which is placed on extrinsic evidence of legislative intent by federal courts has made it relatively easy to draft a statute in broad or ambiguous terms and then to insert a statement in a committee report which will resolve the ambiguity in such a way as to support an interpretation which, if clearly expressed in the statute, might not have been accepted by the Congress. Mr. Dickerson rightly denounces this practice not only as morally indefensible but also as usurping the legislative function.[17]

Other commentators concur,[18] and a census of items of "manufactured legislative intent" would surely show great expansion in recent years. Personally I detect neither immorality nor usurpation of the legislative function. Judges and administrators have become sophisticated in handling extrinsic aids;[19] and with the qualification mentioned above—that the draftsman be loyal to his "legislator clients"—it seems to me that fair interpretations of vague language are legitimate ploys by whoever are authorized to edit the extrinsic documents. That does not imply, of course,

---

Congress to have directed the executive branch to enforce these incomprehensible statutes would not have advanced civil rights. . . . it would have invited the court to legislate, as all sloppy and vague acts of Congress require it to do, and then, when it does state the law—as it must—bring down upon it the condemnation of large sections of the community. . . . The Senate amendments avoid all this.").

[17]*Legislative Drafting: A Review,* 41 A.B.A.J. 76 (1955).

[18]See citations in NEWMAN & SURREY, LEGISLATION 158-78 (1955).

[19]*Id.* at 646-63; *cf.* Nutting, *The Supreme Court and Extrinsic Aids to Statutory Interpretation,* 43 A.B.A.J. 266 (1957); Breuer, *Legislative Intent and Extrinsic Aids to Statutory Interpretation in New York,* 51 L. LIBRARY J. 2 (1958); Ruud, *Legislative History Research Libraries: A Proposal,* 44 A.B.A.J. 887 (1958); Braucher, *The Legislative History of the Uniform Commercial Code,* 58 COLUM. L. REV. 798, 814 (1958) ("The reader may decide for himself . . . whether it would be wise, in the manner of the 1957 Indiana bill, to enjoin judges from reading such an article as this."); *id.* at 808 ("Use of Comments").

that a judge or administrator is bound by those interpretations. On the contrary, his job is to interpret the words of the statute in the light of all available evidence.

The "use [of] means other than those addressed to the reason and understanding."—The quoted words are from Canon 26 of the ABA Canons of Professional Ethics, which reads as follows:

A lawyer openly, and in his true character, may render professional services before legislative or other bodies, regarding proposed legislation and in advocacy of claims before departments of government, upon the same principles of ethics which justify his appearance before the Courts; but it is unprofessional for a lawyer so engaged to conceal his attorneyship, or to employ secret personal solicitations, or to use means other than those addressed to the reason and understanding, to influence action.[20]

Charles Horsky, author of *The Washington Lawyer* and presently chairman of the ABA Special Committee on Legal Services and Procedure, after noting that Canon 26 has had no pertinent official interpretation, concludes:

Fundamentally, there can be no more basis for a lawyer to obtain the vote of a member of Congress on the basis of friendship, or on the basis of past, present or future favors, then there is for a lawyer to obtain a vote from a judge or a juror on the same basis. The lawyer stands on a different footing from his client. John Smith, the voter, and also the man who favors H.R. 10,000, can with propriety tell his Congressman that the price of Smith's next vote or his next campaign contribution is the Congressman's own vote for H.R. 10,000. . . . [But the] Washington lawyer, or any other lawyer, for that matter, is not the voter. He is retained, and paid, for professional advice and services. But when he is retained, or paid, for his influence or his alleged influence over a member of Congress, regardless of the merits of the issue, he is no longer acting as a lawyer.[21]

If those remarks apply only to the case where a lawyer's influence derives from a debt owed to him by the legislator, the conclusion seems sound. What is meant, however, by the statement

---

[20]ABA Committee on Professional Grievances, Opinions 18 (1957).
[21]The Washington Lawyer 57-58 (1952).

that "there can be no more basis for a lawyer to obtain the vote
of a member of Congress on the basis of friendship, or on the basis
of past, present or future favors, than there is for a lawyer to obtain
a vote from a judge or juror on the same basis"? If the favors come
from the client and not the lawyer, is the lawyer governed by the
same proscriptions that apply to judicial cases? Is it truly unethical
for a lawyer to tell a legislator that the price of the client's next
vote is the legislator's vote? Or might it rather be malpractice were
that fact of political life left unmentioned? In general, should we
not argue that for a politician the facts of political life quite properly are included among "those addressed to the reason and understanding"?

The handling of campaign funds.—The Horsky point is more
troublesome when we consider campaign contributions. He says
that a voter but not a lawyer may tell a legislator that the price of
a campaign contribution is a legislative vote. There is, I suppose,
some borderline where campaign gifts become bribes. Two years
ago a committee of the United States Senate, investigating a lawyer's gift of $2,500 to Senator Francis Case, concluded that even
though "the offer of the contribution was for the purpose of
influencing the Senator's vote . . . there was neither a bribe nor
an attempt to bribe."[22] And the lawyer involved was later charged
merely with failure to file under the Lobbying Act. The committee
argued, however (assuming filing), that "lobbying is proper; contributions are proper—but they must not be combined for an
ulterior purpose." "Ulterior" is a queasy word, and hardly illumi-
nates our quest.

There is no doubt that lawyers on behalf of clients are handling
campaign funds, and there is no doubt that in general the campaign fund problem is the Number One problem of ethics in
government today.[23] My own approach to the problem as a whole

[22]S. REP. No. 1724, 84th Cong., 2d Sess. 9, 7 (1956) cf. Perkins, *Sampling
the Evolution of Social Engineering,* 17 U. PITT. L. REV. 362 (1956).

[23]See Peters, *Political Campaign Financing: Tax Incentives for Small Contributors,* 18 LA. L. REV. 414 (1958). For highly informed comment on President

is that we need rules of disclosure rather than rules of prohibition.[24] I suggest that the same approach would in the long run give us the most practicable reforms as to lawyers' conduct.

INVESTIGATING AND INFLUENCE PEDDLING. Legislative work involves jobs other than statute making, and clients' interests are often at stake in those other jobs. Two kinds of clients whose troubles have been notorious in recent years are unwilling witnesses and favor seekers.

Unwilling witnesses.—At an American Law Institute meeting five years ago, Abe Fortas, of Washington, D.C., asked, with respect to the lawyer for unwilling witnesses, "Where does his duty lie: Is it to lend dubious psychological aid to his client by his paralyzed presence; or does he owe it to his profession and to a decent regard for the traditions of the law to decline to lend himself to this distortion of a cherished right?" He suggested that "the bar might well . . . ponder whether it will permit, without protest, the type of degradation of the right to counsel which is taking place in the hearing rooms of the congressional committees."[25]

In 1958 Congress again dramatized for us this fact: Among the people who can be hurt in an investigation are not merely alleged subversives and "Fifth Amendment criminals," but a variety of individuals such as Bernard Goldfine, Richard Mack, Jimmy Hoffa, Sherman Adams, Professor Schwartz, Admiral Strauss, and John Foster Dulles. Those witnesses and hundreds of others who knew that they, too, were to be grilled have demonstrated, I think, that defense attorneys have a good deal more to offer than "dubious

---

Eisenhower's contrasting of vicuna coats with campaign gifts, see remarks of Sen. Neuberger, 104 CONG. REC. 10555 (daily ed. June 19, 1958); *cf.* Schaffter, *Summary of Recommendations Concerning Campaign Funds, Made by Congressional Committees, 1905-56,* in S. REP. No. 395, 85th Cong., 1st Sess. 275 (1957).

[24]See Newman, *The Supreme Court, Congressional Investigations, and Influence Peddling,* 33 N.Y.U.L. REV. 796, 808 (1958), and *Reflections on Money and Party Politics in Britain,* 10 PARL. AFFAIRS 308, 326 (1957).

[25]Quoted in NEWMAN & SURREY, LEGISLATION 404 (1955).

psychological aid." And notwithstanding some reckless statements by a few aggressive investigators, I think we can prove a right to counsel that does comprehend a good deal more than "his paralyzed presence." In short, are we not now ready to agree that lawyers ought not to refuse their aid to witnesses entangled in the investigative net?

By no means, however, are procedural reforms dispensable. On the contrary, we can be thankful for significant reforms already in effect, and we must struggle for more. In brief summary, though, I would argue that the following list, compiled from Mr. Fortas's comments, is too inclusive:

1. The right of the client to notice of the subjects on which he will be examined, and to consult documents to refresh his recollection

2. The opportunity to question one's client, to cross-examine, to call witnesses, and to object to questions that are "loaded or otherwise improper"

3. Protection (1) from questions that are based on documents not previously made available, or that confuse dates, times, and events, and (2) from publication of résumés or dramatic contradiction of secret testimony

4. Protection from abuse reflecting "considerably less than judicial restraint," and from threats of disciplining addressed to counsel

5. In loyalty or security cases, a finding by the majority of the committee of "probable cause to believe that presently or within the past few years—perhaps three or five years—the person has been engaged in activities inimical to the United States."[26]

---

[26]See Fortas, *Methods of Committees Investigating Subversion: A Critique*, 29 NOTRE DAME LAW. 192, 207-09 (1954); speech quoted *supra* note 25 at 406; *cf.* Newman, *The Supreme Court, Congressional Investigations, and Influence Peddling*, 33 N.Y.U.L. REV. 796, 799 (1958).

There is no space here for an analysis of desirable committee rules. I present the Fortas list only to show that he, along with many other distinguished leaders of the bar, would go far in according legislative witnesses the rights of judicial defendants. For me there is too great danger that by copying adjudicative techniques we will imperil legislative goals. Further, in opposition to the dicta in *Watkins* v. *United States*, decided by the Supreme Court in June, 1957,[27] I contend (1) that sometimes there is a legislative purpose in exposing the private affairs of individuals, and (2) that the informing function of a legislature includes much more than merely advising citizens as to the peccadillos of their government servants. I endorse Dean Edward Levi's comment that "the legislative process . . . includes the stimulation of public opinion and it may include the conduct of political warfare. The legislative inquiry functions in such a world."[28]

Favor seekers.—We take it for granted that a lawyer does not ask legislators to help his client in a court proceeding. Are we reversing the assumption for agency proceedings? Are we approaching the point where a lawyer, to assure a client full administrative protection, must seek legislative aid?

Most lawyers would regard that claim as preposterous, on the basis of their own experience with tax cases, corporation commission and SEC cases, Labor Board cases, public utility cases, workmen's compensation cases, and similar proceedings. Over-all, legislative interference in agency matters is still atypical—though in a few fields it is routine, and in many fields there are notorious incidents. Among his first inquiries ten years ago as editor of the *ABA Journal's* Department of Legislation, Professor Harry Jones asked whether modern Congressmen were really legislators or were rather "constituent case-takers." He concluded:

[27] 354 U.S. 178.
[28] *Congressional Investigations: Foreword*, 18 U. Chi. L. Rev. 421-22 (1951).

Pending some forthright attack on the errand-running problem, there is urgent need for greater restraint on the part of lawyers and other responsible citizens in soliciting the personal intervention of members of Congress in administrative and other non-legislative matters.[29]

We now know that constituent case-taking is a function not performed by American legislators alone.[30] My conclusion regarding a "forthright attack on the errand-running problem" is that the bulk of such cases can wisely be limited only by rules that legislators themselves make, to protect their offices from inundation. One such rule would be that requests must be in writing. Another would result in the use of form letters by the legislator, when he forwards the constituent's complaint to the agency and then forwards the agency's reply to the constituent. A third would require, in effect, that administrative remedies first be exhausted.

That last requirement, it seems to me, practicably formulates what Professor Jones had in mind when he called for "greater restraint on the part of lawyers." In the spring of 1958 I witnessed the progress and final denial of a meritorious claim that was prejudiced, I believe, by an unskilled lawyer's assumption that from the start he should exploit a chance to demand special service from two Senators, as well as from two recently retired, high-placed agency officials. The result was that a considerable number of nonretired, non-high-placed officials, some of whom had less than love for at least one of the Senators, bared their teeth and stiffened their spines. One can only speculate as to unwon cases, but surely a good cause is often prejudiced by forcing adjudicators to fret about the political pressures instead of the merits.

[29]34 A.B.A.J. 912, 913 (1948); cf. Newman & Keaton, *Congress and the Faithful Execution of Laws: Should Legislators Supervise Administrators?*, 41 CALIF. LAW REV. 565 (1953).

[30]Concerning Russian M.P.s, "The only similarity with parliamentarians elsewhere would seem to be their constituents' belief that by writing letters to them they can get them to intercede with the 'authorities' on their behalf." Beloff, Book Review of SCOTT, RUSSIAN POLITICAL INSTITUTIONS, 11 PARL. AFFAIRS 372, 375 (1958). For Britain see Newman, *Reflections on Money and Party Politics in Britain*, 10 id. 308, 312 (1957).

Lawyers would do well, I suggest, to restrict their legislative appeals to those cases where administrative error seems clear and judicial relief is inadequate. On the other hand, we should be wary of attempts formally to curtail legislative intervention. When agency action is required to be based on a record, communications from a legislator should be part of that record; and they should be subject to rebuttal, too—like all other communications involving witnesses or advocates. Even when agency action is not on the record, the legislators' letters (and memos of their phone calls) should be in a public file, wherefrom they can be rebutted informally.[31] But these again, like the money-and-politics reforms we discussed above, are rules of disclosure and not rules of prohibition.

The right of citizens to petition legislators and the right of legislators to police bureaucrats are precious. Let us not impair those rights by simple transposition of rules we have worked out to protect judges and juries. Influence can be pernicious, but ignorance is worse. In the words of Woodrow Wilson, "The country must remain in embarrassing, crippling ignorance of the very affairs which it is most important that it should understand and direct . . . unless Congress both scrutinize these things [the acts and the disposition of officials] and sift them by every form of discussion."[32]

LEGISLATURES AND THE PUBLIC INTEREST

As lawyers our interest in the legislative process is not confined to clients' concerns, bar activities, and personal aims to serve in the legislature. Among all citizens we tend to be relatively well informed, relatively articulate, and relatively heeded in our demands that legislators represent their constituents effectively, in the public interest.

[31]In a recent poll of Congressmen, among 155 replies 87.5 percent answered "yes" to the question: "Do you think all communications between members of Congress and members of Federal regulatory agencies on a specific case should be made part of the public file on that case?" 16 CONG. Q. WEEKLY REP. 498 (1958).

[32]Quoted in United States v. Rumely, 345 U.S. 41, 43 (1953).

For making law and otherwise declaring the public interest, recent decades indicate that the basic procedures of the legislature are fixed and unlikely to suffer revision. The most respected champion of change, Woodrow Wilson, preached inconsequentially his thesis that cabinet forms of government should be adapted for use here. George Norris and his partisans achieved only a single success in their campaign for a unicameral system. Even within accepted constitutional frameworks, proposals more than peripheral seem destined for small impact—such as the recent flurry regarding increased party responsibility and the recurring challenges to "rural domination."[33]

Yet to serve the public interest, though we may be spared the burdens of structural change, we shall necessarily deal with crucial questions that relate to power and to function. To illustrate this concluding point I shall briefly discuss three issues: (1) the role of Congress in international and military affairs, vis-à-vis the Executive; (2) the role of legislatures in lawmaking, vis-à-vis courts and administrative agencies; and (3) the role of legislatures in preserving personal freedom, vis-à-vis all other legal institutions.

Congress, foreign policy, and military affairs.—Since World War II there have been times when isolationist voices within Congress seemed powerful as well as shrill. At those times many editors and other molders of opinion argued that the cold war and the H-bomb and missiles all meant that, from now on, we should

[33]See McMurray, *The Responsible Majority: Some Reflections on Political Parties,* 11 W. POL. Q. 175 (1958); Carleton, *Our Congressional Elections: In Defense of the Traditional System,* 70 POL. SCI. Q. 341 (1955); Morstein Marx, *Legislation, Representation, and the Party System,* 14 U. PITT. L. REV. 151 (1953); BAKER, RURAL VERSUS URBAN POLITICAL POWER (1955); Kennedy, *The Shame of the States,* N. Y. Times, May 18, 1958, § 6 (Magazine) p. 12; Wechsler, *The Political Safeguards of Federalism,* 54 COLUM. L. REV. 543, 551 (1954).

"What are the prospects for action . . . on the unfinished business of congressional reorganization? My answer is that they are not bright at the present time. There is scattered support in Congress for particular items on the agenda of reform but no sign of such widespread backing as preceded passage of the Legislative Reorganization Act.' Galloway, *Congressional Reorganization: Unfinished Business,* in THE PHILOSOPHY AND POLICIES OF WOODROW WILSON, 214, 226 (Latham ed. 1958); cf. THE AMERICAN ASSEMBLY, THE FORTY-EIGHT STATES 139 (1955).

put our trust in the President, and not in the national legislature, for leadership in the Nuclear Age.

In 1958 there was little of that kind of talk. I wish the change mirrored a considered judgment that, obviously, *both* the President and the Congress owe us leadership. I fear, though, that it rather reflects some doubts concerning Lebanon and Formosa, some dashed hopes as to South America and India and Indonesia, and some disappointments arising from the presidential handling of the Little Rock and other racial crises.

This nation will always witness attacks on its political institutions that result from citizens' substantive views. I am puzzled, however, by a seemingly general willingness to endorse Executive claims without statement of their congressional counterparts. Thus, "The Commander-in-Chief clearly must be permitted to rank his own officers." But does that mean that Admiral Rickover must be denied a promotion? Similarly, though "it is the President who appoints ambassadors," should the Senate, exercising its power to advise and consent, hesitate to query the qualifications of a Max Gluck for Ceylon or a Scott McLeod for Ireland? And though "military requirements govern our need for more plutonium capacity, and . . . the Department of Defense . . . advises . . . that the necessity for more plutonium for military purposes is not established," does it follow that Congress, exercising its lawmaking power, should not authorize a $145,000,000 plutonium reactor?[34] I say no. For the Congress, as well as the President and his generals and admirals and the Secretary of State, has constitutional duties regarding military affairs and foreign policy; and those

[34]See Time Magazine, July 28, 1958, p. 14; 104 CONG. REC. 15103 (daily ed. Aug. 6, 1958), remarks of Representative Holifield; *cf.* Rep. Vinson's report on accomplishments of the Armed Services Committee, *id.* A7194 (daily ed. Aug. 11, 1958); Barkdoll dispatch, *Anderson Says U.N. Atomic Report Destroys Some "Pet Theories" of AEC,* Washington Post, Aug. 11, 1958, p. A7; Leach, *Comment,* in GOVERNMENT UNDER LAW 224 (Sutherland ed. 1956); Huntington, *Comment,* in *id.* at 228; "104 CONG. REC. 15726 (daily ed. Aug. 12, 1958) (remarks of Senator M. Smith); and see Marcy, *The Legislative Process and Its Relation to Foreign Policy,* The Torch, July 1956, p. 9; Rovere, *Letter From Washington,* The New Yorker, Mar. 23, 1957, pp. 125-35.

duties should be performed effectively, which sometimes means aggressively.

Ernest Griffith, director of the Federal Legislative Reference Service, has referred in *Congress: Its Contemporary Role* to the "myth . . . that in practice the President is almost completely determinative in our international relations except for the Senate's alleged role as obstructor." He suggests by way of refutation that "international policy will succeed only if there is a deep, underlying solidarity in popular support—a solidarity which Congress can develop as well as register. That Congress has been able to do this in large measure is remarkable evidence of its current sense of responsibility and maturity."[35]

A parallel myth is detectable regarding the sanctity of the President's manse and his bureaucrats' rights of privacy. As to those problems lawyers' views have recently become paramount, and the paramount lawyer in the 1950s seems to be the United States Attorney General. Personally, I do not see why we should ascribe to the founding fathers a rule requiring the President's special assistant for science and technology to decline to testify before Congress. I question, too, whether in 1787 the founding fathers had in mind that when called upon to justify his conduct Sherman Adams would appear before congressional inquirers as a matter of courtesy only. Finally, with respect to the privacy of administrative communications and the White House pronouncement of May 17, 1954 (that originated as a tactical weapon in the flamboyant McCarthy-Army hearings but now, apparently, is to be enshrined as a basic document of constitutional democracy), I join with Judge Learned Hand in this inquiry: "Is it not possible to argue that Congress, especially now that the appropriations for the armed forces are the largest items of the budget, should be allowed to inquire in as much detail as it wishes, not only how

[35]GRIFFITH, CONGRESS: ITS CONTEMPORARY ROLE 101, 104 (1956).

past appropriations have been spent, but in general about the conduct of the national defense?"[36]

Legislatures and lawmaking.—Statutes are not ideal laws. They are typically the product of compromise; they are often enacted hastily, without due hearing of evidence and argument; and the crucial votes sometimes bear no relation whatever to the merits.

Nonetheless, there seems to be agreement that legislatures are better entrusted with lawmaking than are courts and agencies. A century ago the courts may have been preeminent, and during the decade that began in 1933 a strong case was made for administrative rules. The judge-backers have been overwhelmed, however; and even the most ardent New Dealers no longer argue that the public interest is best served, consistently, by broad grants of rule-making power bound only by vague standards.

Some areas we still leave to judges, either because there is little choice (as with constitutional law) or because we believe they perform creditably in them (property, tort, and contract law). But for most public law (*e.g.*, licensing and taxation) we accord courts only interpretive powers; and our constant toying with model statutes, uniform statutes, and the various codes of various states demonstrates that with private law, too, we desire at least legislative supplementation. Within the legal fraternity it is not yet even agreed that courts should fix all their procedural rules.[37]

The boldest recent bid for judicial lawmaking came, I think, on May 31, 1955, when the Supreme Court assigned to many

[36]THE BILL OF RIGHTS 17 (1958). "Killian . . . has declined, as a member of the President's staff, to testify before Congress." Time Magazine, July 14, 1958, p. 20. *Compare* Rogers, *Constitutional Law: The Papers of the Executive Branch,* 44 A.B.A.J. 941 (1958), *with Hearings Before Subcommittee on Government Information of House Committee on Government Operations,* 84th Cong. 2d Sess., pt. 3 (1956). See Notes, 18 PUB. AD. REV. 145 and 149 (1958).

[37]*Compare* Joiner & Miller, *Rules of Practice and Procedure: A Study of Judicial Rule Making,* 55 MICH. L. REV. 623 (1957), *The Rule-Making Function and the Judicial Conference of the United States,* 21 F.R.D. 117 (1958), *with* N. J. COMMISSION TO STUDY THE IMPROVEMENT OF THE LAW OF EVIDENCE, REPORT 5 (1956) *and* Louisell, Book Review (MOORE'S FEDERAL PRACTICE), 66 YALE J.L. 164, 166 (1956).

federal district judges the task of prescribing school laws for racial integration. State statutes, local ordinances, school board regulations—all are to be checked for compliance with norms to be set by judicial decree. "The courts may consider problems related to administration arising from the physical condition of the school plant, the school transportation system, personnel, revision of school districts and attendance areas into compact units to achieve a system of determining admission to the public schools on a nonracial basis, and *revision of local laws and regulations* which may be necessary in solving the foregoing problems."[38] Should that experiment be successful, we can at least abandon the doctrine labeled "Difficulty of Supervision," so picturesquely used by law teachers to enliven the course in Equity. Should the experiment be spectacularly successful, we might even acquire new respect for the courts as public-lawmakers.

With respect to lawmaking generally, in the future I hope we shall be better guided in our choice of "enactor" than we have been in the past. We profess a goal that would focus legislative attention on "policy" and not "detail"; yet we complacently accept tax statutes and hundreds of other statutes that seem to ooze details. Ignoring a rich experience, we are almost capricious when we choose statute making instead of rule making. We are similarly unled when we choose adjudication rather than promulgation as the vehicle for lawmaking. Justice Jackson once argued passionately for promulgation, but he had few facts and a fragile theory.[39] On these problems, perhaps more than on any other mentioned in this paper, I feel we might benefit from empirical data and scientifically based theory. Here, particularly, lawyers should seek the aid of behavioral scientists and political theorists.[40] It seems inex-

[38]Brown v. Board of Educ. 349 U.S. 294, 300-01 (1955) (Italics added).

[39]SEC v. Chenery Corp., 332 U.S. 194, 212 (1947), DAVIS, ADMINISTRATIVE LAW 557 (1951).

[40]For recent evidence of the capacity of behaviorists and theorists to aid us on legislative matters in general, see Robinson, *Decision Making in the House Rules Committee*, 3 ADMIN. SCI. Q. 73 (1958); Riker, *The Paradox of Voting and*

cusable that we are still so ignorant on the question, "By whom and how are laws *best* made?"

Legislatures and personal freedom.—Recently, while scanning the legislative history of personal freedoms, I examined Justice Douglas's splendid *Almanac of Liberty.* To my chagrin there was but one entry in the index under the word "parliament," and that read: "Parliament, encroachment on liberties by." Similarly, the first of several entries under "Congress" was "Congress, in contempt of." Other entries included "direct election of Senators" and "immunity of members," but otherwise they led me to hardly inspiring topics such as "The Great Compromise," the Twentieth Amendment, The United States Bank, and "Judicial Supremacy."[41] I suspect that Justice Douglas is not the only scholar who in the 1950s, presumably without design and surely without malice, might review the current legislative history of freedoms under two main headings: "Legislatures, encroachment on Liberties by," and "Judicial supremacy, thank God!"

Fifty-four years ago Justice Holmes cautioned: "It must be remembered that legislatures are ultimate guardians of the liberties . . . of the people in quite as great a degree as the courts."[42] One hundred and eighty-four years ago, the First Continental Con-

---

Congressional Rules for Voting on Amendments, 52 AM. POL. SCI. REV. 349 (1958); Note, *The Roles of Congressional Leaders: National Party vs. Constituency,* 46 *id.* 1024 (1952); *cf.* Kort, *Reply to Fisher's "Mathematical Analysis of Supreme Court Decisions,"* 52 *id.* 339 (1958). Readers should watch for reports now being published by Buchanan, Eulau, Ferguson, and Wahlke for the State Legislative Research Project of the SSRC Committee on Political Behavior.

"The areas of study in Political Science differ significantly in the extent to which they have thus far been subjected to the behavioralist approach. The . . . least studied are perhaps public law, jurisprudence, and judicial affairs." WALDO, POLITICAL SCIENCE IN THE U.S.A. 23 (1956).

[41]AN ALMANAC OF LIBERTY 403 and 395 (1954). To be fair I must concede that under "Parliamentary immunity" Justice Douglas discusses the Peter Wentworth and John Elliot episodes, relating to the Bill of Rights provision "That the Freedom of Speech, and Debates or Proceedings in Parliament, ought not to be impeached or questioned in any Court or Place out of Parliament." *Id.* at 265-66; *cf. id.* at 175 (The English Bill of Rights).

[42]Missouri, K. & T. Ry. v. May, 194 U.S. 267, 270 (1904).

gress resolved, "That the foundation of English liberty, and of all free government, is a right in the people to participate in their legislative council."[43] At this point I will not recount the episodes that have led us now to underplay the legislature, and overplay the courts, in freedom's cause. I will, though, stress a few facts that to me seem disturbing.

Do we not blame legislators for violations of liberties that in fact are the product of executive and adjudicative acts? Police brutality and illegal searches and seizures and vagrancy abuses, for instance, are hardly ever prescribed by statute. And for each case where a censorship law has been held void, are there not scores of other cases holding merely that public officials stretched the words of the law too far? And though the McCarthy, Jenner, and Un-American Activities Committees cruelly caricatured the problems of loyalty and security, is it not true (1) that not Congress but rather three administrations invented and expanded the loyalty-security program, and (2) that the total number of people who have suffered from legislative exposure of their loyalty-security sins is far less than the number who have suffered from agency action?

With respect to judges, we castigate the legislators who are now attacking decisions where the Supreme Court's pro-freedom bias has been noteworthy. But is it not significant that in 1958 the majority of legislators proved their own bias, and again reflected the legislature's great tradition of freedom, by refusing to reverse

[43]Resolution 4 of Oct. 14, 1774, 1 AMERICAN ARCHIVES (4th Series) 911 (1837). This quotation is not indexed in *An Almanac of Liberty*, though others from the Oct. 14th Resolution of the Continental Congress are. See *id.* at 109; *cf. id.* at 121 (" 'The first grand right,' the Letter [of Oct. 16 to the People of Quebec] says, is representative government, making people 'ruled by laws, which they themselves approve, not by edicts of men over whom they have no controul.' "). Also see DOUGLAS, BEING AN AMERICAN 45 (1948); *id.* at 98 ("We are apt to think of legislatures, of the police, or of other agents of the executive as the tyrants to be feared. But judges too can be tyrants."); and *cf.* ANGLE, CREATED EQUAL? THE COMPLETE LINCOLN-DOUGLAS DEBATES OF 1858 at 219 (1958) ("Is not Congress, itself, under obligation to give legislative support to any right that is established in the United States Constitution?").

those decisions? And how well the record of that majority compares with the record of (1) the police and prosecutors and other officials whose views in the specific cases were otherwise, and (2) the many trial and appellate judges who did not have the wit to anticipate the Supreme Court's vigorous stand.

The greatest cost of undervaluing the legislative gift to freedom, I believe, is exemplified by contrasting those energies that are aimed at adjudicative victory with those aimed at legislative reform. Previously I have mentioned Professor Cary's comments, "What is the point of litigating a tax case when we can have the statute amended for the same outlay of time and money?" That observation is by no means limited to tax battles; and what might we have gained for liberty had we learned that lesson! Loyalty-security supplies my best example. For at least fifteen years we have been barraged by editorials, exposés, law review articles, scholarly reports, bar reports, government reports—and some judicial opinions that tend mostly either to endorse the program or to bite at its fringes. But as Justice Traynor has asked in another context, "Where is the infantry that will undertake the task of patient persuasion to convert splendid studies into working laws?"[44] What if those editorialists and scholars and reporters and brief writers had allotted a fair share of their talents to legislative reform? Action in the Congress would not have been assured. But can we criticize the Congress for inaction when there was not practicably available even any draft of reformed law to serve as a base for legislative activity?[45]

CONCLUSION

My arguments here have concerned issues that, more or less, are headline items for law-trained readers. Singly, the items may

---

[44]*Unjustifiable Reliance*, 42 MINN. L. REV. 11, 24 (1957).

[45]Cf. Mankiewicz, Mangum, & Moody, *The Federal Loyalty-Security Program: A Proposed Statute*, 44 CALIF. L. REV. 72 (1956); and see Smith & Cotter, *Freedom and Authority in the Amphibial State*, 1 MIDWEST J. POL. SCI. 40, 58 (1957).

be of less than centennial significance. To mark 1958, perhaps, one should have searched for legislative events to match the Lincoln-Douglas debates in 1858, or for symbols in the history of legislatures such as Queen Elizabeth's succession four hundred years ago and Oliver Cromwell's death three hundred years ago.

Taken together the items here discussed show a great need for refocusing our legal look. Now that we do participate in legislating for our bar associations and our clients and our causes, and not just for personal political gain, we can see that legislative disputes are sometimes like court disputes—that common law parallels are sometimes apt for procedures, techniques, and ethics. What we frequently overlook are immense historical and functional differences. Legislatures must not now be tailored to the habits of court lawyers—just as centuries ago, happily, they were not tailored to the habits of court councilors. Courtesies, respects, moralities, and competencies that are elementary in adjudicating may be quite inapt for statute making. For legislatures we assume a context of politics, elections, lobbying, and parliamentary strategy. The channels of those activities need some governing, and many improvements are practicable. But in designing improvements let us remember that the legislature is a unique legal institution, and a grand one for those who sponsor Bill of Rights ideals and twentieth-century democracy.

Comment

BY CLIFFORD P. CASE
UNITED STATES SENATOR FROM NEW JERSEY

Professor Newman has given us a provocative and useful discussion of our legislative process, one that is especially interesting to a legislator. With his fundamental points I am in general agreement, though on several we differ in degree.

The basic premise of his paper is that the legislature is a unique institution, that is, it is unique as a legal institution. This, of course, is true. Yet, while we agree with the truth of that statement, I think we do not always remember its implications. Very often after we say, "Yes, that's true," we proceed to talk about the legislative process using patterns and approaches which are more appropriate to other fields—the judiciary, for instance.

Now, the uniqueness of our legislative institution is its political nature. Accepting Mr. Truman's definition of a statesman as a "dead politician," legislature members are, first of all, live practitioners of politics, who work in a context of partisanship and always with an election impending. Four years ago I thought six years was eternity, but it seems just tomorrow today.

There is a somewhat snide implication, I think, about the present administration in Professor Newman's paper. It is in the suggestion that perhaps the legislature appears in a good light because the administration looks bad this year. I shall resist the impulse to rebut this point by point, though it could be done on a massive scale. I have spent too much time doing exactly that during the last few months in another more useful context.

From the standpoint of our discussion and related, I think, to the point, I want to take some exception to the suggestion (and I make the assumption only for the purpose of this discussion) that if there is a weak president, the legislature may take his place. It simply is not possible for a strong legislature to take the place of a weak president.

Generally speaking, a legislature cannot lead. Though I state this somewhat out of my personal experience, I have had confirmation of its validity from an article by Max Freedman in the Manchester Guardian. He said, in substance, that in the turbulent areas of Europe and Asia where problems demand swift response, Congress deceives itself if it thinks it can take a leading role. It cannot make policy. It can criticize; it can correct; it can obstruct. It cannot lead.

I think this is true and, while I am a cultist for the legislature, having been in the thick of legislative matters for quite a while, I also see its limitations, both in fact and potentially. I do not want to have legislators charged with more than they can do. Legislators from the beginning of time have been the butt of cartoonists and caricaturists, and I want to add nothing to the fuel they already have by admitting a failure to meet expectations when the expectations are overoptimistic and unreasonable. Legislators can explore, on a long-range basis, and inform public opinion and can define the framework in which policy—long-range policy—must be carried out, but they cannot fix policies.

Even in those cases where it seems that Congress has made policy, by passing laws over the President's veto (the Taft-Hartley Act, for example), I think it will be found that in almost every instance Congress has, in fact, not made policy. It has merely reflected a settled, massive public opinion in a given area. Certainly this was true when the Wagner Act was first adopted and it was true later when Taft-Hartley was enacted. And I suggest that, despite the outcry still made, more or less pro forma, by organized labor about Taft-Hartley, the fact that there has never been a serious effort to amend it shows it was the establishment in law of a well-settled public recognition of the need for just such action as was taken. But this is hardly the making of policy. This is the occasional registering of policy already outlined.

There are many reasons why Congress cannot both make and carry out policy. I think the chief one is probably the nature of our political system in the United States. Our parties do not have the fixed character that many people assume they do. A great part of the public generally does not realize this. It continues to ask, "Why aren't you a good Republican?" or "a good Democrat?"

We are not disciplined. We have no ideology, and I am thankful that we do not. This ramshackle, vague, amorphous operation of ours meets the real test of a political system: it works. To the devil with logic! We have what is right for us. I would not change an iota of it, and I am glad to see that the political scientists are coming around to this view. There is less demand among them for rationality in our political system. Leave rationality to other people and let us keep a system that works.

But our system does mean that Congress cannot be relied on to make policy in any sustained or broad sense. Certainly it cannot be relied on to conduct the operations of foreign affairs except in so far as it can occasionally obstruct, correct, perhaps—and even complain. These are very useful legislative functions, but they follow policy. They do not create it.

I want to make it clear that I am not suggesting that individual members of Congress and the Senate do not have a very great responsibility in all matters of policy. They do—by talking, by making use of their marvelous forum where, if one has anything to say, people will listen. The obligation to use this forum is enormous. Most of us there do not take the obligation as seriously as we should, though there are some who serve it to the fullest extent.

As individuals and as groups we have an obligation to initiate suggestions for policy in all fields, whether it is a new program in the field of education or health, or one in some other area. But as members of parties we have no such obligation. Furthermore, we cannot have one. As an institution Congress can seldom initiate and can never carry out policy, particularly, as Max Freedman pointed out, in such areas as foreign policy.

Because Congress is a political institution, it has many varied problems, most of which are not solely legal. Professor Newman has, rightly, I think, singled out for particular attention in the ethics of statute making: the "use [of] means other than those addressed to the reason and understanding" and the handling of campaign funds. He discusses these means under the heading "Legislatures and Clients." I do not criticize him for his position, for with tongue in cheek he was quoting from the ABA Canons of Professional Ethics. I am sure that Professor Newman would agree that the significance of these means reaches far beyond influence peddling, for the problem of the sources of campaign funds and the purposes of their expenditures runs, if I may use a bad pun, like a golden thread through the whole fabric of our political life. But I am, I may say, in hearty accord with Professor Newman's advocacy of the "need for rules of disclosure rather than rules of prohibition" as the intelligent approach to problems of this sort.

In a way, he may not go far enough. My own experience on the Committee of Rules, working on campaign expenditures legislation, has convinced me that the principle of disclosure should apply more broadly than even he suggests, taking account not only of elections but of primaries and primary campaigns.

I do not think I would place much reliance on the suggestion that Theodore Roosevelt made and that my very highly esteemed colleague, Senator Neuberger, now urges: that we have election campaigns financed at public expense. I am afraid that it would be extremely complicated even for general elections; and for primary elections I fail to see how it could possibly be done. I certainly agree with the intention, but if the freedom of individuals to contribute toward the campaigns of the candidates of their choice is restricted, then the proposal is not feasible, especially in primary campaigns where it is most important.

On the one hand, it is difficult to see why anybody who has a notion that he has the right to campaign should be given money enough to put on a campaign for a party office or for nomination by a party. On the other, I think it essential that individuals be permitted to accept private contributions, since without outside money entrenched party organizations will never be broken into by bright young people, like Nelson Rockefeller, for instance.

Beyond that, I know that Professor Newman would agree to the desirability of requiring all candidates for Federal office, as well as civilian officials, legislative employees, and military officers above a certain level of salary, to file an annual report showing all sources of income, all assets, all dealings in property, and all financial transactions of every kind.

I came to that view with reluctance, but I hold it very firmly now. Professor Newman not only agrees—he wrote to me about it—but suggests that we should make it very clear that though all candidates and other government personnel at a salary level of, say, $12,500 or $15,000 would have to report their financial status, there should be no implication that it is all right for people under that salary level to have their hand in anybody's pocket or in the public till. Of course that is true. It is purely a mechanical matter. If there were too many reports of this kind nobody would ever be able to look at all of them, and they would be buried almost more effectively than if there had not been any.

Disclosure is, of course, the great remedy, and the only one I can think of for the most difficult problem of all, one I have had to face, as a practical matter: the Congressman's relations with the executive departments on behalf of his constituents. It is very difficult to determine what to do in many of these cases. Some people say that a legislator should keep hands off entirely. That is impossible. As with all people, there are some bureaucrats who are lazy. There are also some, like human beings in general, who are subject to other influences, even the relatively benign influences of representatives in Congress from other states. This is the most usual sort, of course, and one finds that he has to fight for his own constituents' interests because the gentlemen from other states are doing the same thing for theirs. But how does one know when and how far it is proper to go? I do not. The only solution I can think of is to have all contacts with the executive departments a matter of public record, so that the public can decide what is proper. I should certainly like to have such help with many of the problems that come to me—and they come all the time.

Commenting in brief, I do think Professor Newman's point on the importance of the legislature as the ultimate guardian of the liberties of the people is valid, but again, I do not want him or anybody else to give us legislators too much credit or to rely on us too much—certainly not exclusively. Since we are the expression of the popular will, so we are, naturally, sensitive to public opinion, which makes us tend to become fearful. Fear of unpopularity and of the unpopular opens the door for intimidation. Nobody wants to be against mother or God. Therefore, nobody wants to appear antiveteran or pro-Communist, antilabor or even anti-small business.

Whenever an issue is raised in these black and white terms, the result is almost a foregone conclusion. Unfortunately the issue can often be put, or can be made to be seen, in those terms, which is almost the same thing. Serious reservations about the conduct and the value of much of the work of some of our committees is never reflected in House votes on appropriations for those committees.

Another example to illustrate why we must not be relied on beyond our capacities as a Congress is the ease with which Congress overrode the veto of the Internal Security Act. I still remember with a rather red face the hours, the many days, as a matter of fact, that the Senate spent in the Second Session of the 85th Congress affirming our determination that the country should never surrender to any foreign power. Taking time and energy for such a meaningless resolution was utterly ridiculous, and yet, the matter was raised and had to be voted on. Naturally everbody voted for it. Many people felt impelled to take the floor to declare our undying resistance to any such notion.

I hope that despite the brevity of the examples I have made clear why we must not be counted on too much. We are subject to the weaknesses of all political officers.

Finally, I should like to demur very lightly to some of the implications in several of Professor Newman's points. I do not think quite as highly as he does of deliberate ambiguity in legislative drafting. I think its value is quite doubtful, on the whole, although it is perhaps all right to have the rule as stated by the people he quotes and then to have an exception once in a while, which, of course, would be the case.

I have even greater doubt as to the soundness of the points he makes about the correctness of the use of means other than those that appeal to reason. I even question whether it is proper for a client, let alone a lawyer on behalf of his client, to suggest to me that my vote on a pending measure will determine his vote in the next election, or, more specifically, his willingness to open his pocketbook to me for a political contribution. In practice I would throw any person who made such a threat to me out of my office, even if I needed the money very much. I know perfectly well, however, that this is just a use by Professor Newman of a peda-gogical device for shocking people into taking some action. It is an old trick, and with it I think he has fired a little bit of a spark in me.

Comment

BY PAUL R. HAYS
NASH PROFESSOR OF LAW
COLUMBIA UNIVERSITY SCHOOL OF LAW

Professor Newman's discussion of the legislative process is a dis-tillation drawn with wisdom from broad knowledge of the field. Some of the points he has made seem to me particularly challeng-ing, and it is on these that I shall comment.

Professor Newman does not foresee for the future any funda-mental changes in the structure and procedures of our legislative tribunals. "Recent decades," he says, "indicate that the basic procedures of the legislature are fixed and unlikely to suffer revision. . . . Even within accepted constitutional frameworks, proposals more than peripheral seem destined for small impact."

He cites the failure of the proposal for a unicameral legislature to win favor outside Nebraska, and what he calls "the recent flurry regarding increased party responsibility and the recurring challenges to 'rural domination.'"

But there are enormous pressures developing as the result of profound readjustments in the distribution of population, pressures which in the course of time must almost inevitably lead to demands for major rearrangements of political structure. The population shift which has resulted from "the explosion of the metropolis" has fathered a host of new political, economic, and sociological problems. New geographical groupings and area arrangements are obviously required. The recent basic reorganization of the government of Miami and the surrounding areas is a case in point. The issue of "rural domination," as that issue has been phrased, may already be outmoded by this even more insistent issue. With the impetus of the 1960 census,[46] the need for regional planning, for areal administration, for political units determined rationally on the basis of demographic, economic, and sociological considerations will tend to lead, I believe, not only to major changes in legislative reapportionment but even eventually to significant reallocations of the legislative power itself.[47] With the advent of regional planning boards and area-wide administrative units there will surely be developments in the direction of legislative autonomy for the new political subdivisions. The governance of a New York metropolitan region, which would include northern New Jersey and southern Connecticut, as well as Westchester County and most, if not all, of Long Island, will clearly not be left to the legislatures of the three states as those legislatures are presently constituted.

[46]On the possibilities of court response to the pressure for reapportionment, see Lewis, *Legislative Apportionment and the Federal Courts*, 71 HARV. L. REV. 1057 (1958).

[47]See Gulick, *Metropolitan Organization*, 314 ANNALS AM. ACAD. OF POL. AND SOC. SCIENCE 57 (1957); Sayre, *"Urbanism and Government, 1957-1977": A Rejoinder*, *id.* at 82.

Professor Newman's very interesting treatment of the subject of the relationship of lawyers to legislation suggests to me another emphasis in legislative development—a development toward what I may call legislative professionalism. I am not referring here to the important function of the technicians in statutory draftsmanship, in which Columbia can so proudly claim the roles of both founder and leader,[48] but rather to the progressive institutionalization of the work of preparing legislation and legislative programs. In this respect we are witnessing a trend which I am certain will have a profound effect not only on the quality of legislation, but on its character, scope, and content.

The importance of the part played in the legislative procedure of Congress by the committee staffs has been constantly increasing since the adoption of the Reorganization Act,[49] and the trend has been the same in several of the states which have made provision for streamlining their committees and for providing them with more adequate staff assistance. When Congress and the state legislatures have adopted appropriate personnel policies,[50] we shall have an increasingly large group of civil servants of long service who are not only experts on legislative procedures but specialists in problems, for example, of education, mental health, highway construction, the ICC, the SEC, the NLRB, or the UN.

Another area of increasing professionalism is in the legislative sections of the various departments and administrative authorities. Most important legislative proposals originate or are prepared in these sections.

The development of these professional legislative staffs has an important bearing on the work of the lawyer about which Professor Newman has written. In great measure that work will consist of consultation with and attempts to convince the staff people who

[48]FOUNDATION FOR RESEARCH IN LEGAL HISTORY: A HISTORY OF THE SCHOOL OF LAW, COLUMBIA UNIVESITY 255-58 (1955).
[49]See GROSS, THE LEGISLATIVE STRUGGLE 280-83 (1953).
[50]See *id.* at 422-23.

are actually preparing or refashioning legislative programs. This part of the lawyer's work will become, if indeed it has not already, far more important in the average case than appearances at committee hearings or conferences with individual legislators. This observation leads me to comment that in the field of legislation our law school instruction seems to tend to assume that all our graduates will be hired by clients interested in the Bricker Amendment or the preservation of the American way of life. We train students on how to recover three hundred dollars in damages in the municipal court for a personal injury, but when it comes to legislation we seem to assume that all of our graduates will deal only with issues of the greatest national importance. Our lobbying lawyer, in fact, is a great deal more likely to have a client who is interested in some report form which is prescribed under the state banking law or in some provision of the Surrogate's Court Act. His intervention will be most effective if he "lobbies" the legal adviser to the Deputy Commissioner in charge of the Banking Department's legislative program or the appropriate clerk of the surrogate's court.

It seems clear that as the professionalization of legislation increases there will be increased institutionalization of lobbying. I am not speaking here of the regulation of lobbying. The registration of lobbyists has had only very limited success,[51] and regulation in any real sense is not likely to succeed anyway. What appears to be needed is more lobbying rather than less. On the one hand, as the staffs of committees and departments become more important in the legislative process there should be more opportunity afforded for consultation on suggestions for new legislation and on pending bills. Legislative proposals should be more widely circulated among the interested parties who should be encouraged to comment and criticize. Public hearings should be held where

[51]See Kennedy, *Congressional Lobbies: A Chronic Problem Re-examined,* 45 GEO. L. J. 535 (1957); Lyon & Stanhagen, *Lobbying, Liberty and the Legislative Process: An Appraisal of the Proposed Legislative Activities Disclosure Act,* 26 GEO. WASH. L. REV. 391 (1958).

they are appropriate. By the time the legislative committee is ready to hold hearings, the bill should have been perfected in form, and the real issues which it raises should have been carefully defined and fully canvassed.

More lobbying is surely necessary in the case of unrepresented or underrepresented groups. With respect to legislation in the fields of criminal law, health, education, recreation, social security, and generally, consumer protection, there is now insufficient provision for making certain that all important points of view are adequately presented to those who are in charge of preparing legislation. Increasing professionalization will of itself tend to improve this situation, but other institutional methods must be devised such as a required prescreening of legislative proposals by designated public and private organizations.

Professionalization will also tend to provide more adequately for the "legislative oversight" that has been of such sporadic and generally unsatisfactory character in the past.[52] Permanent committee staffs will be in continuous communication with the agencies in respect to which their committees function. Specialized agencies such as the New York Banking Board[53] and the Governor's Advisory Committee on Welfare Funds will be charged with the duty of observing the operation of legislation, of receiving and considering suggestions for new legislation, and of initiating legislative proposals. Continuous supervision of the various areas of legislative action will be exercised by permanent official groups with competent permanent staffs, as the Law Revision Commissions[54] now exercise supervision in the field of private law and the Judicial Councils and Advisory Committees in the

[52]See Ginnane, *The Control of Federal Administration by Congressional Resolutions and Committees*, 66 Harv. L. Rev. 569 (1953); Acheson, A Citizen Looks at Congress 34-46 (1957).

[53]See N. Y. Banking Law §§ 13-14.

[54]See MacDonald, *Foreword to the Symposium*, 40 Cornell L.Q. 641 (1955), discussing the impact of twenty years of existence by the New York Law Revision Commission.

field of procedure.[55] The work of such groups can be strengthened and inspirited from time to time by the designation of special commissions in particular fields, on the model of the Royal Commissions[56] in England and the Hoover Commission in this country. In the over-all consideration of legislative programs the development of Legislative Councils with permanent staffs has contributed another new aspect to the growth of legislative professionalism.[57]

A point of particular interest in Professor Newman's presentation is his suggestion for an empirical study of who can best make our laws. I believe that pending such a study much could be accomplished by a careful jurisprudential survey of the material which is already available. If we should take, as an example, the ordering of our federal-state relations, it seems to me that we would surely find areas in which it would appear, on the basis of past experience and of the essential strengths and weaknesses of the legislatures, the courts, and the administrators, that the considerations relevant to the problem of allocation of the power of governance as between nation and state include: questions of constitutional structure, in which the courts are skilled; questions of political desirability and acceptability, as well as fundamental aspects of economic and sociological policy, which are appropriate for legislative determination; and questions of governmental techniques, for which administrative expertness is relevant.[58] Taking

[55]For interesting recent comment on the status of law reform in Great Britain, see POLLARD, SPEED-UP LAW REFORM (The Fabian Society 1958).

[56]For comment on the work of certain recent commissions see Elliott, *Recent English Reports: An Evaluation,* 29 N.Y.U.L. REV. 1043 (1954).

[57]See Asch, *The Legislative Council Movement in the United States,* 31 ST. JOHN's L. REV. 49 (1956).

[58]See THE COMMISSION ON INTERGOVERNMETAL RELATIONS: A REPORT TO THE PRESIDENT 33 (1955): "Under our federal system, the division of responsibilties between the National Government and the States was once thought to be settled mainly in terms of power: either one level, or both, or neither, had the authority to move; and that was enough to settle their functions. Such a decision was usually one for the judiciary. Under current judicial doctrine, there are still limits on the coercive powers at both levels, but the National powers are broad and the possibilities by means of spending are still broader. The crucial questions now are

as another example an area presenting very different problems, that of workmen's compensation, our experience has surely shown, at least, that legislative provision should contain only the most general of guides and that court intervention must be greatly restricted.[59] Professor Newman's references to tax law provide further suggestions for this type of study.

Another type of study, too, is suggested to me by Professor Newman's discussion. The great contributions of Professor Newman and our other outstanding scholars in the field of legislation appear to me to have been largely in the area of procedure. I wonder whether there are principles of legislation which it might be helpful to formulate and to which, if so formulated, we might turn, as we do, for example, to the principles of stare decisis in the common law? Of course, there are rules of interpretation, and Professor Newman's remarks on the manufacture of legislative history and the device of deliberate ambiguity show, as he suggests, that the legislature may well become in fact, as it now is in fiction, the dispositive locus of application of such rules. With the increasing professionalization to which I have referred, not only Professor Newman's sophisticated legislator, but the specialized committee staff, the legislation-minded lawyer, whether representing a government department or a private client, as well as the bill-drafting bureaus themselves, will surely tend generally to make the "legislative intent" more of a reality through the skillful use of the rules of interpretation.

---

questions of policy: Which level ought to move? Or should both? Or neither? What are the prudent and proper divisions of labor and responsibility between them? These are questions mainly for legislative judgment, and the criteria are chiefly political, economic, and administrative, rather than legal. The emphasis is on mutual and complementary undertakings in furtherance of common aims. The task of this Commission, accordingly, is to determine, within the constitutional limits of National and State powers, and in the light of 165 years of practical experience, what division of responsibilities is best calculated to sustain a workable basis for intergovernmental relations in the future."

See also Hays, *Federalism and Labor Relations in the United States,* 102 U. PA. L. REV. 959, 968-71 (1954).

[59]SOMERS & SOMERS, WORKMEN'S COMPENSATION (1954), particularly Chapter Eight, "Workmen's Compensation at the Crossroads."

But in my reference to legislative principles I have in mind a rather broader area of investigation of which I will give only two or three examples. Professor Newman suggests one of these areas by his support of the use of publicity[60] or disclosure, with relation both to lobbyists and to the problem of the ubiquitous Congressman. Would a general study of the advantages and weaknesses of regulation by required disclosure be useful? In a broad sense this concept cuts across many fields. There has been, for example, considerable discussion of whether the SEC principle, as it is called, provides adequate regulation[61] for pension and welfare funds.[62] Much of the proposed legislation directed at the misconduct of union officials relies upon disclosure. Disclosure of prohibited activity has been tried in a limited way under the tax law.[63] Carried to its logical end, some of the thinking behind certain types of disclosure proposals would lead to the conclusion that crime generally could be controlled by annually handing out forms to everybody, requiring everyone to list all felonies and misdemeanors committed by him during the past year. Perhaps a study of the uses and the limitations of the disclosure principle would be helpful.

Another area in which it seems to me that a consideration of principles might provide guidance for future legislative action is the area of the relationship between legislation and the common law. The old maxim reads that legislation in derogation of the common law will be strictly construed. Whether or not such a rule ever ought to have been applied, the fact is that most legislation is

[60]On the use of publicity as an administrative sanction, see CHAMBERLAIN, DOWLING & HAYS, THE JUDICIAL FUNCTION OF FEDERAL ADMINISTRATIVE AGENCIES 111-21 (1942).

[61]See the newly adopted Welfare and Pension Plans Disclosure Act, Pub. L. 85-836, 72 Stat. 997 (1958).

[62]See e.g., Note, *Protection of Beneficiaries Under Employee Benefit Plans*, 58 COLUM. L. REV. 79 (1958); Note, *Taft-Hartley Regulations of Employer Payments to Union Representatives: Bribery, Extortion and Welfare Funds Under Section 302*, 67 YALE L.J. 732 (1958).

[63]See United States v. Kahriger, 345 U.S. 22 (1953).

in derogation of the common law. And yet there are certain common law principles which might be very useful adjuncts of legislation, particularly in view of the specialized knowledge and skill which the courts can bring to bear on the application of such principles to cases arising under statutes. What I have in mind is an exploration of the possibilities in legislation for strengthening or modifying common law concepts instead of supplanting them. The New York Law Revision Commission some years ago adopted certain legislation which instead of abolishing the doctrine of consideration sought to do just that.[64] There is today much discussion of the inadequacy of the law of trusts to cover the cases of defaulting corporate directors, union officials, and trustees of welfare and pension funds. Instead of supplanting the trust concept, perhaps it would be wise to seek by legislation to shore it up so that it would be adequate.[65] Before we decide to take automobile accident cases out of the hands of the courts,[66] perhaps we ought to study not only the deficiencies of the workmen's compensation systems, but also the possibility that the applicable common law concepts can be made to serve by effecting changes within a traditional framework which has certain enduring values. By these examples I mean to suggest the possibility that by our headlong rush into the age of legislation we may be sacrificing some of the values which we have thought of as the particular glories of the common law, and that a study of the principles of legislation might reveal material as beneficial to our legal system as that produced in the past by studies, like Professor Newman's, of the procedures of legislation.

[64]See 1941 LAW REVISION COMM'N REP. 345-414; Hays, *Formal Contracts and Consideration: A Legislative Program*, 41 COLUM. L. REV. 849 (1941).

[65]See Note, *Regulation of Employee Benefit Plans: Activate the Law of Trusts*, 8 STAN. L. REV. 655 (1956); cf., Note, *Protection of Beneficiaries Under Employee Benefit Plans*, 58 COLUM. L. REV. 79, 92-95 (1958); N.Y. BANKING LAW §§ 60-75 (Supp. 1958); N.Y. INS. LAW §§ 37 to 37-p (Supp. 1958).

[66]See *e.g.*, Richardson, *Policy-Oriented Legislation in Accident Litigation*, 44 KY. L.J. 172 (1955); Kaye & Breslow, *Legislation To Replace Adjudication-Planned Compensation for Auto Accident Victims*, 35 B.U.L. REV. 488 (1955).

The Administrative Process

BY WARNER W. GARDNER

SHEA, GREENMAN & GARDNER
WASHINGTON, D. C.

To assay the present and portend the future of the administrative process, it will be useful to have a bench mark. It seems appropriate to choose our station in deference to the occasion which this Conference commemorates, the Centennial of the Columbia Law School. Let us look briefly, then, at the federal administrative process in 1858, as soon as we have defined what we are looking for.

I conceive the administrative process to embrace all formal rule making and all adjudication of conflicting claims not undertaken by the legislature or the courts. I consider the administrative agency to be either an independent authority or a bureau or office within an executive department, which to a significant degree performs rule-making or adjudicatory functions.[1]

The First Session of the 35th Congress sat from December 7, 1857, to June 14, 1858. It created two administrative agencies: one to conduct the vote on admitting Kansas to the Union[2] and the other to fix the boundaries and the value of land to be taken for

---

[1]Some organizations, such as the Fish and Wild Life Service, are administrative agencies in so far as rule making is concerned and executive agencies in so far as their other responsibilities are concerned. Others, such as the Tax Court or the National Labor Relations Board, are adjudicatory agencies without substantive rule-making functions.

[2]Act of May 4, 1858, ch. 26, § 2, 11 Stat. 271.

the Washington aqueduct.[3] It made routine amendment of two special land commission acts.[4] One of the most enduring administrative processes in our nation, that built about the Registers of the Land Office established in 1800,[5] received its normal quota of legislative action: the appeal procedure to the Commissioner and the Secretary of the Interior was refined[6] and new land offices were created in California and New Mexico.[7] The Light House Board received its annual appropriation,[8] and additional expense money was voted the two commissioners appointed to inquire "into processes and means claimed to have been discovered by J. T. Barclay for preventing the abrasion, counterfeiting, and deterioration of the coins of the United States."[9] Mr. Barclay or his successors seem to have solved well the problems of abrasion and counterfeiting.

The administrative process was, then, by no means a novelty when the Columbia Law School was founded. In the disposal of public lands it was already more than a half-century old. In customs appraisals and veterans pensions it can, by stretching a

[3]Act of April 8, 1858, ch. 14, 11 Stat. 263-64. The members of the "agency" were called "jurors" but were to conduct their valuation on the site and without the presence of the judge. Their $150,000 valuation was made in July and in November, 1858, was set aside, apparently by a state court rather than the federal court prescribed by the act. There followed arbitration, in 1862, and suit in the Court of Claims when the $15,000 arbitration award was not paid. Its judgment on the arbitration award was affirmed in 1884. United States v. Great Falls Mfg. Co., 112 U.S. 645, 659 (1884). Payment was appropriated in 1885 (Act of March 3, 1885, ch. 359, 23 Stat. 446, 452), twenty-seven years after the original act.

[4]These were the commissioners to determine titles in Missouri, established by the Act of July 9, 1832, ch. 180, 4 Stat. 565, and the California Land Commission, whose thoroughly sophisticated procedures were established by the Act of March 3, 1851, ch. 41, 9 Stat. 631, and Act of May 11, 1858, ch. 35, 11 Stat. 287.

[5]Act of May 10, 1800, ch. 55, 2 Stat. 73.

[6]Act of June 12, 1858, ch. 154, 11 Stat. 326-27.

[7]Act of March 29, 1858, ch. 12, 11 Stat. 262, and Act of May 24, 1858, ch. 44, 11 Stat. 292.

[8]Act of June 2, 1858, ch. 82, 11 Stat. 295, 299, 300. The Board was established by the Act of Aug. 31, 1852, ch. 112, §§ 8-17, 10 Stat. 119. Its duties seem to have been largely executive but to have called for an administrative agency because they cut across the work of several departments.

[9]Act of June 12, 1858, ch. 154, 11 Stat. 319, 324, supplementing Act of Feb. 26, 1857, 11 Stat. 254.

point, be traced back to the First Session of the 1st Congress[10]
The administrative agencies were created then, as they are now,
not in consequence of any theory of proper governmental organization, but simply in response to a particular problem.

As a rule, I believe, an administrative agency is created whenever governmental action is required in an area presenting three
awkward features in combination: (1) The required action is
too complex, or requires too much factual investigation, for confident action by the Congress. (2) It presents conflicting interests,
either between individuals or between an individual and the
government, which could not appropriately be resolved by the
summary methods of the executive process.[11] (3) Finally, along
with the conflict of interests there is something which is sufficient
to make unsatisfactory a purely judicial solution of the conflict.
The feature which makes judicial administration inappropriate
can be, for example, the need for rule making, a governmental
interest in the furtherance of a program, the volume of business,
or else a conflict which is outside of the usual case or controversy
pattern. When these three features coincide, making inappropriate
either legislative, executive, or judicial solution of the problem,
we ordinarily have another administrative agency. When one of
them is absent, the job is more likely than not to be done by one
of the original branches of the government.[12]

The particular, practical problems not easily handled by the
regular branches of government have from the beginning been

[10]Act of July 4, 1789, ch. 2, 1 Stat. 24, and Act of Sept. 29, 1789, ch. 23, 1
Stat. 95.

[11]Sometimes, too, an administrative agency is created to perform essentially executive functions simply because of the difficulty in placing the job in any of the established departments. Examples are the Light House Board in 1852 and the National
Aeronautics and Space Administration in 1958.

[12]For example, the Fair Labor Standards Act, 52 Stat. 1060 (1938), 29 U.S.C.
§ 201 (1952), left its major enforcement functions to executive inspection, and judicial prosecution and private suit. Except for the transitional work of the industry
committees in raising the initial wage minima, see Opp. Cotton Mills, Inc. v. Administrator, 312 U.S. 126 (1941), there were no major delegations of legislative authority, and no particular gain to be had in administrative rather than judicial proceedings
for violation.

met by reliance on the administrative process. As our society and its government have grown more complex, and our population has become more interdependent, the number of these specialized problems has very greatly increased. Probably a majority of the major issues now faced by the Congress are too complicated in their details to admit of more than a general policy direction by the legislature. If not a majority, a very considerable fraction of these issues will now involve an area of conflict too serious for summary executive disposition. The inevitable result is a proliferation of administrative agencies at all levels of government.

If anyone knows how many administrative agencies there are in the government of the United States alone, I have not found that indefatigable and omniscient man. If we take only the narrowest count, that of agencies which adjudicate private rights, we find some fifty-four agencies listed in the *United States Government Organization Manual*, 1958-1959. Of these, two are found within the legislative branch, twenty-six are independent, and twenty-six are housed in the executive departments. The Office of Administrative Procedure in the Department of Justice[13] believes that there are about one hundred and fifteen to one hundred and twenty agencies with adjudicatory functions.

When we turn to the rule-making or quasi-legislative side of the administrative process, we find, in addition to every independent agency, virtually every department and bureau of the executive branch engaged in this subordinate legislation. The Code of Federal Regulations takes up nine feet on our library shelves, while the codified statutes occupy but twelve inches.

The really important statistic cannot be had. That is the number of people who have major issues in their lives settled by operation

[13]This Office was created by order of the Attorney General in 1957 (22 Fed. Reg. 998), in response to the somewhat more thoroughgoing recommendations of the PRESIDENT'S CONFERENCE ON ADMINISTRATIVE PROCEDURE REPORT 3-4 (1955) and of the COMMISSION ON ORGANIZATION OF THE EXECUTIVE BRANCH OF THE GOVERNMENT, REPORT ON LEGAL SERVICES AND PROCEDURE 82-84 (1955). It collects data and offers advisory services.

of the administrative process. Viewed in terms of government operation and organization, the same statistic would be described as the volume of business. We can, however, isolate some suggestive parts of the aggregate statistic.

The Social Security Administration receives over 2,000,000 applications for old age and survivors benefits a year; in 1957 it assigned 12,737 appeals for hearing.[14] Hearing examiners in twenty-one departments and agencies concluded 16,849 cases in 1957,[15] to which should be added the 15,158 hearings of the Veterans Board of Appeals,[16] plus an indeterminate number which escaped capture by the statisticians.

These large numbers refer, in general, to what is known as small matters. But the widow who seeks her only source of income in a social security payment would not consider her case either small or unimportant. And when the annual multiplier is a seven-figure number, not many governmental functions can be so important as this type of case.

Other matters are of major significance in our government and in the life of our nation even though the multiplier be but one. Examples are the difficult decisions as to the necessarily exclusive choice of the sort of color television transmitting equipment to license;[17] fixing the Federal Reserve rediscount rate; whether by the rail rate structure to recognize the carriers' lower costs in moving the heavy traffic of the industrialized areas or to grant the Western and Southern territories an uneconomic equality of rates and thus an equal opportunity for development;[18] whether the non-scheduled air carriers would be eliminated or continued in existence

[14]1956 DEP'T OF HEALTH, EDUC. & WELFARE ANN. REP. 28; 1957 DEP'T OF JUSTICE OFFICE OF ADMINISTRATIVE PROCEDURE ANN. REP. 12.

[15]*Id.* at 14.

[16]1956 ADM'R OF VETERANS AFFAIRS ANN. REP. 134.

[17]See Radio Corp. of America v. United States, 341 U.S. 412 (1951); *followed by* In the Matter of Rules Governing Color Television Transmission, 10 P. & F.R.R. 1501 (1953).

[18]Class Rate Investigation, 1939, 262 I.C.C. 447 (1945), *modified*, 264 I.C.C. 41 (1946); New York v. United States, 331 U.S. 284 (1947).

under new standards of control;[19] and whether the enormous hydroelectric potential of the Snake River is to be developed by public or by private power.[20] Our illustrations could be multiplied. In many, though by no means all, of these major decisions, the administrative discretion is in practical effect final and beyond revision by the courts, the Congress, or the executive.

Even within the fairly limited area of administrative action which is open to judicial review, the administrative agencies contribute the largest category of the Supreme Court's work, with review of their actions now comprising one third of the total cases decided on the merits.[21] The late Justice Jackson has speculated that "perhaps more values are affected by their decisions than by those of all the courts."[22]

It gains nothing to debate whether all this is good or is bad. The complexity of the twentieth century means that, in any democratic form of government, most of the actual governing must be done by specialized agencies which can prescribe the rules and decide the conflicts which cannot practicably be handled by the legislature or the courts and cannot appropriately be disposed of by the executive. At an accelerating rate, we have been developing a fourth branch in our government. It is with us now, and will remain with us into the indefinite future.

The administrative process has grown up outside the pale of eighteenth-century political theory, and is thus without recognition in our Constitution. It is now profitless to trace the literary and constitutional controversies which accompanied not the birth but rather the tardy recognition of the administrative process.[23] It

[19]Large Irregular Air Carrier Investigation, CAB Docket No. 5132, Nov. 15, 1955, *remanded for further proceedings,* American Airlines v. CAB, 235 F.2d 845 (D.C. Cir. 1956).

[20]See National Hell's Canyon Ass'n v. FPC, 237 F.2d 771 (D.C. Cir. 1956), *following* United States *ex. rel.* Chapman v. FPC, 345 U.S. 153 (1953).

[21]Frankfurter, *The Supreme Court in the Mirror of Justice,* 44 A.B.A.J. 723, 802 (1958).

[22]Federal Trade Comm'n v. Ruberoid Co., 343 U.S. 470, 487 (1952).

[23]DAVIS, ADMINISTRATIVE LAW 4-34, 41-54 (1951), gives an excellent summary.

would seem more fitting that we make a practical, nontheoretical examination of the administrative process, which itself is a nontheoretical improvisation to meet the practical necessities of government.

I am not sure that even this modest objective lies within reach. For nearly a quarter of a century I have been concerned with the federal administrative agencies. That concern has been various. I have advised some and tried to supervise others. I have conducted some and have litigated before others. I have defended them and attacked them in the courts. I have assisted those who sit in judicial review of the agencies. I have once, by midsummer courtesy of the Columbia Law School, taught about them. I have not, however, adequately thought about them.

When I received the invitation to participate in this Conference, I expected that upon proper reflection twenty-five years of minor crises, each crowding on the heels of another, would sort themselves out, as jumbled filings can be marshaled by a magnet. The result, I hoped, would be an edifice of some indigenous utility, with each one of its blocks linked solidly into the governing pattern.

I have been disappointed in my expectations. My reflections have brought forth no basic concept of the administrative agency, and no ordered philosophy of its procedure. To the contrary, they have led me to doubt the validity of any generalization about administrative agencies, their functions, or their procedures. In considerable measure each administrative agency is an *ad hoc* improvisation, designed to operate within a specific practical context. Similarities between agencies can be found, but the differences are likely to be greater. The differences are those of function, of tradition, of personnel, and of volume of business. It is an obvious non sequitur to reason that (*a*) no administrative agency is a court, a legislature, or an executive, and so (*b*) all administrative agencies are the same. Yet because of that non sequitur we find persistent efforts to have universal administrative procedures prescribed by the Congress, and all of us, scholars and practitioners alike, tend to approach the administrative process as though every agency were cut by the same die and molded by the same press.

I reach this conclusion without making any claim to rights of discovery. It is laid bare in the agency studies and the Report of the Attorney General's Committee on Administrative Procedure (1941). This study, directed by Professor Gellhorn of the Columbia Law School, has for almost two decades been the starting point for anyone who wished a particular and pragmatic study of the administrative process, and for any who wished to understand the administrative agency rather than merely to have opinions about it. Yet, the contemporary literature gives some reason to fear that the lessons of this study have been forgotten, and that there is occasion again to emphasize its teaching.

It is necessary, of course, to generalize about the administrative process if we are to think about it at all, or if we are to develop any control of or any check or balance to the administrative agency. But it seems to me imperative that we remember that no generalizations about the administrative process can claim universal validity. Only some can sustain the more modest claim of statistical probability.

My hypothesis is perhaps best tested by looking first at the general nature and over-all operations of the administrative agencies and then at a few of the salient steps in the administrative process as they have been described in the Administrative Procedure Act. In both phases, my examination of the administrative process will of necessity focus somewhat more sharply upon its shortcomings than upon its solid achievements. The great bulk of the work of the administrative agencies is done intelligently, fairly, and well. But the law paper, as the newspaper, would find more tedium than profit if it ignored the bizarre and the wicked because it was as a statistical matter submerged by the workaday good of the world. My concern is, therefore, more with the pathology of the administrative process, with the areas where it does not work as well as it might, than with the much larger areas where it works either adequately or exceedingly well.

In my general examination of the agency itself I shall touch upon its expertise, its speed of action, and the sources of control over or influence upon it.

The courts, perhaps more than the scholars, pay fairly consistent tribute to the "expertise" and to the "informed discretion" of the administrative agency.[24] This quality is bestowed on the administrative agency by judicial fiat and I know of no instance in which a litigant has yielded to the temptation to submit evidentiary proof of the contrary. The proposition should be tested at two levels, the agency head and its staff.

In a few agencies, such as the Atomic Energy Commission, there has been a conscientious effort to appoint at least some of the Commission from among those with specialized and expert qualifications.[25] There are other less prominent examples.[26] In some agencies, such as the Interstate Commerce Commission and the Tax Court, the tenure of office is ordinarily sufficiently long for an acquired expertise to develop;[27] these, too, are exactly the

[24]E.g., Panama Canal Co. v. Grace Line, Inc., 356 U.S. 309, 317 (1958); Federal Maritime Bd. v. Isbrandtsen Co., 356 U.S. 481, 498 (1958); Railroad Comm'n Bd. v. Rowan & Nichols Oil Co., 310 U.S. 573, 583 (1940). The tribute leads both to a narrowing of direct review and to the insistence upon the primary jurisdiction of the administrative agency.

[25]The Atomic Energy Act requires that upon nomination of a commission member, "the President shall set forth the experience and qualifications of the nominee." Atomic Energy Act of 1954, § 21, 68 Stat. 924, 42 U.S.C. § 2032 (Supp. V, 1958).

[26]Among those which might be mentioned are the Federal Coal Mine Safety Board of Review, at least intermittently the Federal Reserve Board and the National Mediation Board, and without doubt the various Corps of Engineers boards such as the Beach Erosion Board and the Mississippi River Commission.

[27]Compare the average period of three to four years of service by the members of the Maritime Commission, Securities and Exchange Commission, Civil Aeronautics Board, and Federal Communications Commission, reported in 1949 by the TASK FORCE OF THE COMMISSION ON ORGANIZATION OF THE EXECUTIVE BRANCH OF THE GOVERNMENT, REPORT ON REGULATORY COMMISSIONS 24. The current period of longevity is probably even shorter.

agencies most likely to receive new members who have prior experience in the field. One of the most effective agency heads now in office is a lawyer who had specialized in the field before he took office. But in most agencies the commissioner or the head is in no sense an expert. In more cases than not he will to one degree or another have a political background, and in more cases than not his qualifications would point to government service in general rather than to the particular agency to which he is appointed.[28] This is not a bad thing. I, for one, believe we get better government from nonspecialists, indeed from politicians, than we get from experts. And with the passage of enough time in office, the nonexpert is likely to become at least experienced, if not expert. But even though it be a good thing to have nonexpert agency heads, it is not also a good thing to build up our law and our thinking on the fiction of their invariable expertise.[29]

The agency staff, in contrast, can more often than not be described as expert.[30] It is an expertness based usually upon a good many years of familiarity with the regulation of the industry, and only rarely upon any substantial experience in the operation of the industry. It is, therefore, ordinarily true, as John Dickinson has said,[31] that they "are experts as students or analysts, observing, but always from the outside and with a touch of unfamiliarity." But, as expertise goes in the world of government, we must grant it to the usual agency staff.

The staff expertise will not always be transferred to the agency when it makes its decisions. Sometimes this may be because of

[28]Consider the breadth of the "expertise" of the Hon. G. Joseph Minetti, who on May 23, 1956, was an expert on ocean shipping and the next day, having moved to a different board, an expert on air transport.

[29]None can read, for one example, Mr. Justice Frankfurter's opinion *dubitante* in Radio Corp. of America v. United States, 341 U.S. 412, 421 (1951), without being convinced, at least when history has proved the Justice right, that a most fallible judgment was being immunized from review by the fiction of expertise.

[30]U.S. ATTORNEY GEN.'s COMM. ON ADMINISTRATIVE PROCEDURE, FINAL REPORT 21 (1941), draws careful distinction between the specialized skills of the staffs and those of the agency heads.

[31]Dickinson, *Judicial Review of Administrative Determinations*, 25 MINN. L. REV. 588, 602 (1941).

the technical complexity of the problem. Agency heads as well
as reviewing courts will often or even ordinarily take on compulsory
faith the more technical and complex proposals of the staff. At
other times it may be because our search for disinterested justice
has, by a vigorous separation of functions, insured only that we
have an uninformed dispensation of justice. But let us assume
that the expertise has been transferred, and that the agency
decision reflects the accumulated information and insight of the
staff. There is no reason, even in that event, to pay the same
deference to the expertise of the agency when it determines
whether a book is "obscene, lewd or lascivious"[32] as when it
decides an issue of oil proration, touching "matters of geography
and geology and physics and engineering."[33]

However technical the field, there should be suspicion of the
"expertise" which is asserted and advanced without explanation.
As Mr. Justice Douglas has said, "Unless we make the requirements for administrative action strict and demanding, *expertise,*
the strength of modern government, can become a monster which
rules with no practical limit on its discretion. Absolute discretion,
like corruption, marks the beginning of the end of liberty."[34]

The administrative agency was once supposed to have the
enormous benefit of informal and expeditious action.[35] The recent
commentators are probably swinging too far in the reverse
direction, and may be unduly critical of the inordinate delay
which attaches to the administrative process.[36]

[32]Roth v. Goldman, 172 F.2d 787, 788, 789 (2d Cir. 1949); Anderson v. Patten,
247 Fed. 382 (S.D.N.Y. 1917); One, Inc. v. Olesen, 241 F.2d 772, 775, (9th Cir.
1957). In *Roth* the Postmaster General had held one book obscene and the rest of
the material unmailable because fraudulently advertised to be obscene.

[33]Railroad Comm'n v. Rowan & Nichols Oil Co., 310 U.S. 573, 583 (1940).

[34]New York v. United States, 342 U.S. 882, 884 (1951) (dissenting opinion).

[35]The current proposal to obtain "swift, sure and economic" disposition of automobile cases by an administrative agency is discussed in Peck, *Do Juries Delay
Justice?,* 18 F.R.D. 455, 458 (1956).

[36]*E.g.,* Parker, *Why do Administrative Agencies Exist?,* 45 Geo. L.J. 331, 355
(1957); Nathanson, *Administrative Law,* 51 Nw. U.L. Rev. 174 (1956); Kintner,
The Administrative Process Comes of Age, 16 Fed. B.J. 539 (1956); Schwartz,
Administrative Justice, 30 N.Y.U.L. Rev. 1390, 1401-02 (1955).

It is easy to understand that criticism. Some random samples of its occasion are: In 1946 I encountered a letter granting, after three and a half years of deliberation, an Indian girl's request to use restricted funds to buy a named heifer calf. The Court of Claims not long ago took jurisdiction of a case because the Armed Services Board of Contract Appeals had consumed two and a half years without getting any closer to trial; it acted in response to a brief organized about the proposition that "Plaintiff Has Been Sufficiently Exhausted by Its Administrative Remedies."[37] I am told that the effort to achieve a uniform rail freight classification, initiated by the Interstate Commerce Commission seventy years ago,[38] is nearing completion. The Securities and Exchange Commission quite early in its life found it desirable, to obtain speedier and less expensive action, to transfer some classes of its enforcement work from the agency to the courts.[39] The Federal Communications Commission has taken seventeen years to resolve a channel interference dispute between two stations.[40]

The one and a half years it takes the National Labor Relations Board to reach decision in an unfair labor practice case[41] is said by one with long experience in that field to mean that, apart from the cases being conducted under the shelter of a preliminary

[37]Southeastern Oil Florida, Inc. v. United States, 127 Ct. Cl. 480, 484-85, 115 F. Supp. 198, 201 (1954). It took, fittingly, four years from date of petition to entry of judgment in the Court of Claims.

[38]The history of this undertaking is narrated in Class Rate Investigation, 1939, 261 I.C.C. 447, 459-465 (1945), 5th Supplemental Rep., I.C.C. 171 (1952).

[39]U.S. ATTORNEY GEN.'S COMM. ON ADMINISTRATIVE PROCEDURE, FINAL REPORT 6 (1941).

[40]See American Broadcasting Co. v. FCC, 191 F.2d 492 (D.C. Cir. 1951), followed by a September 27, 1956 order giving the Commission sixty days to take action, since: "When in our prior opinion we sanctioned preservation of the status quo 'for such reasonable period as may be necessary to make "a valid determination . . . with all deliberate speed," we did not intend to countenance a continuation of KOB's infringing status for five years beyond the ten that had then passed'."

[41]The average time from filing complaint to decision in the last half of 1957 was 457 days. Hearings on Union Finances and Administrative Practices, Senate Committee on Labor and Public Welfare, Subcommittee on Labor and Public Welfare, Subcommittee on Labor, 85th Cong., 2d Sess. 820 (1958).

injunction, the ultimate decision almost never makes any practical difference to the labor relations between the parties. The surveys of the Second Hoover Commission have suggested that a year is a fair median figure for administrative hearings which require a decision between competing claims.[42]

We can all agree that the administrative process is slow, and often much too slow for effective government. The reasons are not hard to find: some of the issues are enormously complicated; there are often rising work loads coupled with static or dwindling appropriations; there is too much desk-to-desk movement producing certain delay and only uncertain supervision; and in some instances there is simple incompetence. These, however, seem to me to be vices inherent in government generally, not in the administrative process alone. A fifth reason, the willingness of most of our profession to harass and delay the tribunal which may favor an opponent, is a cross borne chiefly by the administrative agency.

Before we condemn the administrative agencies as unconscionably slow, we must consider the enormous mass of business which they complete. There would have to be a score of federal judges for every one now in service if all the administrative adjudications were to be made by the courts.

Perhaps the most significant procedural contribution of the administrative agency is its ability to dispose of business by informal discussion and decision. This includes not only differences between the agency and the citizen but between adverse parties before the agency. The procedure is so much taken for granted that I had to be reminded that in my own experience probably more disputes with which I was involved had been resolved after

---

[42]COMMISSION ON ORGANIZATION OF THE EXECUTIVE BRANCH OF THE GOVERNMENT, TASK FORCE REPORT ON LEGAL SERVICES AND PROCEDURE 184 (1955). One cannot use a verb stronger than "suggested," for the Commission's statistical appendix—which might for some have been more valuable than their recommendations—"has not been published and is not available."

a conference of an hour or so before the agency head or a ranking official than had been put to formal hearing and decision. Such disposition is not, however, usually possible of issues for which the statute requires a hearing. In those cases the administrative agency is about as helpless as is the court in preventing the litigation which the statute protects.

The available statistical data on administrative and judicial expedition, where hearings are held, cannot be put to sensible use, since they include indifferently the easy, short case and the long, complex one. I experiment with such numbers in the note below,[43] but end up with an unverifiable and nonquantitative judgment. It is my belief that the pretrial or prehearing period is normally much shorter for the administrative agency than for the court. But, once the trial or hearing stage is reached, I believe the cases of any substantial complexity will move more rapidly in the courts than in the agencies. I suggest below what the reason for this may be. At this point it is sufficient to record my unprovable conviction that the easy cases move much more quickly through the administrative agency, and the hard ones somewhat more quickly through the courts.

[43]My data on the courts is taken from the 1957 DIRECTOR OF THE ADMINISTRATIVE OFFICE OF THE UNITED STATES COURTS ANN. REP., and on the administrative agencies from the 1957 DEPARTMENT OF JUSTICE OFFICE OF ADMINISTRATIVE PROCEDURE ANN. REP. Each looks to the median, and neither undertakes the impossible task of separating the easy from the hard case. For what it is worth, in F.Y. 1957 the median court case took 14.2 months from filing to judgment after trial (Table C-5). The median administrative proceeding took about 2.4 months from assignment to examiner to his decision (pp. 25-27); the arithmetic is my own, since the Department wisely avoids derivation of any over-all median. There are no current data available as to the time from examiner's decision to agency decision. Each set of data indicates speed beyond what it has been my own lot to encounter. The administrative data, for example, is heavily distorted by showing 20 percent of the total cases in two fast-moving categories, suspension or revocation of marine licenses, and ICC certificates of public convenience and necessity. The official surveys in 1941 and in 1955 show that the considerable majority of contested administrative proceedings are concluded within a year of their institution; uncontested matters seem to range around a typical period of a month or two. U.S. ATTORNEY GEN.'S COMM. ON ADMINISTRATIVE PROCEDURE, FINAL REPORT 327-64 (1941); COMMISSION ON ORGANIZATION OF THE EXECUTIVE BRANCH OF THE GOVERNMENT, op. cit. supra note 42.

Turning to the sources of control over the administrative agency, I have found impossible any general formulation of the extent to which the agency is subject to control by any branch of the government. The theory is simple: the executive department has general control of the agencies within the departments and only budgetary control of the independent agencies;[44] the judiciary has control of procedure and statutory interpretation and of abuses in discretionary decision; and the legislature has—by appropriation, amendment, and investigation—as much control as it wishes to exercise. Yet in practice the theory dissolves into a multitude of particular contradictions, and into an aggregation of subtle influences which make elusive even the particular judgment.

Since I discuss judicial review below, it is sufficient here to note that it cannot operate at all with respect to many agency activities and that, as a rule, it can go beyond statutory construction and procedural fairness only with respect to the agencies which decide controversies that are of a sort similar to those which judges decide.

Legislative control is a far more various problem. Professor Schwartz, writing shortly before his own spectacular field experience, thought that the Congress should and could accomplish as a regular matter an effective control of the agencies to which it had delegated its powers.[45] This, I believe, is quite unrealistic if advanced as a general proposition. Yet we must recognize that any other general proposition is equally unrealistic.

Some agencies are subject to a fairly sustained and continuous supervision by a congressional committee. The foremost example is the relationship between the Atomic Energy Commission and the

[44]The recent decision in Wiener v. United States, 357 U.S. 349 (1958), that the President cannot remove a War Claims Commissioner even in the absence of statutory tenure, proceeds upon the premise that agency functions of a quasi-judicial nature are quite incompatible with executive control.

[45]Schwartz, *Administrative Process and Congressional Control*, 16 Fed. B.J. 519, 526-27 (1956).

Joint Committee on Atomic Energy.[46] Other agencies are subject to a somewhat random supervision by congressional committees with a particular interest in their activities: examples are those in the Department of Agriculture or the Maritime Administration. Still others are subject to an even more episodic supervision and direction by particular members of the Congress, either chairmen or ranking members of their legislative or appropriation committees. Still others—and probably the majority in number—are freed of any effective or sustained control by the Congress.

If it is difficult to generalize about legislative control, it is doubly so with respect to executive control. It is easier by far to name the tools than to judge their efficacy. There is the direct order, which may not always be obeyed,[47] with respect to the agencies which are a part of an executive department. There are a host of collateral influences which can operate with respect to the independent agency: budgetary control through appropriation requests, support or indifference to legislative programs, the power of reappointment, vulnerability to the prestige of White House conferences, and the simple hope of promotion to a more important post.[48] The aggregate impact of these controls when exercised will vary from complete to negligible, and they will be exercised up and down the range from very frequently to never according to the executive interest in the agency's work.

[46]The activities of the newly organized House Committee on Legislative Oversight could lead to a fairly sustained procedural control of the administrative agency, but it now seems more likely that it will devote its attention to the more stimulating search for sensation.

[47]I have discovered to my cost that the directions of an Assistant Secretary of the Interior to the Bureau of Reclamation, with its wide congressional and popular support, can hardly be more than hortatory. I have been consoled by the discovery that the same may be said of the directions of the Secretaries of War as to the civil work of the Corps of Engineers.

[48]We have, as suggested rather forcibly by the so-called "Goldfine Investigation," come some distance toward standards of propriety since the time President Harding visited a meeting of the Interstate Commerce Commission, uninvited and unannounced, to urge his view on a pending matter. See Arpaia, *The Independent Agency*, 69 HARV. L. REV. 483, 488 (1956).

If there are one hundred twenty administrative agencies, then there are, I believe, one hundred twenty separate answers as to whether they are independent or controlled. The answer in each case will depend more upon the accidents of personality and of tradition than upon formal organization.[49] Of only one generalization can we be confident: whatever degree of control there may be—whether by executive, legislature, or court—will be episodic and unpredictable, and will not be the systematic line-of-command supervision which is typical of the executive process.

To the extent that the administrative agency is in fact freed of control, how is it guided or influenced? I believe its chief sources of guidance are three, and that since they are more often opposed than united the result is tolerably good government.

The main source of guidance is the agency's permanent staff. In the course of a quarter of a century in Washington I have encountered only one clear instance where the head of an already established agency or department succeeded in subjugating his employees to the point that the clear preponderance of the departmental actions, where there was room for choice, reflected his views rather than those held by his staff when he took office. That was done by Harold Ickes. He had a strong will, a quick temper, and thirteen years of tenure as Secretary of the Interior. All three ingredients are, I believe, necessary for success in this unusual venture.

This is no reflection either on the agency heads or the staffs. It is instead inevitable. The permanent staff knows the technical subject, it knows the statute and the regulations, and it knows the precedents—in each case far better than its superior officer. Since

49The Federal Maritime Board, in one respect less "independent" than other agencies, "shall be guided by the general policies of the Secretary of Commerce with respect" to its subsidy functions. *Reorganization Plan No. 21 of 1950* § 106, H.R. Doc. No. 526, 81st Cong., 2d Sess. 8. Its chairman recently explained that "we receive policy guidance in these matters from the Secretary of Commerce, but we are not bound to follow that guidance." *Hearings on Superliner Passenger Vessels Before a Subcommittee of Senate Committee on Interstate and Foreign Commerce,* 85th Cong., 2d Sess. 79 (1958).

we are by definition in that large area where there is freedom to choose, it is inevitable that the expertise of the staff will be directed toward the end it considers best. The unhappy agency head who has under him two or more administrative organizations with conflicting aims can hardly fail to envy the lucky man who is presented only homogeneous papers to sign.[50]

Some agencies, but only a minority of them, have developed techniques permitting even on routine administrative matters an informal appeal by personal appearance before the agency head from a distasteful staff decision. This I have found to work quite well in fields which the agency head understands or has an interest in, but, since the staff recommendation will inevitably be taken as prima facie correct, it serves to produce only delay in the case of technical issues outside his area of interest, such as accounting, engineering, safety regulations, or law.

The countervailing influence upon the agency which regulates a particular industry is the industry itself.[51] It operates to a lesser degree in the agencies which cut across many industries. But it is not, I would be bold enough to guess, negligible even there. The "industry-mindedness" of the established administrative agency has been deplored.[52] But, as Professor Jaffe reminds us, this may be just what the Congress wanted when it gave the agency the job not only of regulating but of supporting and developing the industry.[53] And certainly, to the extent that the executive process

[50]One Secretary of the Interior, unable to resolve a four-cornered dispute between two bureaus, one industry, and one group of governmental beneficiaries, undertook in 1946 to waive technical defenses to an equity suit. That waiver was repudiated by the Department of Justice, which thought that the government ought not to be sued even when it wanted to be, but was effectively restored by the Supreme Court. Hynes v. Grimes Packing Co., 337 U.S. 86 (1949). The result was more authoritative but took three years longer than would have been possbile had the official been able to find both reliable advice and adequate resolution to impose his decision.

[51]Cragun & DeSeife, A Skeptic Views Twenty-five Years of Administrative Procedure, 16 FED. B.J. 556, 561 (1956).

[52]Parker, supra note 36. Huntington, The Marasmus of the I.C.C., 61 YALE L.J. 467 (1952).

[53]Jaffe, The Effective Limits of the Administrative Process, 67 HARV. L. REV. 1105, 1107-09 (1954).

may be fairly analogous, we expect the Department of Agriculture to be the guardian of the farmers' interests, and we hope, if we do not always expect, that the Office of Indian Affairs will do the same for its wards. I believe it in any case to be inevitable. One cannot spend his time immersed in the problems of a single industry without becoming both aware of these problems and sympathetic toward their solution.

For reasons which I cannot adequately explain, my own experience indicates that the sympathy for the regulated industry is more likely to be found at the top of the agency than in its staff. Possibly it is because each staff member is concentrating on his own job in one field, naturally seeking to increase his own effectiveness in that field, and will not often have the over-all perspective which affords understanding and thus breeds sympathy. In any case, I view the agency's frequent sympathy toward the regulated industry as offsetting the staff's otherwise largely uncontrolled interest in the farthest reasonable reach of their regulatory powers. As these drawbacks to perfect government ordinarily operate in opposing directions, I believe we have better government than if either were absent while the other remained.

The third major influence upon the administrative agency is, I believe, and certainly hope, the bar which practices before it. The agency's work must inevitably be better done if it has the benefit of careful research, thoughtful consideration, and effective advocacy on behalf of the interested parties. Its work must inevitably be more quickly dispatched if its practitioners can move with speed, can understand what is both relevant and important, and can discharge their responsibilities without the wrangling which no court would permit.

It seems to me in this regard to be unfortunate that there has developed so much specialization in the Washington administrative bar. A good proportion of the Washington attorneys who practice before the administrative agencies have no extensive experience either with courtroom practice or before more than a very few of the other agencies. I know of no cure for this, and can only deplore this further fragmentation of an increasingly specialized society.

I have not included "politics" among the significant sources of influence upon agency action, because I do not believe it to be one. To be sure, we have recently had a most unpleasant example of how one major regulatory agency, the Federal Communications Commission, has operated in a tradition by which each litigant seeks to outbalance the personal and congressional pressures which his adversary could bring to bear upon the agency, and by which some of the commissioners' votes were successfully lobbied in advance of argument. This I do not believe to be statistically typical of the administrative process generally. At the same time, I do not know of any contemporary agency which has shown the flamboyant resistance to political pressures offered by Secretary Ickes; he once, for example, issued a formal order barring, from any subsequent entry past the Department's doors, one who advised a Land Office adjudicator that he was counsel to the Democratic National Committee as well as attorney for the applicant. I do not know of any major, contemporary agency which one can confidently say will invariably discharge its responsibilities without regard to political considerations. I do not know of many agencies where the large, front-page issues will be certainly decided on wholly nonpolitical grounds. But in the large, and by statistical rather than moral measures, I believe politics to be a significant determinant in only an exceedingly minute fraction of agency decisions.

An incomparably more frequent and more important source of influence upon the agency is the simple fact that in most cases it has a program which it is responsible for forwarding. Whether prescribed by Congress or developed by the agency on its own, it is equally a consideration of prime importance to the agency. This is not necessarily bad. It is obviously proper and desirable in rule making. Even in adjudication, it has been said that the Federal Communications Commission's troubles may arise from the fact that it has never been given and never has developed an affirmative program, and so is left without internal guidance in the choice of whom to endow with permits of great value.

Whether for good or bad, the role of the agency's program seems to me one of the central features of the administrative process. Most contested agency proceedings will involve facts permitting at least two ultimate conclusions. The ambiguities of the controlling statute are legion, when cast in terms so broad as those establishing and regulating administrative agencies. We have learned to expect that almost every ambiguity will be resolved in favor of "the program." This was very frankly suggested by Interstate Commerce Commissioner Arpaia, who chided the Second Hoover Commission Task Force because it "was unmindful of the fact that the adjudicatory process of the I.C.C. is merely a tool, use of which facilitates the exercise of its legislative or regulating functions."[54] The Federal Maritime Board once, with all gravity, introduced a decision with the unusual observation that, as the matter had been left it for decision to which the party had agreed to be bound, "our consideration of the matter should be from a judicial point of view."[55]

It is easy to deplore this attitude. As Judge Prettyman has put it, "the function of an agency is the administration of law: no more, no less."[56] The agency ought, certainly, to call the facts as it sees them and ought to apply the law as the Congress enacted it. It is responsible not only for its own program but also to the citizens of the nation generally. But, after deploring the matter, I feel we must recognize it as inevitable. Probably the Tax Court and the two accident compensation agencies, being

[54]Arpaia, *supra* note 48, at 498.
[55]*A.P.L.: Applicability of § 802, M.M. Act, 1936*, 3 F.M.B. 675.
[56]Prettyman, *The Nature of Administrative Law*, 44 VA. L. REV. 685, 689 (1958).

without responsibility for a program, do proceed without this sort of built-in bias. I have known of no other examples, even when I look to the agencies for which I have borne some responsibility, of a consistently disinterested and judicial approach, and certainly do not expect it from an agency with an affirmative program to further.

Whatever ought to be the case, the agency with a program is in fact like a lawyer with a client. It has not a blind and unreasoning commitment, but certainly a strong predisposition to wish success to one rather than the other side of the issue. I have no recollection of being troubled by this attitude when I was within an agency, but find it profoundly distasteful when I practice before one of them.

When we turn from the agency itself to its detailed procedures, we must at the outset recognize that the Administrative Procedure Act,[57] enacted in 1946, has made an enormous contribution to the administrative process. This I believe to be because it has set largely hortatory standards, and has overlaid its prescriptions with broad exemptions and general escape clauses.[58] I may borrow, somewhat out of context, Mr. Justice Frankfurter's judgment that "it is fair to say that in all this Congress expressed a mood. And it expressed its mood not merely by oratory but by legislation."[59] The result is a happy one: we have standards of agency action but have left what is in fact if not in theory a fairly complete freedom to adapt procedure to particular need.

I believe the legal profession is generally of the contrary view, considering the act of value only in so far as it prescribes definite procedures without exceptions, and so has given generously of its time and talent to develop tighter and more far-reaching procedural controls. We find the Task Force of the Second Hoover Commission, and the Commission itself, delivering stern

[57]60 Stat. 237 (1946), 5 U.S.C. § 1001 (1952).
[58]See Parker, *The Administrative Procedure Act*, 60 YALE L.J. 581 (1951).
[59]Universal Camera Corp. v. NLRB, 340 U.S. 474, 487 (1951).

judgments: "The more closely administrative procedures can be made to conform to judicial procedures, the greater the probability that justice will be attained." "A serious deficiency in the administrative adjudicatory process is the absence of any uniform method of evaluating evidence and proof."[60] The American Bar Association has developed a somewhat modified version of the Commission recommendations and has proposed a carefully considered but—for want of exceptions and want of vagueness—a probably unworkable revision of the Administrative Procedure Act.[61]

All of this I consider on balance to be a mistake, and believe with the song writer that the legislators "have gone about as fur as they can go." My reasons might be illustrated by some of the major provisions of the Administrative Procedure Act.

The act in Section 3 requires, with some broad exceptions, that all procedural and substantive rules be published, and that all public records shall be disclosed. All this is good. Secrecy is the first defense of sloppy[62] or malignant government. But the Administrative Procedure Act has not made the affairs of government public, nor has it ensured that the citizen knows the administrative law by which he is governed.

This is not to say that the Administrative Procedure Act has been enacted in vain. Many agencies have moved into almost complete compliance with both its terms and its spirit. Others have not, and refuse to make public either their reasons for or the comment received on their rule making, refuse to make available the opinions of their general counsel, and deny access to the staff rec-

[60]COMMISSION ON ORGANIZATION OF THE EXECUTIVE BRANCH OF THE GOVERNMENT, REPORT ON LEGAL SERVICES AND PROCEDURE 71 (1955); COMMISSION ON ORGANIZATION OF THE EXECUTIVE BRANCH OF THE GOVERNMENT, TASK FORCE REPORT ON LEGAL SERVICES AND PROCEDURE 138, 191 (1955). Davis, EVIDENCE, 30 N.Y.U.L. REV. 1309 (1955), has demonstrated that few sentences have been more compact in error than the Delphic pronouncement last quoted.

[61]S. 4094, 85th Cong., 2d Sess. (1958).

[62]Counsel for one administrative agency resisted disclosure of the reasons for a rule because it would put "everybody in the position of second guessing the staff of the agency." F.M.B. Docket No. S-57, Tr. 222.

ommendations leading to their administrative actions. Today, equally with the period before 1946, many administrative agencies conduct a large part of their business behind a wall of secrecy.

I am not able to make a statistical inquest into the degree of adherence to Section 3. I can only say that it is very far from universal and that, where the agency adheres to a tradition of secrecy, its practice is almost beyond challenge. By the time judicial review had been completed the need for the information would ordinarily long since have vanished. This conclusion seems borne out by the fact that the reports contain not a single court decision under Sections 3(b) or (c) of the Administrative Procedure Act.

At the other end of my roster of complaints is the foolish consequence when Section 3 is applied to a situation such as the Congress never envisaged. The catch of Alaska salmon is regulated by administrative action, taken in Alaska, which lengthens or shortens closed periods according to a count of the salmon entering the river on the way to spawn. The run is of very short duration; hence, the regulation has to be changed from week to week, if not from day to day. Announcement is made by radio. A willful violator with actual notice of a lengthened closed period was excused because the Fish and Wildlife Service had three days before fixed the closed period by radio announcement instead of by publication in the *Federal Register*.[63] By correlative folly, an Idaho farmer was conclusively presumed to have known of a regulation, published in the *Federal Register* but not known to him or the government agent, which meant that his policy of crop insurance was worthless.[64]

Section 4 of the act requires generally that there be notice of proposed rule making, with an opportunity to submit comment

[63]Hotch v. United States, 208 F.2d 244, 250 (9th Cir. 1953). The argument had not occurred to his counsel until petition for rehearing in the Court of Appeals. One practitioner has defended the decision on grounds better than those selected by the court: it is not unreasonable to require that the published regulations provide for radio announcement of amendment before one goes to jail for violating a radio command.

[64]Federal Crop Ins. Corp. v. Merrill, 332 U.S. 380 (1947).

which shall be considered by the agency, and that substantive rules shall not be effective until after thirty days. It also provides a goodly selection of exceptions, including a general power for the agency to find the requirement impracticable or undesirable.

This is good legislation, and has made a large contribution to improved administration. But it has done so by providing a standard of governmental conduct, not a law. Quite apart from the necessary escape clause, the rule-making procedure is often simply ignored. One administrator, sorely tried by what he considered inexcusable litigation, in August 1953, decreed by letter that, effective January, 1946, seven and a half years before, the expenses of a broadly defined category of litigation were not allowable for the industry which he regulated. The National Labor Relations Board in 1954 amended its jurisdictional standards, to exclude the smaller third of its cases, by retroactive announcement and without opportunity to comment.[65] I believe, too, the *Chenery* cases[66] represent an ill-advised effort to accomplish by retroactive adjudication what were better done by prospective rule making.

Yet, even with these complaints, I believe the rule-making process has been greatly improved by operation of the Administrative Procedure Act. In general, rules are prospective in effect and are promulgated only after receiving, and usually considering, public comment. While there are some rather gross departures from the legislative standard, they are the exception rather than the rule.

It would be profitless in such an essay as this to try to follow through each of the provisions of Sections 5, 6, 7, and 8 of the Administrative Procedure Act with respect to adjudication. I shall therefore, content myself with some general observations on a few of the salient aspects of the adjudicatory process.

[65]It resulted, prior to judicial reversal, in dismissal of a case where the Trial Examiner had already found the complainant to be discharged solely because he gave testimony before the Board. See Pedersen v. NLRB, 234 F.2d 417 (2d Cir. 1956).
[66]SEC. v. Chenery Corp., 318 U.S. 80 (1943); SEC v. Chenery Corp., 332 U.S. 194 (1947).

I consider it wholly illusory to suppose that a common procedure can be adopted for all agency hearings required by statute. Consider two types of administrative hearings, each covered by the same statutory procedures. One is a Natural Gas Act contest between competing applicants for a certificate of public convenience and necessity; as I understand these proceedings, the participating lawyers will be numbered by the scores, the exhibits by the hundreds, and testimony will be accumulated over months of hearing. In contrast, the Indian Service Probate Examiners,[67] at least as they functioned a decade ago, move about from reservation to reservation. Upon arrival they assemble a meeting—in a church, or a tent, or around a log—and ask who has died and who were his heirs; the latter issue is as likely as not to be decided by the weight of opinion at the community meeting. Proceedings are often in the native tongue; transcripts are rare and then only imperfectly made. I do not consider either procedure perfect, but I do suggest that no statute can be so cunningly contrived as to cover both. The Administrative Procedure Act has, I suspect, worked quite admirably in matters such as Indian probate for the simple reason that no one has ever paid a great deal of attention to it.

The contrasts could be expanded indefinitely. An Interstate Commerce Commission territorial rate proceeding has no procedural point in common with a Longshore and Harborworker's award for a broken finger. The appeal from a denial of veteran's insurance benefits to an allegedly illegitimate son has different procedural requirements from a statistical inquest into the adequacy of United States-flag liner service. The Supreme Court has said that the Secretary of Agriculture must, if he is to decide, personally turn enough of the tens of thousands of pages of a stockyard rate

[67]The Secretary is directed to determine heirs upon notice and hearing. 48 Stat. 647 (1934), 25 U.S.C. § 372 (1952). Since 1954 the appropriation acts (collected in 25 U.S.C. § 372-1 (Supp. V, 1958)) have exempted the appointment of examiners from the Administrative Procedure Act.

record to say that it was his own decision.[68] The Court might have been on more compelling ground if it had been considering a deportation proceeding.

The Administrative Procedure Act has nevertheless worked reasonably well in its regulation of agency adjudication. To a considerable degree this has been so because its categorical requirements are comparatively few, and have largely been ignored when they are both imperative and inconvenient. The last thing we can want, to use a word as repellent as its objective is unrealistic, is to "judicialize" all administrative adjudications. This may be made more specific by looking at a few of the detailed provisions of administrative procedure as now defined by statute.

Subject to a variety of exceptions, Section 5(c) insulates the hearing officer and the agency from all officials and employees concerned with investigative and prosecuting functions. The objective is, of course, commendable; none could wish ex parte consultation between those who decide and those who prosecute. But the work of a number of agencies has, I believe, been impeded, and that of others might be frustrated, if Section 5(c) were fully obeyed.

The ordinary agency will have a series of technical bureaus under it, usually including law, accounting, engineering, and some others reflecting the agency's specialty. While the provision is inapplicable to agency members, its prohibition against consultation applies to the officers they might consult. In result, the agency is expected to make its determinations without consultation with its technical staff, but only with its personal assistants. This in turn produces the massive duplication of function by which each member of the National Labor Relations Board has a staff of about twenty personal assistants and the more common situation where

[68]Morgan v. United States, 298 U.S. 468, 481-82 (1936); cf. Morgan v. United States, 304 U.S. 1, 17-18 (1938). But cf. United States v. Morgan, 313 U.S. 409, 422 (1941).

the agency opinions are written in the first instance by young lawyers without supervision or check from the agency's technical experts. In all, I believe Section 5(c) causes an impairment of efficiency and a divorcement from expertise which far overbalances the advantage of insulated impartiality which it seeks.

I have not had any experience within an agency after the Administrative Procedure Act had actually become reflected in agency procedures. I cannot, therefore, speak with confidence but only out of suspicion. But I have the gravest doubt that this thorough separation of functions has been, or can be, or should be, actually applied in any agency.

If a hearing has dragged on for several years, should the agency ignore current statistics because they are available only from an office with investigative functions, or should it be required to reopen the hearing in order to use even uncontrovertible data? If the examiner cannot understand a technical exhibit in the record, it seems better to consult the technical staff of the agency than to guess. If either an examiner or an agency wishes to relate the particular case to the over-all program of the agency, they ought to be able to explore the policy and extent of that program with their experts. I believe that in practice this is very frequently done, not in conscious and deliberate violation of Section 5(c), but without thought of the act and because it is the natural and sensible thing to do. In any case, with the basic and inevitable bias toward its program, which I have already noted, I find it unimportant to be concerned with whom the agency consults in order to effectuate that bias. The result is chiefly an enforced separation from the expertise and the efficiency which the agency is supposed to supply, with no significant gain.[69]

[69]When carried to the point, as with the National Labor Relations Board, that the General Counsel is wholly independent of the Board, and can measurably control the sort of work done by the agency, insistence upon the separation of functions can be a major threat to the agency's effectiveness. Labor Management Relations Act § 3(d), 61 Stat. 139 (1947), 29 U.S.C. § 153 (1956). See Klaus, *The Taft-Hartley Experiment*, 11 IND. & LAB. REL. REV. 371 (1958).

The whole theory of separation of functions, at least apart from the purely prosecuting activities, seems to me to be beside the point. The vice is not consultation, but rather secret consultation. Procedures, which would have to vary from agency to agency, could probably be devised to ensure that there was knowledge of and an opportunity to rebut the advice which the examiner or the agency derived from elsewhere in the agency. Even these should properly be confined to the sort of advice which admits of useful countervailing evidence or argument. If this were done, the considerable inefficiency imposed by separation of functions could without injustice be avoided.

I am skeptical, too, about the supposed advantage of the agency's freedom from the technical rules of evidence. I believe most practicing lawyers will agree that almost anything of real value which can be introduced in an administrative proceeding could also be introduced in a trial before a judge without a jury. There will very rarely be found any administrative use of judicially inadmissible evidence which affects the result.

What is needed in administrative process is not a restriction upon the type of evidence which is admissible, as proposed in some of the current drafts of procedural reform, but rather trial examiners with the confidence and the competence to exclude the unimportant and the repetitious. It is a rare administrative hearing, when the issues are contested and of any complexity, which does not take considerably more time than that which would be allowed by the ordinary experienced and impatient judge. I believe the general verdict of the practicing lawyers is that the curse of any reasonably complex administrative hearing is not its summary but rather its dilatory nature.

The cure for this is not to be found in any statutory words. It can come only from the agencies themselves. It should take two forms: exhortation of their examiners to take the lead in shortening hearings and a scrupulous care, in their review of examiner decisions, to establish a firm rule that the exclusion of evidence is discretionary, reversible only for real abuse.

One of the major contributions which the administrative agency has made to the process of government is the development of short cuts to prompt decision. "Canned testimony" is an enormous time-saver in statistical presentations. The "shortened procedure," by which the parties consent to serve their statements of fact and of arguments in lieu of hearing, could make an even heavier contribution to expedition were it not for the reluctance of the bar of many agencies to leave anything of consequence to a written submission alone. That reluctance does not rest upon a desire to talk out loud, but rather upon a skepticism as to how carefully papers are read. The examiner who listens is a captive audience, while the one who reads is not captive and may not even be an audience. Possibly the agency should be given discretionary power to impose the shortened procedure, but I could not bring myself to advocate the grant of such power.

Turning now to judicial review of the administrative process, like other aspects of administrative law, it seems to me to have some elements of the paradoxical. I shall suggest below what I consider the salient aspects of judicial review. Each in some measure is inconsistent with its predecessor.

The central fact about judicial review is that it cannot often reach to the substance of the administrative action. The reviewing court can supervise the agency's procedure in the case at hand, and can put aside its interpretation of the law. In some agencies, such as the Tax Court, the Federal Trade Commission, and the National Labor Relations Board, the adjudications are sufficiently akin to those of the courts so that there will be a fairly broad and close review of the merits of their decision. But more often than not, and most notably in the agencies regulating a particular industry, the heart of the administrative process is beyond revision or correction by the reviewing court.

It does not matter greatly how one describes this central decision of the agency. It can be said to be exercising its delegated legislative power,[70] or to be exercising its discretion. It is in either case doing something the courts cannot well supervise. No court can be expected to review agency action in, for example, determining the areas where wild geese cannot be hunted,[71] or in whether a grain rate system, permitting storage in transit, should be applied to all or only to primary markets.[72] Whether the decision reflects expertise or not, it remains the agency's solution to a complicated practical problem committed to its care. If the procedures are fair and the statutory law not in issue, no responsible court is going to substitute its own practical judgment for a reasonable conclusion reached by the agency. Perhaps because of this substantial immunity to revision of discretionary action, or perhaps because the agencies as a rule do a fair and creditable job, the fact is clear that judicial review will only rarely result in the reversal of their action.

Judicial review of most agencies cannot, therefore, ordinarily be expected to control more than procedure and statutory interpretation. But even in the agencies where the heart of the administrative process is virtually impregnable to judicial control, it does not seem to me that judicial review is unimportant. To the contrary, I am convinced—and so, I believe, are most of my fellow practitioners—that the availability of judicial review is by far the most significant safeguard against administrative excess which can be contrived. Its efficacy derives from three sources.

There will inevitably develop, in an administrative proceeding of any moderate complexity, a number of procedural or legal issues of some substance. Those issues, assuming at least one or two are fairly balanced, are likely to be decided one way if the reviewing court considers the complainant fairly treated, and another if the

[70]United States v. George S. Bush & Co., 310 U.S. 371, 379-80 (1940), contains a vigorous exposition of this approach.
[71]Lansden v. Hart, 180 F.2d 679, 683 (7th Cir. 1950).
[72]Board of Trade v. United States, 314 U.S. 534, 548 (1942).

administrative action seems unfair. This leaves direct judicial protection for issues of procedure and of law, with an oblique and indirect weight given to the fairness of discretionary decisions which could not be reviewed directly.

A second and more important source of the efficacy of judicial review is its preventive value. None can prove, and certainly none can disprove, the conviction of the bar that the administrative agency will proceed more carefully and more dispassionately if it recognizes the possibility that a defeated party may seek judicial review. Its members, I believe even its partisans will concede, are subject to ordinary human frailties. Inevitably then, the possibility advantage by delay, not many administrative issues warrant the reasons given, and to the statutory words which are used to support the agency's action.

Finally, the courts seem to be increasingly alert to the necessity that—even in fields where they cannot substitute their judgment —the administrative agency articulate its reasons with care and with particularity.[73] This affords a limited opportunity for control of the discretionary decision which is remanded and, to the extent the agency mends its ways, a valuable prophylactic influence upon future agency action.

I am convinced, therefore, that judicial review is a necessary ingredient of a wisely conceived administrative process and that it ought to be available to all interested parties in virtually every type of administrative proceeding. But still we cannot expect too much. In addition to the necessary immunity of administrative discretion which I have already mentioned, there is the very practical and very serious bar of delay and expense.

Anyone who considers judicial review of agency action must allow about a year if he has access to direct review by a court of appeals and about two years if he must file in a district court and then carry the controversy to the court of appeals. If a

[73]E.g., Schaffer Transp. Co. v. United States, 355 U.S. 83 (1957); United States v. Carolina Freight Carriers Corp., 315 U.S. 475, 489 (1942).

certiorari question should develop which would warrant Supreme Court review, another year should be added. If the result of the review should be to require further agency proceedings, yet another year or so must be added. Except for the litigant who advantage by delay, not many administrative issues warrant an investment of time such as this. In probably a majority of the circumstances, it would be sounder business practice to adjust at once to the agency decision and go on from there, rather than to endure several years of uncertainty in order to try to improve the result.

The matter of expense is closely related to that of delay. It is not possible to be precise, and surely it is not polite to mention money. Yet none can discuss realistically judicial review unless he recognizes that an issue of average complexity cannot adequately be carried to the courts except at a cost which will range upward from $5,000.

These factors together exclude the great mass of administrative proceedings from effective judicial review. Only major controversies warrant several years delay plus a good many thousands of dollars simply to pursue the chance of improving the result. But the saving feature of these practical barriers to review is that their operation is never entirely certain in advance. The agency may not have any clear idea of the dollars and cents worth of the controversy. The party, or his attorney, may feel strongly enough to seek even an uneconomic vindication of his position. In consequence, the preventive or prophylactic value of judicial review is only partially dissipated by the fact that it is not often an economically prudent remedy to pursue.

Section 10 of the Administrative Procedure Act contains, to the casual reader, some bold and forthright words about the availability of judicial review. This is not the place to attempt a detailed description of the erosion which twelve years have worked on these phrases. It should be sufficient to note that one may count on the fingers of his two hands the cases which because of the enactment of Section 10 have afforded a judicial review otherwise denied.[74]

Most assuredly the Administrative Procedure Act has worked no miracles upon the attorneys who defend the administrative agencies. In one typical case the government's answer denied the availability of judicial review because: a cash payment of more than $3,000 was not involved, there was no justiciable controversy, no statutory right to sue was shown, the suit was one against the United States, an unincorporated agency could not be sued, the matter was committed to the discretion of the board, the action was premature, and the plaintiff was guilty of laches.[75] Although I am by no means a disinterested commentator, yet I believe it would be better were the Department of Justice to welcome rather than to obstruct judicial review of the federal agencies. It did begin, fifteen or twenty years ago, to take some small and hesitant steps in that direction.[76] Had that movement continued, there might

[74]So far as my incomplete researches show, they include only Homovich v. Chapman, 191 F.2d 761, 764 (D.C. Cir. 1951); Air Line Dispatchers Ass'n v. National Mediation Bd., 189 F.2d 685, 689 (D.C. Cir. 1951); American President Lines v. Federal Maritime Bd., 112 F. Supp. 346, 348-49 (D.D.C. 1953); Pacific Inland Tariff Bureau v. United States, 129 F. Supp. 472, 478 (D. Ore. 1955); Fischer v. Haeberle, 80 F. Supp. 652, 654 (E.D.N.Y. 1948); Unger v. United States, 79 F. Supp. 280, 284-86 (E.D. Ill. 1948); Snyder v. Buck, 75 F. Supp. 902, 906-08 (D.D.C. 1948); and possibly Friend v. Lee, 221 F.2d 96, 102 (D.C. Cir. 1955). The declaratory judgment in deportation cases is a new form of suit, but not a new access to the courts. See McGrath v. Kristensen, 340 U.S. 162 (1950); Shaughnessy v. Pedreiro, 349 U.S. 48 (1955).

The two most vigorous opinions, both by Judge Holtzoff, did not fare well. *Snyder* was vacated on appeal because of the failure to keep abreast of changing official defendants, Buck v. Snyder, 179 F.2d 466 (D.C. Cir. 1949), *aff'd*, 340 U.S. 15 (1950). *American President Lines* was subjected to gratuitous disapproval by the Court of Appeals, in that a condemning dictum was inserted after the slip sheets and before the reporter's text. Kansas City Power & Light Co. v. McKay, 225 F.2d 924, 932 (D.C. Cir. 1955).

[75]American President Lines v. Federal Maritime Bd., *supra* note 74 (D.D.C. 1953).

[76]See, *e.g.*, Perkins v. Elg., 307 U.S. 325, 349-50 (1939), in which the government conceded that the Declaratory Judgment Act was an appropriate remedy if the Secretary of State erroneously failed to recognize citizenship, and Brooks v. Dewar, 313 U.S. 354 (1941), in which the government virtually conceded that the official

be less need of corrective legislation. As the Department has not taken that sort of leadership, there is much attraction to that part of the American Bar Association proposal which, so far as categorical words may be able to do it, would revise the Administrative Procedure Act to mean what it seems to have meant in 1946.

Having presented my bill of particulars, I am not sure where it leaves us. The administrative agency discharges a very large part of the government's business, and ordinarily does a very creditable job where no other branch of the government could even attempt the task. Each agency, arising from a particular practical context, is different from the others, and no procrustean code can be applicable to all. So far as the Congress has sought to press all agencies into a common procedural mold, it has done much good in enacting a hortatory standard of fair procedure and some harm in so far as it has encouraged a debilitating formalism and delay. The agencies on the whole do a fair and efficient job, but are usually beyond any systematic control by the legislature or the executive, while judicial review of most agencies can operate only on the edges and not at the center of the administrative process.

As the administrative process of the present can be seen only dimly, and displays an uncertain and contradictory pattern, I shall put it behind me, and turn to the comparative precision of hope and prophesy as to the future of the process.

As I have made plain by now, we will, in my judgment, see no future diminution of administrative agencies or their powers. Instead, the accelerating complexity of modern life will force a corresponding acceleration in the growth of administrative agencies and powers.

---

could properly be sued without joining his superior, and that the doctrine of suits against the United States was confused beyond rationalization. (The concessions are reflected in the government briefs, not in the opinion of the Supreme Court. Brief for Petitioner, Brooks v. Dewar, *supra*).

Accompanying the growth, there will probably be in the years immediately ahead a considerable revulsion against the powers of the administrative agency, comparable to that which led to enactment of the Administrative Procedure Act in 1946. As with most such ground swells in a democracy, it will be based partly on fact and partly on fiction. It will be realized by the Congress that the agencies are in fact beyond organized and effective control. An accumulating series of separate and dubiously justified complaints against one agency or another will play its part. The current congressional investigation of White House inquiries, the payment of hotel bills, and who boasted to whom about what commissioner he had in his pocket, while statistically irrelevant in the larger operation of the administrative process, will probably prove the main compulsion toward the reform bill I expect of the 1960s.

I cannot predict whether the reform will take the form of the American Bar Association proposal, of the somewhat more naive absolutism of the Second Hoover Commission report, or of something as yet undrafted. It will probably turn upon whether the originating storms are of gale or hurricane intensity.

To the precise extent that the coming reform bill is precise, categorical, and without saving exceptions, to just that extent will it break down in practice. This will probably not produce a legislative retreat, but rather a judicial rounding of the sharp corners, accompanied by a growth in legislative exception of whole agencies from all procedural regulation.

A decade from now I should expect to find a little more judicial review, and a little less official secrecy, than now. Otherwise, I expect no discernible variation from the overreform followed by necessary reaction that I now anticipate.

If we look beyond the coming decade, we depart from our bench marks, and hopes then replace predictions. They would run as follows.

At the core of this new administrative procedure would be a liberal sprinkling of first-rate personnel: men with energy, vision, and fairness; men who could effectively make minor (although not major) sacrifices of reason and statutory command to advance the program which the Congress might have wanted had it thought of it; and men who would remember that their job was to serve, preferably with distinction, the whole people and neither a particular industry nor a particular party.

If the administrative process were in the hands of men like this, it would, to me, be a matter of comparative indifference what form the statutory procedures might take. I want, in short, the very situation deplored by one of our more prolific authors in the field of administrative law. He quotes,[77] with the sympathy one feels for the missionary among savages, a letter from an English barrister, who complained, "Administrative law is in a mess in England because nobody there believes that a British Civil Servant could do anything seriously wrong." If we could get our law into the same mess, for the same reason, we could put aside most of our worries about the administrative process.

Governor Harriman recently made the same point, more perceptively, when he said[78] that "the prestige of the British civil servants was not given them by the system, but rather brought to the system *by them*, as members of the educated, governing class.

I do not, in all candor, believe that we are moving very rapidly toward top-notch agency personnel. My judgment is, of course, as worthless as that of everyone who has deplored the deficiencies of the present generation as compared to his own. Still, it seems to me to be true that we have, ever since the close of the Second World War, done everything possible to make government service unattractive to men of talent. We have hounded government servants to distraction about their personal beliefs; we have made

[77]Vom Bauer, *Impact of Administrative Process in Executive Branch*, 16 FED. B.J. 453, 480 (1956).
[78]Harriman, *Better Public Servants*, Harpers Magazine, Sept. 1958, pp. 55, 56.

recruitment near to impossible by having months of field investigations interposed between offer and employment; we have, for a brief but catastrophic period, driven out of government service men who were appointed without a thought to their politics but who served under a defeated party; we have steadfastly refused to reward superior talent by superior pay; we have persisted in leaving the Civil Service Commission classification clerk in charge of the destinies of men whose work he does not understand; and—probably most compelling of all—we have afforded consistently brighter opportunities in industry than was done in the days of the Great Depression.

I do not mean to say that the administrative agencies are staffed by incompetents or by hacks. Their level of capacity is astonishingly high, when all things are considered, and every agency of any size will have a few men of unusual talent who have given their lives to government service either because of a sense of public service or because of the challenge of the extraordinarily large responsibilities that are theirs. With that recognition, my judgment remains that the general level of agency competence is substantially lower than it was prewar, and a great deal lower than it ought to be to achieve the most effective government.

A considerable improvement of personnel is not impossible of attainment. We had an effective system of recruitment for a few years, from 1941 to 1944, when government lawyers were recruited through a discerning and workable system, under the Board of Legal Examiners, first directed by Professor Wechsler of the Columbia Law School.[79] I am encouraged to note that the Second Hoover Commission, while subscribing in general to a somewhat primitive belief that it should and could "judicialize" administrative procedure, did recommend a thoughtful and ap-

[79]Exec. Order No. 8743, 6 Fed. Reg. 2118 (1941), in response to *President's Committee on Civil Service Improvement Report*, H.R. Doc. No. 118, 77th Cong., 1st Sess. (1941). The system was terminated by a rider on an appropriation act. Act of June 27, 1944, ch. 286, 58 Stat. 361, 364.

parently workable system for establishing a superior career service for lawyers and examiners.[80]

It will, of course, take more than a good system of recruitment and promotion to bring agency personnel to the high level of competence which is commensurate with their responsibilities. Government service must be made as attractive to the young lawyer of talent as is private practice or corporate counseling. If the government does its part, there yet remains the necessity that the law schools by the guidance of their students, and the community by its respect, give to government employees and officials the prestige which they have earned.

Whether we will develop the sort of personnel the job requires I cannot know, and can only hope. I expect in any event that the administrative process will develop along two somewhat contradictory routes. In time, I believe, we will tire of trying to impose identical and rigid procedures upon all agencies, however dissimilar their functions. Of necessity, the Administrative Procedure Act of the reasonably distant future will enact some very general standards of procedure and leave it to the agency to fill in the details appropriate to its particular function. I expect, in other words, an eventual relaxation rather than a tightening of the present legislative prescription of agency procedure.

I expect a simultaneous move toward an expanded rather than a restricted judicial review. It will probably come by legislation, although it could just as well come under a broad-gauged leadership by the Attorney General. We are not likely to leave the administrative agency indefinitely without any systematic method of control, and judicial review is the only available method of control which can operate across the whole range of agency action and yet preserve the agency-to-agency and case-to-case flexibility which the job requires. I do not expect an expanded scope of judicial review. For the reasons already developed there are in-

[80]It was introduced as S. 932, 85th Cong., 1st Sess. (1957).

herent limitations upon judicial review of administrative discretion. But I do expect that it will not be too long before anyone who is actually injured by an administrative decision or regulation will be able to carry his complaint to a court.

I see in that connection no notable advantage to a special administrative court such as is proposed from time to time, and do not expect that one will be created. The purpose of judicial review is not to find a better expert, but to subject the agency's action to independent scrutiny as to its fairness. For that purpose I do not think it likely that, with all their occasional limitations, we can find a better group than the regular federal judges. It is possible, indeed, that a specialized administrative court would inevitably come to consider itself as the Old Commerce Court is said to have done,[81] a superagency with jurisdiction to revise policy as well as law. That, I think all can agree, would be thoroughly unfortunate.

Over-all, the administrative agency, today and tomorrow, represents the practical effort of practical men to deal with the many problems of our industrial society which present too many conflicts of interest for summary executive action. If it is staffed with a reasonable proportion of intelligent, conscientious and fair-minded men, the development of the administrative process will take care of itself. To the extent that it is staffed with ordinary humans, some broad legislative control of its procedures, and some case-to-case scrutiny of its fairness, will always be necessary.

The quality of the administrative performance will reflect not only that of the men who run it, but also that of the men who appear before it. It is hard for any agency to measure up to its responsibilties if its practitioners and its critics seek to submerge it in guerrilla warfare against either the substantive or the procedural program which the country has elected to enact. More significantly, it is not often that an agency can find the leisure to do the work that should have been done by the parties before it, or that

[81]Arpaia, *supra* note 48, at 486.

it can effectively speed its procedures without the cooperation of the attorneys at its bar.

In the end, then, the future of the administrative process, as of the rest of our law rests to a substantial degree in the hands of the law schools. I believe those hands to be good hands.

Comment

BY KENNETH CULP DAVIS

PROFESSOR OF LAW
UNIVERSITY OF MINNESOTA LAW SCHOOL

With conciseness I can express my main reaction to Mr. Gardner's paper in two words: I agree. Multiplying verbosity fivefold, I can say: I agree with every one of Mr. Gardner's seven main propositions.

Perhaps I might quarrel with him slightly over one of the seven, for I believe that an agency can have its own affirmative program and still be entirely fair in the adjudication of cases.[82] But instead of arguing that, I prefer to discuss the need for affirmative suggestions for reform. Mr. Gardner does not really sound a call to action, and I think a good many reforms relating to the administrative process are needed. The closest Mr. Gardner comes to an affirmative proposal is his seventh main proposition, namely, that judicial review of administrative action should and will be more often available. I agree with that proposition, but believe that it needs amplification.

Whenever a legislative body or a court has given an answer to the question whether particular administrative action should be

---

[82]The Supreme Court has programs, such as getting rid of police abuses in criminal cases, and desegregating the public schools, but I do not believe that its sense of fairness is affected by these programs. Nor do I believe that the SEC's program of promoting truth in the sale of securities upsets its balance when it adjudicates a case.

reviewable or unreviewable, I think that the answer has usually been a good one. For instance, when Congress provided that certain Veterans Administration decisions should be unreviewable, it did so on the basis of a full consideration of the problem, and its answer seems to me both reasonable and sensible. When the Supreme Court held in *Chicago & Southern*[83] that a determination by the President concerning an international air route is unreviewable because of resort to confidential diplomatic information, the decision was a close one, five to four, but the majority had substantial reasons for its conclusion. At the same time, the push of the American Bar Association to legislate in wholesale fashion that every final agency action shall be subject to judicial review unless "expressly precluded by Act of Congress later enacted" is much too undiscriminating, and I am opposed to the ABA program on this point.[84]

This being so why do I say that I agree with Mr. Gardner that the availability of judicial review should be expanded? What I have in mind primarily is the extremely unsatisfactory bodies of law which deny review for such reasons as lack of standing, lack of ripeness, and sovereign immunity.

[83]Chicago & So. Air Lines v. Waterman S.S. Corp., 333 U.S. 103 (1948).

[84]S. 4094, 85th Cong., 2d Sess. § 10(a) (1958): "Every . . . final agency action . . . shall, except as expressly precluded by Act of Congress hereafter enacted, be subject to judicial review under this Act." § 1001(h) provides: " 'Action' includes the whole or any part of any agency rule, order, license, sanction, relief, or the equivalent or denial thereof, or failure to act." § 1001(f) provides: " 'Relief' includes the whole or any part of any agency (1) grant of money, assistance, license, authority, exemption, exception, privilege, or remedy, (2) recognition of any claim, right, immunity, privilege, exemption, exception, or remedy, or (3) any other action upon the application or petition of, and beneficial to, any person."

Some examples of administrative action that would become reviewable under these provisions are: (1) a commanding officer of a domestic military post denies a leave; (2) the President or Secretary of State exercises discretion in conducting foreign affairs; (3) an agency denies a stenographer a parking space in the basement of the building; (4) the President removes a cabinet officer; (5) the Post Office buys X's property and refuses to buy Y's; (6) a prosecuting attorney refuses to prosecute; the NLRB refuses to prosecute; (7) the Antitrust Division chooses a criminal proceeding instead of an equity proceeding; (8) the Budget Bureau recommends increasing or decreasing an appropriation; (9) the President refuses to commute a sentence; (10) the Customs Bureau refuses to mitigate a fine.

Let us take a basic fact Mr. Gardner has given us and build on it. He states that the average cost of taking a case from federal agency to federal court is $5,000. What should a party get for his $5,000, and what does he get? He should normally get a determination of the merits, within the proper scope of judicial review. What he often gets is nothing more than a chance to litigate such questions as standing, ripeness, and sovereign immunity, and if he loses on any one of those questions he pays his $5,000 and fails to get a determination of the merits of his case. The ABA in its proposed legislation overlooks this problem.[85]

Let me give a few random examples. United Airlines provides service to Catalina Island, thirty miles off the California coast. It operates under a certificate from the CAB in Washington. The California Public Utilities Commission instructed United to file its schedules with the state commission. Failure to comply was subject to $500 to $2,000 fine. After seeking informally to persuade the state commission that it did not have jurisdiction, United sought a declaratory judgment in federal court. The district court sensibly held that the flight was partly over the high seas, that this gave the CAB jurisdiction, and that therefore the state commission was without jurisdiction. The Supreme Court, without opinion, reversed, citing a ripeness case.[86] The airline paid for judicial review and even paid for going to the Supreme Court, and it came out with nothing. In my opinion, the Court's failure to consider the case on its merits was both injustice and bad government.

In *International Longshoremen's Union* v. *Boyd*,[87] the Supreme Court held that a statute was not ripe for challenge even though an officer had threatened to enforce it. The union and

[85]See S. 4094, 85th Cong., 2d Sess. § 1009 (1958).

[86]Public Util. Comm'n v. United Air Lines, 346 U.S. 402 (1953). The case cited is Public Serv. Comm'n v. Wycoff Co., 344 U.S. 237 (1952), which is clearly distinguishable in that the state agency in the Wycoff case had threatened no action, whereas the state agency in the United case had "instructed" United to file its schedules.

[87]347 U.S. 222 (1954).

several alien members sought injunction and declaratory judgment against the District Director of Immigration, who had announced that aliens going to Alaska would be treated on return as if they were entering the United States for the first time (aliens may be excluded for many reasons that would not justify deportation). These men go to Alaska each summer to work in the fish canneries. The District Director's announcement meant that either they had to risk loss of their right to remain in the United States or they had to give up their jobs. They were confronted with a real and immediate dilemma, not a hypothetical or remote one. The district court sensibly decided the merits. The Supreme Court held that the question of statutory interpretation was unripe for judicial consideration. Without even bothering to state the facts concerning the official threat of enforcement or the effect of the threat upon the plaintiffs, the Court effectively prevented the aliens from getting relief from the real and present dilemma in which the machinery of the law had put them. Again, I think the Supreme Court's refusal to decide the merits at the instance of parties who are so importantly and so immediately affected is both injustice and bad government.

For an example of a Supreme Court holding on standing, let us take *City of Atlanta* v. *Ickes.*[88] A city that consumed a large amount of coal was denied injunction and declaratory judgment against an order of a federal agency fixing minimum prices for coal. The effect of the order was to compel the city to pay more for the coal it was purchasing. The city asserted that the order was invalid. The district court sensibly decided on the merits. The Supreme Court held, in a per curiam opinion misciting four cases on standing, that the city had no standing to raise the question. Mr. Justice Frankfurter has proudly cited the case in support of the statement: "This Court has held that a consumer has no standing to challenge a minimum price order."[89] I think denial to

[88]308 U.S. 517 (1939).
[89]Stark v. Wickard, 321 U.S. 288, 319 (1944) (dissenting opinion).

the city of standing to challenge the order causing it to pay more for the coal it purchases is another instance of both injustice and bad government.

For an example of judicial use of the doctrine of sovereign immunity as a reason for denying judicial review of administrative action, let us take the *Larson* case, probably the key case.[90] A government agency sold coal to the plaintiff, and a complex controversy arose over the facts and the law of sales, the law of contracts, and the law of property. The plaintiff sought to enjoin the officer from selling the coal to a third party, and to obtain a declaratory judgment that the coal belonged to the plaintiff. Never could there be a question more appropriate for a court to determine. But the Supreme Court, seemingly losing sight of what courts are for, refused to reach the merits because of a lot of technical reasons about sovereign immunity. Once more, refusal to decide the merits seems to me both injustice and bad government.

The four examples I have given are fairly representative of an attitude that often prevails in the Supreme Court, although it does not always prevail. One cardinal observation about the law of standing, ripeness, and sovereign immunity is that the case law is contradictory. Indeed, some of it is more than contradictory; for instance, on ripeness questions the Supreme Court sometimes closes the judicial doors to real and present controversies and sometimes opens the doors to abstract or hypothetical or remote questions.[91]

The Supreme Court has recently called the law of standing "a complicated specialty of federal jurisdiction."[92] That is exactly what it has become. But why should it be that? The state courts are confronted with the same problems of standing, and they

[90]Larson v. Domestic & Foreign Commerce Corp., 337 U.S. 682 (1949).

[91]See the full analysis of the cases supporting this statement, 3 DAVIS. ADMINISTRATIVE LAW TREATISE § 21.10 (1958). For discussion of the law of "Standing," see ch. 22 of the Treatise; for "Ripeness," see ch. 21; and for "Sovereign Immunity in Suits Against Officers for Relief Other Than Damages," see ch. 27.

[92]United States *ex rel.* Chapman v. FPC, 345 U.S. 153, 156 (1953).

have not produced a body of law in the nature of a complicated specialty. Instead, relatively speaking, they generally do what the Supreme Court should do, namely, they follow the simple, natural, and sound idea that the judicial doors should normally be open to plaintiffs who are in fact substantially hurt by governmental action.[93] This is what the Supreme Court itself did until recent decades. I think it is fair to say that the law of standing and ripeness has become so technical and complex that the Supreme Court has lost sight of the ultimate reality that it is often closing the judicial doors to plaintiffs who are in fact immediately hurt.

A study of the cases in which the Court has divided on issues of standing and ripeness quickly reveals that Mr. Justice Frankfurter, the oldest of the Justices, is the leader on the Court in favor of closing the judicial doors. Without the Frankfurter influence, the judicial doors would more often be open to plaintiffs who are in fact adversely affected. But now Mr. Justice Harlan, one of the youngest, has shown in two cases that he may be inclined to go at least as far as Mr. Justice Frankfurter. In the *Storer* case, the Court held that a broadcasting company having the maximum number of stations permitted by the FCC's rules could challenge those rules. The Court's reason seems completely persuasive: "The Rules now operate to control the business affairs of Storer."[94] But Justices Frankfurter and Harlan wrote separate dissenting opinions.

In the *Frozen Food* case,[95] the Court held, eight to one, that carriers of commodities declared by the ICC to be nonexempt from ICC regulation could challenge the order. Mr. Justice Harlan dissented alone, asserting the extreme view that because the order was merely declaratory and not a command, it was

[93]For discussion of state law of standing and ripeness, see 3 TREATISE §§ 21.09, 22.10.
[94]United States v. Storer Broadcasting Co., 351 U.S. 192, 199 (1956).
[95]Frozen Food Express v. United States, 351 U.S. 40 (1956).

not reviewable. The Harlan position is akin to saying that a declaratory judgment of a lower court ought not to be reviewable by an appellate court because it does not command anything. The position was too extreme even for Mr. Justice Frankfurter.

That the Court might on its own motion get rid of its extreme attitude of closing the judicial doors is entirely conceivable. Even so, a little prodding with legislation seems desirable. Present legislation seems to be largely disregarded. The Administrative Procedure Act provides that except so far as statutes preclude review, or agency action is by law committed to agency discretion, any person adversely affected shall be entitled to judicial review. Committee reports of both Senate Committee and House Committee say that this means adversely affected in fact.[96]

On the law of standing and ripeness, all that is needed is that any party adversely affected in fact by administrative action should be entitled to challenge it. The ABA bill moves backward instead of forward on this issue, however, since, while the Association provides that a party adversely affected shall be entitled to review, its bill provides that such a party "shall have standing to seek judicial review,"[97] not that such a party shall have standing to obtain judicial review.

What is needed on sovereign immunity seems rather odd. The Supreme Court's case law is quite contradictory. The Court was indulging in understatement when it said in 1947 of its past decisions on sovereign immunity that "as a matter of logic it is not easy to reconcile all of them."[98] What is needed is nothing more than that the Court, on any problem on which its cases are in conflict, should follow the cases which open the judicial doors to a determination on the merits.

For these reasons I agree with Mr. Gardner's last main proposition, that availability of judicial review ought to be expanded.

[96]S. Doc. No. 248, 79th Cong., 2d Sess. 212, 276 (1946).
[97]S. 4094, 85th Cong., 2d Sess. § 1009(b) (1958).
[98]Land v. Dollar, 330 U.S. 731, 738 (1947).

The barriers to such review ought to be broken down. The main barriers are the bodies of artificial law concerning standing, ripeness, and sovereign immunity.

Comment

BY WILLIAM T. GOSSETT
VICE PRESIDENT AND GENERAL COUNSEL
FORD MOTOR COMPANY

Unlike the legislative and judicial processes, the administrative process has not yet been wholly accepted as an institution. We still feel restless about it, even though, as Mr. Gardner has pointed out, it has been with us in minor applications almost since the establishment of the republic, and in major applications for almost a century.

A great deal of this discomfort stems from the fact that historically the administrative process, although it was the product of progressive views and certainly was based on positive hopes, bears some of the aspects of a counterrevolution. For example, we have had from the beginning strong devotion to the doctrine of the separation of powers. Yet the most commanding institutional feature of the administrative agency is that it unites and centralizes executive, legislative, and judicial powers over broad areas of our society. Even more profoundly, the idea of the administrative process seems akin to ancient and rejected ideas of the law. The struggle for the overthrow of these ideas, indeed, forms the substance of much of Western civil history. Both Magna Charta and the American Declaration of Independence, in their legal effects, were rejections of systems of administrative law.[99]

[99]Cf. COOPER, ADMINISTRATIVE AGENCIES AND THE COURTS (1951); PLUCKNETT, CONCISE HISTORY OF THE COMMON LAW (2d ed. 1936); POUND, ADMINISTRATIVE LAW (1942).

Yet in a dynamic society of much vaster complexity than the Constitution makers envisioned, the administrative agency provided an immediate if imperfect answer to pressing needs that could not wait for the slow evolution of old institutions to accommodate them—even if those institutions ever could do so.

Today, then, our position is approximately this: we have the administrative process with us; and as society moves on at an ever faster pace we are likely to have rather more than less of it. There is, on the other hand, a general realization that in the speed of its growth and in the nature and scope of the burden put upon it, it has some inherent weaknesses and dangers. The problem ahead of us would seem to be to minimize these, to retain and improve those characteristics of the administrative process that are useful and necessary, and to get rid of those that can be damaging to our fundamental ideal of a society based upon law.

In general, I agree with Mr. Gardner that we can rely upon external procedural reforms, including judicial review, only to a certain point. We know that legal issues will arise with sufficient frequency that the agencies, despite the marked restraint of the courts in reviewing substantive matters, will not be operating completely beyond the kind of judicial checks to which the Executive and the Congress are subject. But Mr. Gardner has pointed out that, in practice, the litigant seeking judicial review of administrative actions must be content to spend both time and money before he will get it, and could easily be discouraged on that account.[100]

Mr. Gardner seems, however, to be put somewhat at ease on this score by the possibility that it may be enough that judicial review is available if anyone were to insist upon it, and that this

[100]There is the additional consideration, less tangible but more pervasive, of risking almost certain adverse public reaction to judicial action by or against a government administrative agency. For example, stop-order proceedings by the Securities and Exchange Commission, formal investigatory actions by the Federal Trade Commission, and unfair labor charges by the National Labor Relations Board are to be avoided if at all possible.

in itself may have some considerable restraining effect on the agencies. I should think that we would not want to lean on so slender a reed as that. If we find imperfections in the administrative process, we ought to be concerned with making it better and not worrying solely about the relative impotence of the courts or the practical considerations that impede judicial review when it is available.

The question of the role of expertise—the *sine qua non* of the administrative agency—is one of those with which we must deal; and it seems to me that in an increasingly complex society, that role is going to be enlarged rather than diminished. The wiser use of expertise is certainly a major frontier along which the progress of the administrative process ought to move. It can come about safely, I think, only through internal procedural discipline. As Mr. Gardner has noted, Mr. Justice Douglas has used emphatic language on this point: "Unless we make the requirements for administrative action strict and demanding, *expertise*, the strength of modern government, can become a monster which rules with no practical limits on its discretion. Absolute discretion, like corruption, marks the beginning of the end of liberty."[101]

Mr. Gardner puts ultimate reliance here upon the caliber of men that might be recruited for service in the administrative agencies. Although the need for highly qualified personnel is beyond dispute, I must admit to some astonishment at his professed indifference to statutory procedures if he could have "a liberal sprinkling of first-rate personnel." As a point of view, this is, in my judgment, full retreat from government by law. If we had men of such inscrutable wisdom as those whom Mr. Gardner would rely upon to run the administrative process, we would be such a community of supermen that we would have no need of any government at all. But we are not such a

[101]New York v. United States, 342 U.S. 882, 884 (1951) (Douglas, J., dissenting).

community. We are human beings, subject to all kinds of failings, living together in a voluntary democratic experience, seeking solutions to our problems as they arise, trying to construct new instruments to meet new challenges as we go along.

Although I agree with Mr. Gardner's conclusion that the general level of agency competence should be higher, I do not believe that the essential dilemma with which we are now confronted with regard to the administrative process has centered, on the whole, in the men who have served in the agencies. The difficulty consists in the nature of the job that has been thrust upon them and perhaps, in the unprecedented faith we have put in the capacity of administrative mechanisms to launch themselves and to evolve perfectly with only perfunctory guidance.

It is true that if government is to function efficiently, great reliance must be placed upon the wisdom and good faith of administrative officials; and they must be given sufficient discretionary power to accomplish the legislative purpose. But if private rights are to be protected, discretionary grants should not be overgenerous; and we should employ such checks and balances as can be done without unduly hampering administration.[102]

To the extent that a statute employs vague, general terms in granting discretionary authority, to that same extent do we risk being subjected to the exercise of arbitrary power by government agencies. This may come less from an intrusion upon the courts than from an invasion of the legislature. It can occur in a very subtle way as the agency begins to define public policy on its own initiative. It may be expressed in nothing that the agency does or says but only in what the industry and the public conclude is the policy of the agency. Then it becomes a fixed standard of refer-

---

[102]Cf. COMMISSION ON ORGANIZATION OF THE EXECUTIVE BRANCH OF THE GOVERNMENT, TASK FORCE REPORT ON LEGAL SERVICES AND PROCEDURE 133-36 (1955). In the report it is suggested that Congress should establish a special legislative group to review existing statutes to assure that legislative standards are as specific and precise as circumstances permit.

ence that everyone in the industry has at the back of his mind
before he takes any significant action. It is never tested in the
courts, because it is never violated. It is not always even articulated, because it is simply a felt conviction. It is something that
the regulated industry learns to live with and avoids risk by
respecting.[103]

Examples are difficult because of the very nature of the condition. Let me venture one, however, from the history of the Communications Act of 1934. Congress has never made—either in the
Communications Act of 1934 or elsewhere—any declaration that
it is public policy to restrict free journalism because it is broadcast
rather than printed; and there is, of course, grave doubt that any
such effort by the Congress, when viewed against the First
Amendment, would survive judicial scrutiny. In 1941, however,
the Federal Communications Commission, on its own initiative,
decided that it was public policy to prohibit editorializing by
broadcasters. This meant that in contrast with the printed press
no principles or points of view on matters of public interest,
whether the building of a new school or the extension of foreign
aid, could be advocated by broadcasting stations.[104]

In 1949, the Commission modified its view, saying that editorializing was permitted but licensees were "required" to see that
"different opposing positions" on public issues were presented.[105]
This, in effect, still prohibited the broadcasting stations from expressing editorial policies with the same vigor as a newspaper does;
and it is an accepted rule in the broadcasting industry that if you

[103]"When, as in some of these instances [of arbitrary action through the exercise
of supervisory and other administrative powers] and in many others, administrative
discretion is not susceptible of control either through procedural safeguards or
through judicial review, other means must be studied with a view to minimizing
arbitrary action. This area of administrative law has had virtually no attention either
from reform groups or from the commentators. Yet in no branch of administrative
law is scholarly inquiry likely to pay higher dividends." DAVIS, ADMINISTRATIVE
LAW 183 (1951).
[104]Mayflower Broadcasting Corp., 8 F.C.C. 333 (1941).
[105]1, Part Three, Pike & Fischer, Radio Regulation 91:201.

permit someone to urge statehood for Hawaii over the air, you must let someone else use the same facilities to oppose it.

This is a clear instance of an agency's defining public policy, thus exercising a function of the Congress on a matter of sweeping dimensions. Yet there is no avenue of relief readily available to broadcasters. If a broadcaster failed to present "different opposing positions," his license could be revoked or simply not renewed. The grounds empowering revocation are so broad and general that the editorializing need not even be mentioned by the Commission. And in renewal hearings the applicant could be turned down if the Commission were to decide that another applicant could do a better job. As realistic managers, then, the members of the broadcasting industry have no recourse but to accept the dictum.

Now I am not prepared to concede that because in some respects "the agencies are beyond effective control," they ought to remain so. I suggest that it is possible to improve the structure of the administrative process; to devise means of supervisory control; and to have a more disciplined legislative approach. The problem is one of many facets and its solution will not be written in simple terms. But it certainly will not be solved by an across-the-board application of the doctrine of laissez faire.

Manifestly, some areas of administrative discretionary power are beyond the reach of effective supervision. But there are certain areas in which the recognized need for improvement is such as to present a resistless challenge to a profession that is sufficiently resourceful and forward-looking to justify its existence.

We should try to improve the process of institutional decision. The American Bar Association's proposed new code[106] would, I think, contribute materially to the accomplishment of this goal. It would not impose technical, legalistic, or procedural limitations;

[106]Introduced as S. 4094, 85th Cong., 2d Sess. (1958) under the title "Code of Federal Administrative Procedure."

nor would it attempt to "judicialize" the agencies.[107] It would, rather, have the effect of importing into the administrative process some of the more desirable of the trial techniques employed in the federal courts.[108] But more fundamentally, by eliminating many of the exemptions in the Administrative Procedure Act and by the addition of provisions drawn in the light of twelve years of experience under the act, the code would bring about general adherence to such fundamentals of procedural due process as those involved in the right to notice and opportunity for fair hearing, the publication of rules and orders, and adequate judicial review on the full record. These have already been accepted in practice by many of the agencies, but not, unfortunately, by all.

Mr. Gardner has reminded us that administrative agencies are not just policing bodies or regulatory offices. They are supposed to regulate and encourage the healthy growth of industries and services necessary to the public interest. He has emphasized that they have "programs" to that end, and that such programs—and not abstract questions of justice nor any absolutes—are the standard against which they exercise their vast discretionary powers.

Now this is essentially a managerial task, and management talent is not chosen for its skill in administering justice. Its role is one of advocacy—advocacy and advancement of its own program. Here we have another impediment to Mr. Gardner's search for "first-rate" men. What he really needs are men equally gifted in judicial mind and managerial talent. Those of us who have been concerned with both the law and the conduct of enterprises

[107]Mr. Gardner notes that sympathy for the regulated industry, to be found "at the top of the agency," tends to offset "the staff's otherwise largely uncontrolled interest in the farthest reasonable reach of their regulatory powers." Perhaps some degree of "judicializing" of the agencies would be less damaging to the administrative process than the rough justice involved in the clash of the opposing forces described by Mr. Gardner.

[108]"It would greatly clarify our thinking if it were admitted, once and for all by bench and bar, that administrative agencies can be and are vested with true judicial power, which, in its legal effects, is exactly like the power conferred upon the courts." Schwartz, *Administrative Justice and Its Place in the Legal Order*, 30 N.Y.U.L. Rev. 1390, 1397 (1955).

know that a man truly gifted in either way is rare and that frequent combinations of the two are most unlikely. But in addition to possessing judicial and managerial talents, the perfect man in the administrative process would be required to shift easily from a judicial to a managerial approach to the same problem. I cannot see the wisdom of putting such a strain upon the perfectability of man and giving up so easily on the perfectability of the institution.

We will wait a long time, I think, before we can be sure of enough of that kind of genius to justify the conclusion that the problem will be solved by personnel alone. I would rather see whether we cannot reexamine the structure of the agencies and try to improve the architecture. In some of the agencies, for example, it has become the practice to separate staff personnel functionally; managerial personnel, enforcement personnel, and adjudicatory personnel do not have overlapping functions.

Further study of the possibility of similarly defining and separating the powers of commissioners should be undertaken. If nothing else, such a separation of powers within the agencies would make for a felt, even if not a statutory, definition of standards for the guidance of those making appointments.

Mr. Gardner expects to find in a decade, he says, "a little more judicial review, and a little less official secrecy, than now."[109] I would add only the hope that the administrative process would also be graced with more effective legislative guidance than at present.

Certainly a minimum of official secrecy in the administrative process is essential to more effective judicial review. Whether the

[109]Even with respect to questions of statutory interpretation, the courts have exercised a high degree of judicial restraint. "Beginning with Gray v. Powell, 314 U. S. 402, and NLRB v. Hearst Publications, Inc., 322 U. S. 111, the courts have developed a doctrine whereby in some instances statutory interpretation in the course of administrative agency adjudication, especially where there is involved 'specific application of a broad statutory term,' is subject only to strictly limited judicial review, i.e., is to be accepted by the reviewing court 'if it has warrant in the record and a reasonable basis in law.'" Special Committee on Legal Services and Procedures, Report, 81 A.B.A. REP. 491, 507 (1956).

reviewing court is governed by the substantial evidence rule or by some other formula, it can do no more than examine the record. If the record is incomplete, there can be no adequate judicial appraisal of the fairness of the agency's action.[110] Abuse of discretion and other errors of law may be indiscernible.

In spite of a general attitude of disapproval of secrecy in the administrative process, Mr. Gardner characterizes as a "foolish prohibition" the provisions of Section 5(c) of the Administrative Procedure Act, purporting to deprive the agency of full opportunity to consult with its technical staffs. Such a prohibition, he argues, interferes with obtaining the highest degree of "technical expertise." The time has come, I think, when a choice must be made between the right to obtain technical expertise through secret conferences outside the hearing room and the requirement that all such technical information be presented in open hearing and made a part of the record.[111] The latter alternative, always open,

[110]"The inexorable safeguard which the due process clause assures is . . . that no finding shall be made except upon due notice and opportunity to be heard; that the procedure at the hearing shall be consistent with the essentials of a fair trial; and that it shall be conducted in such a way that there will be opportunity for a court to determine whether the applicable rules of law and procedure were observed." St. Joseph Stock Yards Co. v. United States, 298 U.S. 38, 73 (1936) (Brandeis, J., concurring).

[111]In commenting on the proposed "separation of functions" provisions (§ 1005(c)) of the American Bar Association's proposed Code of Federal Administrative Procedure, S. 4094, 85th Cong., 2d Sess. (1958), Advisory Group 2, in the Draft of April 13, 1957, made this explanation of the proposal: "The asserted need for the application of so-called expertise in technical and complex agency proceedings is recognized; the need is fully met by allowing and encouraging, as the draft does, that the expert knowledge be exhibited upon the record in public proceedings and thus made known to the interested and affected parties. Only in this way can the law safeguard the rights of the parties to test, by cross-examination and by rebuttal, the truth and probative value of the assertedly expert statements. Secret consultations in decisional proceedings undermine the opportunity for ascertaining true facts, and similarly transgress the judicial tradition that justice requires the application of the law to the case as *made on the record*. . . . A staff advisor, a hearing officer, a 'disinterested' attorney or expert, an agency member, and an agency might variously confer about decisional facts and issues of law with a dedicated intent to find the most just solution, but human error might, and in many cases surely does, occur which the light of public scrutiny would show up. Such errors in institutional decisions remain obscured from the test of refutation—by cross-examination of rebuttal or argument—and are not available for judicial review."

involves elements of essential fairness that should not be over-looked.

As Mr. Gardner points out, under present procedures in most agencies, counsel for the parties are permitted to appear only before the hearing officer or (sometimes) the agency members. This is unfortunate because the original responsibility for decision often rests neither with the hearing officer nor with members of the agency themselves, but rather with the staff. The staff is inaccessible to counsel for the parties. The result is that the decision makers do not have the benefit that can come only from actual face-to-face discussion of issues with counsel. There are at least two ways to correct this procedural defect: (1) by granting to the hearing officer full power to make the initial decision[112] (this is the recommendation of the Hoover Commission); or (2) to permit oral argument by counsel before the staff members who will actually make the decision.[113]

Mr. Gardner closes his paper with confident expressions of faith in the ability of counsel to improve the "quality of the administrative performance." If, however, counsel is not permitted to participate effectively in the work of the agency by presenting their arguments before the individuals who actually make the decisions, the contribution of counsel will not, I think, fulfill Mr. Gardner's hopes. Only by full participation can counsel be expected to correct serious misapprehensions under which the deciding officer may be laboring.[114]

---

[112]Professor Cooper has suggested that the doctrine of the Morgan case (Morgan v. United States, 298 U.S. 468 (1936)) could be more adequately satisfied if the decision made by the hearing officer who originally presided at the trial were accorded the same status as that given the decision of a trial judge, with appeal to the commission limited in scope to that of an appellate proceeding. Cooper, *Administrative Law: Let Him Who Hears Decide*, 41 A.B.A.J. 705 (1955).

[113]"The cardinal principle of fair hearing is not that all facts must be in the record or that all facts must be subject to cross-examination but that parties must have a chance to meet in the appropriate fashion all materials considered." Davis, ADMINISTRATIVE LAW 519 (1951).

[114]Cooper, *Administrative Law: The Process of Decision*, 44 A.B.A.J. 233 (1958).

It is Mr. Gardner's conclusion that nothing can or should be done to change the statutory formula that defines the scope of judicial review. He suggests that judicial review must be limited in the main to fundamental questions of statutory interpretations and to corrections of procedural devices so lacking in due process as to shock the judicial conscience. This is the interpretation given by some courts to the "substantial evidence" rule. Others have equated it with the "clear error" test, applied by the courts of appeal in passing upon determinations of fact by United States districts courts in civil nonjury cases.[115]

Administrative adjudication being part of a larger regulatory process, no statutory formula should permit a reviewing court to interfere with the respect properly accorded administrative expertise. On the basis, however, of the experience gained during the past twelve years in applying the "substantial evidence" rule in various types of cases arising in a number of the agencies, I agree with Professor Cooper, and with the Special Committee on Legal Services and Procedure of the American Bar Association, in advocating the substitution of the "clear error" test for the "substantial evidence" rule. Perhaps it would not change the result in most cases, but it would eliminate confusion among lawyers and judges alike, and would provide a "time tested, workable device, capable of comparatively uniform application in all circuits and in all types of cases."[116] Thus, it would improve the effectiveness of judicial review.

Looking to the future, I can see no easy resolution of the vexing problems posed by the administrative process. I believe that the

[115]"The substantial-evidence rule under the Administrative Procedure Act and the 'clearly erroneous' tests urged by the reports are, in practice, so nearly alike that only the scholastic mind of the hypercritical law-review writer presumes to see any real difference between them." Chief Justice Vanderbilt, SYMPOSIUM: HOOVER COMMISSION AND TASK FORCE REPORTS ON LEGAL SERVICES AND PROCEDURE: INTRODUCTION, 30 N.Y.U.L. REV. 1267, 1268 (1955).

[116]Cooper, *Administrative Law: The "Substantial Evidence" Rule*, 44 A.B.A.J. 945 (1958); Special Committee on Legal Services and Procedure, Report, 81 A.B.A. REP. 491, 493, 506 (1956).

uneasiness will continue but that it may be modified by such procedural improvements as can be devised. I think, however, that what we are faced with essentially is the solemn responsibility of recognizing that in constructing the administrative process we made only a beginning toward coping with the problems to the solution of which our Constitution provided no convenient institution. The one we invented has not been unworkable. But neither has it sprung overnight into a perfect answer to our needs. As time has gone on we have discovered that it has been too naively hopeful to assume that, given enabling legislation creating the agencies, they could somehow attain, of their own swift making, methodologies that in all other human affairs have been the achievement of centuries-long evolution.

If the administrative process were solely an adjudicating machinery, our problems would be infinitely reduced. But it is not. Administrative agencies are political entities, standing up to their heads in that great ill-defined desideratum, "the public interest." And yet their parent statutes have for the most part simply expressed the legislature's constructive intent in creating them, staking out a broad area in which they were to make regulations, and, then turning them loose. They have, of course, not been wholly immune to legislative oversight. The appropriate committees of the Congress review their activities not only in connection with appropriations but in relation to specific legislation involving their respective fields. But this is not enough to prevent a drift, on the part of the agencies, toward the definition of public policy on their own initiative. And this seems to me a matter for the correction of which we must look to the legislature rather than the courts.

What, then, is the corrective? In my judgment, it lies in the assumption of greater responsibility by the legislature. Enabling acts are written in language that is far too broad and general. Far from defining public policy with regard to the regulated industries, for example, they are content merely to state that it is public policy to regulate them—and no more. Reexamination and revisions of the acts, in accordance with the shifting context in which they are supposed to be operable, are too infrequent and, again, insufficiently specific. No one expects that Congress can ever take over the task of framing all of the rules and regulations that are necessary to give force to the parent statutes. But Congress can and should spell out national policy and not just hint at and suggest it.[117] It is not enough to stake out an area in such general terms and hope that somehow all will be well under any conditions and at all times. We should rather employ some professional expertise in the drafting of enabling statutes.[118]

[117]"The responsibility for fashioning a policy, not only of great economic importance but also one that has divided the faiths and loyalties of classes of people, cannot appropriately be intrusted to the administrative." LANDIS, THE ADMINISTRATIVE PROCESS 55 (1938). Dean Landis was discussing a provision of the House bill which would have empowered the Securities and Exchange Commission to grant exemptions "consistent with the public interest" under the "death sentence" provisions of the Public Utility Holding Company Act of 1935. Of this standard, Mr. Landis said (p. 56): "The House amendment, however, turned over the whole burning issue of the future of the holding company in the public utility field to the Commission itself without any indication of what it should do with it other than that the public interest should be the guide for the Commission action. It was obvious at once that, for the Commission, this was an impossible responsibility. It meant nothing less than that the Commission, rather than the Congress, would become the focal point for all the pressures and counter-pressures that had kept the Congress and the press at a white heat for months. Instead of the controversy being concluded, it would have been protracted interminably with the rooms of the Commission the place of debate rather than the halls of Congress."

[118]In the fifth of his Thomas M. Cooley Lectures, delivered in 1950 and soon to be published, E. Blythe Stason, Dean of the University of Michigan Law School, has suggested the following program:

"We should proceed with caution and discrimination to confer [administrative discretion] only where needful, instead of dispensing it with an open hand thoughtlessly wherever and to whatever extent the pressure of the moment seems to insist. But at the same time we should not withhold it where necessary to effectuate essential objectives.

"To this end we must scrutinize the policy and draftsmanship of the enabling acts and so formulate our grants of power that we confer the needed discretion but no more. It calls for drafting skill of a high order.

"Then, in the second place, when public interest actually compels conferring discretion, it is our task to seek and apply, if we can, an adequate system of supervisory controls appropriate to each situation, balanced to allow the necessary freedom of choice to serve the real needs, but curbed at the same time by supervision to prevent the discretion that must be conferred from running away into arbitrary bureaucracy.

The fact is that there are few spheres in which Congress legislates that are so sensitive to change and development as these economic areas. Technological innovations, changes in the interplay of economic forces, even population and geographic trends can upset premises almost overnight. There seems to me to be no remedy for anachronisms, unrealistic limitations, and unanticipated restrictive pressures, except in legislative attentiveness.

The future of the administrative agency as a governmental device in a modern industrial democracy is promising if the agency is to become more clearly a servant of the public; but there are implications of a hazardous nature if it is allowed to drift into mastery. Although procedural reform can minimize some risks, it is not the complete answer. For the rest, we must turn to legislative meticulousness, with regard both to intent and to surveillance. The evolution of all democratic institutions involves an enormous amount of trial and error, of resolution and compromise, of hopes and regrets. There is no doom in all this. The doom comes only when we forget that this constant process is always unfinished business.

Hold as tight a rein as possible. This calls for a wide understanding of administrative law and the means available both here and elsewhere in the world. The mere presence of supervisory procedures serves a good purpose, not only because of the direct action of the mechanism for correcting error, but also as a result of its indirect influence in inducing wise exercise of its powers by administration.

"Finally, in the third place, if discretionary powers are an essential tool in any particular situation, and if supervisory controls cannot be made available, or if they are inconsistent with the public interest, then grant the power without controls rather than doing greater harm by withholding it, but grant it to the most responsible available public official—not to the lower echelons."

Comment

BY PAUL M. HERZOG

EXECUTIVE VICE PRESIDENT
AMERICAN ARBITRATION ASSOCIATION

Mr. Gardner is eternally right in saying that one cannot generalize very much about administrative agencies or, indeed, about the process itself. As a matter of fact, I am not sure that there is *an* administrative process. There are a series of processes, as Mr. Gardner points out in his paper, processes which, perhaps, bear more resemblance to one another than to anything else, but still not too much to one another. Those processes vary, and they should vary, in accordance with the social problems and the practical needs which particular agencies were established to handle. Their strengths and their weaknesses, it seems to me, can only be judged by practical experience, and not by any particular logical criteria dependent upon blueprints, whether administrative or constitutional.

At the American Arbitration Association we have a motto on our shield which reads, "Speed, Economy and Justice." These words are not wholly unrelated to the motivation of the men who have attempted to apply the administrative process to the solution of social problems. Those who favor the administrative process tend to stress the first two—speed, although it does not always apply, and economy, not in the sense in which we use it at the AAA, but in the sense of increasing the effectiveness of government. According to its opponents, the advocates of the administrative process tend to be a bit careless about the third item—justice. These opponents not only contend that the third is often lacking, but they also find the presence of the first two—speed and economy—not to be particularly advantageous to their interests.

Of course, it must be obvious that all three are essential if the administrative process is to achieve the twin goals that we demand of it: effectiveness *and* fairness.

The advocates of the process and its opponents are rarely disinterested. They are likely to be much more concerned with substance than with form, although their comments, favorable or critical, are more often directed to form rather than substance. That sounds less controversial. Both the proponents and the opponents realize, instinctively as well as intellectually, that just as the substance helps to determine the form—a point made by Mr. Gardner—so, by modifying the form they can influence the substance.

Those who want to get something done—to regulate a particular industry or a particular course of conduct—naturally favor the administrative process as efficient. Those who prefer to limit governmental control over some course of conduct, or some economic interest, will tend to question the fairness of procedures, procedures which may, indeed, prove a bit too efficient for their purposes.

Going back a moment in history, this helps to explain the attitudes of labor and management during the debates about the structure of the National Labor Relations Board during the 1940s, an issue which seems to be relatively quiescent today. We can look at these problems more calmly now because the issue is less fraught with emotion.

I still believe that the creation of an independent general counsel at the Board was, taking it all in all, a mistake. But I am less sure than when I argued the point in 1947 and again in 1950 that it was a mistake on principle, looking at it abstractly from the point of view of a public administrator, to have singled out just one agency to try the experiment of bifurcation. That that particular agency was singled out, I regretted and still regret. But looking back on it now in the light of history, I am disposed to think that the experiment was worth trying as an experiment. However limited its success at the NLRB, it was consistent with the American pragmatic method to try it out on one agency at a time, rather than either to leave it untried or to apply it universally without testing step by step.

If either the proponents or the opponents of the administrative process take an extreme position on procedural issues, and do it primarily for substantive reasons not always admitted, they not only will stimulate the arguments of their adversaries; much more important, they will also make those arguments that much more valid. Conversely, if they do not hearken to their adversaries' reasonable arguments, they will decrease the chances of improving the administrative process, something which none of us can afford. That would be suicidal, because without doubt the administrative process is here to stay. It would be self-defeating not to do something to improve it by working together, regardless of divergent interests and opinions. We simply must try to be objective, no matter what our particular interest may be. As one witness said before me many years ago, "What is sauce for the goose depends on whose ox is gored."

So, those of us who favor expansion of the administrative process should not only continue to urge our more conservative brethren to move toward our point of view. We should, I believe, also be grateful to them for not permitting our passion for more efficient regulation to override the great truths inherent in certain eighteenth-century concepts about the separation of powers.

I do not concur in that famous quotation from Alexander Pope which rings constantly in all our ears: "For forms of government let fools contest,/Whate'er is best administered is best." That is just not so. "Whate'er is best administered" is simply "best administered." That does not mean that it is best. After all, Mussolini made the trains run on time.

Mr. Gardner alludes to methods by which the legislative,

judicial, and executive branches each seek to control one another by controlling the administrative agencies. In a way that is what happens. And it is right that each should exercise some control over that particular segment—but only that particular segment—of an agency's activities which is, respectively, legislative, judicial, or executive. Questions of the extent of judicial review, or the application of the Administrative Procedure Act, correctly go to the courts. The legislature may properly inquire into an agency's exercise of rule-making powers or make changes in its authority. The executive quite rightly can examine closely, if it wishes, into operative efficiency.

Other problems arise where the executive or the legislature seeks to infringe upon the independence of administrative agencies when they are exercising judicial or quasi-judicial functions. When they are deciding cases—and recent revelations make this point all the more important—interference is intolerable. I doubt whether a joint legislative committee—appropriate perhaps to overseeing the Atomic Energy Commission—should supervise the activities of a quasi-judicial agency like the National Labor Relations Board. That was attempted for a while in 1948. There were no disasters, but on theory and in retrospect, I believe it was a mistake. It provided a potentially dangerous opportunity for interference with decisional processes. It was not worth the risk. I say this in spite of very happy experiences with a committee of that sort, headed by the then future Senator Ives, in New York State twenty years ago.

Increased executive control over the administrative agencies has been recommended by the Hoover Commission, by providing that the President designate the chairmen of the commissions instead of maintaining the traditional practice of some of the commissions to elect their own, or to rotate the chairmanship annually. By and large, this recommendation is the best way to fit sound administrative practice into a theory of judicial independence.

One virtue of the administrative process which, I believe, was somewhat understressed by Mr. Gardner is its informal, non-adversary quality. It is sheer gain when a regulatory agency, through consultation or through settlement before the issuance of a formal complaint, can lessen litigation. The most useful function, surely, of the administrative process is preventive. It does not lie in the active exercise of power. The very existence of unused potential power has the same prophylactic effect on the parties that Mr. Gardner says judicial review has over the administrative agencies themselves.

The greatest value of the informality of the administrative process is really educational. The gains that matter most are of that sort. The process provides a unique forum in which people can talk rather than argue, in which they can learn to find solutions rather than contend for the evanescent victories so often sought in adversary proceedings.

The Bar as Lawmaker

BY WHITNEY NORTH SEYMOUR
SIMPSON, THACHER & BARTLETT, NEW YORK CITY

It is proper that the organized bar be included in a review of law-making agencies. This is especially true when law is defined broadly to include not only judicial decisions and statutes but also administrative regulations and those customs and traditions which gradually become a part of institutions. Inherent in this definition is the wise admonition that the measure of a civilization is the extent of its obedience to the unenforceable. In this broadly defined area of law the organized bar has played, in recent years, an increasingly more important role. In fact, it is through bar associations and other professional organizations, rather than through efforts of individual lawyers, that the legal profession has made its greatest contribution to lawmaking. Of course, this is not to say that individual lawyers have not made important contributions as judges, legislative draftsmen, and advocates. For example, the advocate has played a part in the lawmaking process through the persuading of judges to decide cases in particular ways. Thus, in any treatment of Marshall's contribution to American constitutional law, it would be wrong to omit reference to Webster and the other great advocates whose arguments were accepted and became a part of the ultimate warp and woof of the law. However, this subject and the other contributions made by individual lawyers are beyond the scope of this paper.

Perhaps it would be well to be a little more specific about the nature of the lawmaking which will be discussed. Lawmaking has been primarily an educational activity on the part of the bar. A need for change has become apparent to the bar; it has then usually educated its brethren, the public, and the proper authorities as to the need for reform. It has then often, usually on their request, placed its talents at the disposal of the authorities to do the technical drafting or other work necessary to accomplishment. It has not been engaged in propaganda but in the broadest sort of public service of an educational nature. And the profession can take pride in the fact that with few exceptions all of these things have not been primarily for the benefit of the bar but of the public, with the bar benefiting only as a part of the community.

Before turning to some of the specific contributions that the organized bar has made to the process of lawmaking, it is well to sketch in a little of its development. First must be the historical background from which the organized bar emerged in this country. This has been so thoroughly covered by Dean Pound in *The Lawyer From Antiquity to Modern Times* that it need only be given the briefest treatment here. Prior to the Revolution most of the young men who studied law were trained in the Inns of Court. These English-trained lawyers became the leaders in their respective communities and owing to their influence, the caliber of the American Bar was kept at a fairly high level following the Revolution. However, after the turn of the nineteenth century, the spread of democratic notions resulted in a growing hostility toward special privileges granted by government, which, in turn, led to a lowering of the standards for admission to the bar. In Indiana, for example, any voter of good moral character was entitled to practice law in any of the courts of that state, and this remained so until, within the present generation, its constitution was amended to permit the adoption of higher standards. During this period the very loosely organized local bar groups, as such, had little influence, as the bar was subject to widespread suspicion as a sort of secret trade union of a privileged class. The result was a thorough deprofessionalizing of the bar and the advent of what has been called an "Era of Decadence," which was to last until about 1870. Dean Pound has said "there had come to be, not a bar, but so many hundred or so many thousand lawyers, each a law unto himself, accountable only to God and his conscience— if any."

The formation of The Association of the Bar of the City of New York in 1870 marked the end of the decline and has been recognized as the beginning of the "revival of professional organization for promoting the practice of a learned art in the spirit of a public service and advancing the administration of justice according to law." This great Association, which was originally formed by a small group of leading New York lawyers, principally to combat the Tweed Ring's corruption of the New York courts, has throughout its history provided leadership for the organized bar. Its purpose is set forth with great clarity in its constitution, which has formed the pattern for those of most later associations:

The Association is established for the purpose of cultivating the science of jurisprudence, promoting reforms in the law, facilitating the administration of justice, elevating the standards of integrity, honor and courtesy in the legal profession, and cherishing the spirit of brotherhood among the members thereof.

The revitalization of the organized bar was given impetus as a country-wide movement by the formation of the American Bar Association in 1878. This Association has grown from an original complement of 75 members, enjoying the Saratoga waters and related pleasures, to its present membership of approximately 95,000, and it is today twice the size it was ten years ago. By 1923 there was an active state bar association in every state and territory of the Union. In addition, many local bar associations were organized. Of course, these associations are of varying strength and effectiveness. Some are purely social, meeting annually for purposes of comradeship. Others, however, like The Association of the Bar, today have fifty or more active committees vigorously dealing with problems of law reform, discipline, reviews of legislation, quality of judges, and so forth. In a city like New York, a lawyer feeling some obligation to participate in the activities of the organized bar would ordinarily belong to the American Bar Association, the New York State Bar Association, The Association of the Bar of the City of New York, the New York County Lawyers' Association, The American Judicature Society, and probably several other professional organizations. Thus the individual lawyer now participates in many choruses of professional opinion and the organized bar speaks with increasing frequency and authority.

Some brief review of American legal education is also useful. Prior to the founding of a modern law school at Harvard under Professor Langdell, most neophytes received their legal education by apprenticing to practicing lawyers, some of whom probably had limited pedagogical skill. Only a few were fortunate enough to sit at the feet of such inspired teachers as Wythe, Reeve, Kent, and Story. Beginning with the new ideas of Professor Langdell, who is rightly considered to be the father of modern legal education, the case system spread through the leading law schools of the country. New law schools were established in almost every state, but many of these schools were proprietary or part-time schools; there was little, if any, similarity in the educational background requirement for entrance and great disparity in the quality and type of legal education. While the greatest schools were already requiring a substantially full college background, many required none. In 1921 the American Bar Association, under the leadership of Elihu Root and Chief Justice Taft, established new standards for legal education which were ultimately approved by most of the states. These standards have been increased from time to time so that today a minimum of three years of college training is required by almost all approved law schools. The schools have gone far beyond the original Langdell case method, having incorporated legislative, administrative, and other sources of law as part of their regular curricula—indeed all of the other disciplines find greater or less hospitality in the various schools. The part played by the humanities and natural science in legal education is being increasingly recognized. The whole process of legal education is under constant review and scrutiny. Furthermore, legal educators are participating in all of the activities of the organized bar and this mutual relationship is resulting in the most productive cross-fertilization. While there is still some pulling and hauling between lawyers and legal educators about the relative importance of practical training, there is just enough of this to keep the controversy alive, and to keep their respective weapons from becoming rusty. A practical accommodation satisfactory to both educators and practicing lawyers has been reached in most schools.

The last preliminary subject that needs mention relates to the position of the lawyer in American society. This topic is of importance because the influence of the lawyer, and, hence, the organized bar, is affected by it. The position of the lawyer has fluctuated with the economic, political, and social tides of American life. Yet there is little reason to suppose that it is substantially different from what it was in the earliest days of our nation's history, although we take great comfort in all reports that it is improving. Lawyers have, at least from Shakespeare's time, been the subject of jokes and criticism. It is extremely unlikely that the jokes about lawyers or mothers-in-law will ever disappear, nor should they, because some of them are quite good. However, the lawyer's place in our society seems to bear a direct relationship to the quality of the leadership which the lawyers provide. When they behave in accordance with their greatest traditions, the profession seems to stand highest in public favor. When lawyers in the news disregard these traditions, the position of the lawyer is naturally lowered. DeTocqueville noted the high place of the lawyer in American society, as did Bryce a half century later. The fact that the legal profession has always attracted able and ambitious young people is strong evidence of its high standing; American parents have always regarded the law as a worthy objective for their talented children. Thus, there has never been any reason to take a pessimistic view about the basic standing of the legal profession. The question has been, and remains, whether the profession is living up to its full responsibilities in the light of the exclusive franchise which it enjoys. Here the organized bar has been struggling hard to meet the challenge, and while no doubt it has fallen short it has made great strides. The fact that thousands of lawyers recognize the challenge, and have spent vast effort in trying to see that the profession meets it, is encouraging and deserves recognition.

The organized bar has participated in lawmaking in a wide variety of fields. I will attempt to touch upon most of the major fields, but they will not exhaust the list of these activities.

It is appropriate to touch first upon those activities which most intimately concern the quality of the bar itself. Incidentally, it is impressive to note that, here as elsewhere, almost all of the activities in which the organized bar engages are in the direction of insuring greater responsibility on the part of the bar to the public rather than merely adding new advantages to those now enjoyed by members of the legal profession. Where the latter is arguably the case, as in the growing movement to suppress unlawful practice by laymen, there is nevertheless the important factor of insuring to the public the benefit of responsible professional help in place of nonprofessional help operating without the protection of required training or ethical standards.

The development of legal education to its present high state has resulted from the cooperative effort of the organized bar and the law teachers. Very shortly after the foundation of the American Bar Association, it created in 1893 a Section on Legal Education, which since that time has been its principal arm for improving American legal education. This Section was active from the beginning and, as previously noted, successfully carried forward a program of sharp improvement in educational standards. The Association of American Law Schools, the teaching profession's complementary organization to the Section on Legal Education, was formed under the aegis of the American Bar Association in 1900. Ever since, it has worked in close cooperation with the organized bar. Improvements in legal education have in some instances been embodied in court rule, in others they have been made the subject of statute; but all have been important in building a strong bar, increasingly willing to shoulder its obligations to the public.

The statement and enforcement of explicit ethical standards has been and is of primary concern to the organized bar. The first Code of Ethics in the United States was formulated and adopted by the Alabama State Bar Association in 1887. By 1908 this Code, which was based on Sharswood's *Professional Ethics* and Hoffman's Resolutions, had been adopted with slight changes in ten other states. In that same year, the American Bar Association promulgated its Canons of Ethics, which by 1914 had been adopted by thirty-one of the forty-four existing state bar associations. Since 1914 many additional states have adopted the Association's Canons, substantially intact. Thus, this code serves as the controlling guide on matters of ethics in practically all jurisdictions. It is the keystone of disciplinary action, and the subject of appeal where lawyers are in doubt as to the propriety of their conduct and desire advice.

The organized bar did not stop with laying down a code of ethics for the practicing lawyer, but in addition, promulgated Canons of Judicial Ethics. These Canons were prepared in 1922 by a committee headed by Chief Justice Taft, and were adopted by the American Bar Association in 1924. Since they have been subject to occasional amendments to keep them abreast of modern developments. For example, in 1952 the American Bar Association adopted the report of a Special Committee headed by the late John W. Davis that the Canons be amended to provide that the "telecasting of court proceedings are calculated to detract from the essential dignity of the proceedings, degrade the court and create misconceptions with respect thereto in the minds of the public." This Canon is now the subject of widespread discussion between the bar and some of the media. But generally this amendment as well as the other Canons are accepted by the bar, and furnish a guide to conduct where formerly guides were lacking.

Along with the Canons of Professional and Judicial Ethics came the development of examinations into character and fitness. Originally bar examinations were entirely inadequate, and there was no semblance of uniformity in the several states. The following story, which is probably not apocryphal in origin, is related in Professor Hurst's notable book about *American Law Makers,* concerning an examination conducted by Abraham Lincoln while reclining in a bathtub:

Motioning me to be seated, he [Lincoln] began his interrogatories at once, without looking at me a second time to be sure of the identity of his caller. "How long have you been studying?" he asked. "Almost two years," was my response. "By this time, it seems to me," he said laughingly, "you ought to be able to determine whether you have in you the kind of stuff out of which a good lawyer can be made. What books have you read?" I told him, and he said it was more than he read before he was admitted to the bar.

He asked me in a desultory way the definition of a contract, and two or three fundamental questions, all of which I answered readily, and I thought, correctly. Beyond these meager inquiries, as I now recall the incident, he asked nothing more. As he continued his toilet, he entertained me with recollections—many of them characteristically vivid and racy—of his early practice and the various incidents and adventures that attended his start in the profession. The whole proceeding was so unusual and queer, if not grotesque, that I was at a loss to determine whether I was really being examined at all or not. After he had dressed we went downstairs and over to the clerk's office in the courthouse, where he wrote a few lines on a sheet of paper, and, inclosing it in an envelope directed me to report with it to Judge Logan, another member of the examining committee, at Springfield.

The next day I went to Springfield, where I delivered the letter as directed. On reading it, Judge Logan smiled, and, much to my surprise, gave me the required certificate without asking a question beyond my age and residence, and the correct way of spelling my name. The note from Lincoln read: "My dear Judge:—The bearer of this is a young man who thinks he can be a lawyer. Examine him, if you want to. I have done so, and am satisfied. He's a good deal smarter than he looks to be."

In 1931, the organized bar led the way to the creation of a National Conference of Bar Examiners. This organization has steadily improved the quality and uniformity of bar examinations. While a perhaps excessive tolerance for repeaters sometimes permits a candidate, whose outstanding quality is persistence, to slip through after failing many examinations, the reasonable effectiveness of the modern testing procedure is generally recognized.

The bar has also been concerned with trying to screen out candidates whose character (aside from educational training) makes them unfit for the profession. Today, such examinations are generally conducted after graduation from law school and just before admission. While some character committees are equipped with adequate investigatory staffs, others are not so fortunate. There is a general feeling that improvement in these character examinations is possible and desirable. Furthermore, there is a growing feeling that character should be screened earlier than after graduation from law school. There is a tendency to deal overtolerantly with the possible deficiencies of those who have already invested three years in law school study. Many of the law schools are now using questionnaires intended to facilitate the early detection of those whose character records may present problems. This is a matter which is now under careful study by the law schools and the bar, and everyone recognizes the difficulties of the problem. If it were possible to devise a foolproof character examination before law school study begins, it would be of great advantage to the public, the schools, and the bar.

Closely related to these problems has been the movement for an integrated bar, which has been successful in a number of states. Such bars provide more effective control over admission and better disciplinary supervision, and undoubtedly give the organized bar a larger voice in public affairs within their special competence. Consideration of the creation of funds to indemnify the public against losses due to the occasional cases of lawyers' misconduct, which exist in England and most Canadian provinces, is now underway and seems particularly appropriate in integrated bar states.

The organized bar everywhere is deeply concerned with these problems. It is evident that the recalcitrance of a few members of the bar reflects on the balance, and adversely affects the public's acceptance of the positions of the organized bar on many questions. The fullest and most comprehensive enforcement of standards at every stage of professional study and practice is recognized as essential to fullest acceptance of the authority of the bar. The progress in the last couple of generations has been very notable.

One of the difficulties with all discussions of these serious matters is that they tend to chill and obscure consideration of the equally important spirit of comradeship which has always been one of the traditional joys of the profession. In the old circuit-riding days in America, the bar of the circuit had such an intimate relationship that professional ostracism as a penalty for misconduct was easy to invoke. Undoubtedly the traditionally high standards of conduct of the English bar are still maintained in part by the intimate associations of the assize messes and meals at the Inns of Court. Concern for the good opinion of one's professional brethren to whom one is sufficiently exposed may be as effective a regulator of conduct as enforced rules of ethics. One of the problems of the organized bar as it grows in size and scope is to maintain the spirit of comradeship while enforcing standards against those who refuse to recognize their obligations to their brethren and their clients.

Occasionally in America a period of public hysteria and failure of the bar to conduct necessary public education has seemed to lead to some brief decline in the independence and courage of the bar. It has been a tradition of the American bar, as of the English bar, that the most hated individual could procure adequate representation. Memories of Andrew Hamilton and Peter Zenger, Erskine and Tom Paine, John Adams and the English soldiers remind American lawyers of the duty to be bold in defense of unpopular individuals and causes. Occasionally public detestation of defendants or their views has led some members of the public and press to attribute to lawyers their clients' misdeeds. Lawyers have then been subject to economic and social penalties for courageous representation. This has caused deep concern to the organized bar. In 1953, at its annual meeting in Boston, the American Bar Association adopted the following resolution:

1. That the American Bar Association reaffirms the principles that the right of defendants to the benefit of assistance of counsel and the duty of the bar to provide such aid even to the most unpopular defendants involves public acceptance of the correlative right of a lawyer to represent and defend, in accordance with the standards of the legal profession, any client without being penalized by having imputed to him his client's reputation, views or character.

2. That the Association will support any lawyer against criticism or attack in connection with such representation, when, in its judgment, he has behaved in accordance with the standards of the bar.

3. That the Association will continue to educate the profession and the public on the rights and duties of a lawyer in representing any client, regardless of the unpopularity of either the client or his cause.

4. That the Association request all state and local associations to cooperate fully in implementing these declarations of principles.

Following that resolution, the organized bars of Philadelphia, Cleveland, Denver, and other cities provided counsel in some Smith Act cases, and the general applause which greeted the recognition by the bar of its duty to assure defense of the unpopular shows that the public actually understands and supports the tradition of the bar in this regard.

Recent years have seen a growing appreciation by the bar and the public of the duty to provide counsel not only for the unpopular but more broadly for the poor and those of moderate means who do not have access to legal advice. This has created the great legal aid and legal referral programs which, particularly in the last decade, have been important parts of the program of the organized bar in this country. Organized legal aid stems from the predecessor of the New York Legal Aid Society, which was originally formed to aid poor German immigrants. Such a narrow objective was soon replaced by the concept of providing counsel to all poor people. That objective has never been realized even in New York, which has been the most forward-looking city in this regard. However, steady progress has been made. Legal aid societies are now flourishing in dozens of cities and an active national organization is forwarding the cause everywhere. The number of private legal aid groups on the civil side has doubled in recent years, but legal aid on the criminal side still lags despite the devoted efforts of the leaders in the legal aid field. Private legal aid is supplemented or made unnecessary in some states and localities by public defenders, maintained at public expense. There is now great pressure to adopt the public defender system in the federal courts, a matter which is to be considered by Congress. It is to be hoped that this procedure will not supplant active legal aid societies where they are in a position to render adequate service in particular federal districts.

Within the last twenty years, and particularly in the last ten, the movement to maintain panels of lawyers able to advise and help those of modest means who lack counsel has spread throughout the United States. Originally suspected of endangering the independence of the bar through what was regarded as a socialistic trend, it has now been recognized as a very useful additional public service by the bar. It is clear that there are still many people in this country who are unable to obtain lawyers because of poverty or ignorance, and many more who have not learned to identify their problems as those which lawyers could cure. The bar is making steady progress in helping both groups.

Improvement in the adminstration of the courts has been of prime concern to the organized bar. This concern brought the bar to grips with questions relating to the character of the judiciary, the organization of the courts, and the procedure used in the courts.

It was concern for the character of the judiciary that brought about the modern development of the organized bar. The Tweed Ring had corrupted judges in New York City to the point where leaders of an outraged profession in 1870 formed The Association of the Bar primarily to drive out judicial corruption. Eventually it was successful and went on to many other things. Throughout its history the organized bar has been concerned not only with the removal of unfit judges but with the improvement of standards of judicial selection. This has run all the way from pious observations about the importance of character and learning on the bench to detailed proposals for methods of insuring that desirable result.

The so-called "Missouri Plan," and similar devices in other states, were intended to subordinate political considerations in the selection of judges to those which concerned professional competency and character. There has never been agreement on any particular method of selection but there has been general agreement that there is room for improvement. One of the never-ending debates is whether the appointive or the elective system is preferable. Both systems have provided good judges; however, in both there have been some exceptions. The elective system came in with Jacksonian democracy and only a few states have abandoned it. However, many lawyers believe that there is a good deal of hypocrisy about the continued defense of the elective system if it is based upon the theory that the people actually have any large voice in the selection of judges under that system. All those sophisticated in its actual operations understand that political leaders select those to be submitted to the electorate. The voters rarely have any actual knowledge about the professional qualifications of candidates. In New York, for instance, a recent survey indicated that an infinitesimal number of voters knew the names of any of the judicial candidates for whom they were called upon to vote. The highest judicial officer in New York State is the Chief Judge of the Court of Appeals who is elected by the voters on a state-wide basis. This survey indicated that only about 1 percent of the electorate knew the name of this important judicial officer. Such studies have led to consideration of departure from the elective system. Some have urged the creation of a nomination commission which would aid the Governor in appointments. There is no unanimity but change is in the wind, and the organized bar is much concerned with the problem.

A comparatively recent development in connection with federal judicial appointments has stemmed from the activities of the organized bar. For a long period prior to 1952 the bar had been advocating that federal judges be selected from a list provided by the organized bar, or that at least the names of those under consideration should be submitted for scrutiny as to their professional qualifications. Occasionally an appointment, like that of Judge Medina, was based largely on the advocacy of the organized bar. Although other appointments have had the support of the bar, no general procedure for professional scrutiny had ever been adopted.

In 1952, when the present president of the American Bar Association, Ross L. Malone, was Deputy Attorney General, a most desirable development took place. The Attorney General agreed to submit to the American Bar Association for its approval the names of the candidates most likely to be appointed to a particular judicial office. The procedure established was that such names would go to the Commitee on Federal Judiciary of the American Bar Association which, in turn, obtained the cooperation of the appropriate state and local associations. This procedure has been followed ever since. Dozens of judicial appointments have been made only after such approval. In a few cases names have been disapproved and then other names have been submitted. In a very small number of cases the Administration has felt constrained, probably by political pressure, to disregard the disapproval of names submitted, but generally the grounds of disapproval in such cases can fairly be said to have been arguable. Originally President Eisenhower did not treat this procedure as applicable to appointments to the Supreme Court. However, in his most recent appointments the procedure has been used, and he has stated that he intends to follow it in the future.

For many years the organized bar was concerned with the inadequacy of federal judicial salaries. They were not only inadequate by comparison with some state court salaries and the income of private practitioners but the low salaries were prejudicing the availability of qualified candidates in metropolitan areas. Prior to 1953 the bar had pressed for legislative relief for many years. It became evident that judicial salaries could only be increased if congressional salaries were similarly increased. A commission was created by joint action of the two Houses of Congress to study the problem of congressional and judicial salaries. The organized bar had a substantial part in the creation of this commission; a former president of the American Bar Association was chairman and another was counsel. The American Bar Association brought to Washington approximately sixty witnesses, representing substantially every walk of life including industrialists, labor leaders, housewives, farmers, truckers, doctors, and so forth, to testify in support of the need for increased salaries. The hearings so overwhelmingly supported an increase that Congress voted substantial increases forthwith. The quality of lawmaking must certainly have been affected by the reduction of financial concern which these increases insured.

The bar has been concerned with the need for improved organization of the courts. The courts in most of our states were set up early in the nineteenth century, many of them in a patchwork manner. It was clear that in most states the structure could be improved by streamlining, and that most, if not all, required some centralized administration to assure efficient housekeeping. The Section of Judicial Administration of the American Bar Association brought forward a so-called "American Bar Association plan" in 1938. The essential suggestions for the managing of the business of the courts were: (1) a unified judicial system with the power and responsibility in one of the judges to assign other judges to particular tasks which would relieve docket congestion and utilize the available judges to the best advantage; (2) the strengthening of the judicial councils with representation accorded to the bar and the judiciary committees of the legislatures; and (3) the compiling of quarterly judicial statistics.

In New Jersey, under the driving leadership of Arthur Vanderbilt, which required the mobilization of the entire community over a period of some fifteen years, a constitutional amendment ultimately insured streamlining of the courts. In New York, under the leadership of the organized bar, the legislature in 1953 created a Temporary Commission on the Courts (the so-called "Tweed Commission"), of which I had the honor to be a member, to recommend improvement in the organization of the New York courts. After careful study the Commission recommended a reorganization plan; however, political, judicial, and some professional opposition persuaded the legislature to kill the plan and the Commission. Further substantial progress will require a fresh mobilization of public opinion. Progress has been made in Illinois, Pennsylvania, and other states toward the streamlining of their judicial machinery. Where the bar has been bold enough to take a look at the problem, it has generally been forthright in advocating the need for improvement.

In connection with the federal judiciary, the organized bar has made contributions of a negative sort which have helped to preserve the independence of those courts. Thus at the time of the so-called "court-packing" plan, the bar led the fight against such devices for changing judicial decisions. This was a valuable form of public education. While there are those who say, like the witty English correspondent, that "a switch in time, saved nine," there is no doubt that the bar's fight was significant. Some ten years ago the bar pressed for adoption of the so-called "Butler Amendment" to the Federal Constitution, which would have prevented Congress from tampering with the Supreme Court's power of review in cases arising under the Constitution. Most recently, opposition to the Jenner-Butler proposals to restrict review by the Court in some areas has been led by the bar, and indeed it is not too much to say that its opposition has been decisive.

Inundation of the courts by accident cases is a universal phenomenon. Everywhere it has resulted in some delay. In some courts the delays have become so critical as almost to paralyze the judicial machinery. Friends of the courts have asserted that unless the bar and the judges find a way to overcome the consequences of this new flood, some other system of adjudication will be demanded by the public. Here is an area which challenges the best thought and devotion of the organized bar. Mr. Chief Justice Warren issued a call to mobilize the bar to deal with delay in the courts in his notable address to the American Bar Association meeting in Los Angeles in August, 1958.

At the instance of the organized bar in Pennsylvania, that state has been conducting an interesting experiment dealing with the compulsory arbitration of trivial cases. In many of the counties the courts may transfer minor cases to arbitrators, preserving the ultimate right of trial by jury if the litigants are dissatisfied with an award. Hundreds of cases are now so dealt with and apparently with general satisfaction. Similar ingenuity in relieving courts should in time commend itself to consideration elsewhere.

The organized bar has always played an important role in the development of methods of centralized judicial administration. Much progress has been and is being made in this area. A federal administrative office has functioned in the federal courts for two decades. The present head of that office has recently said that its creation was largely due to the advocacy of the organized bar, particularly The American Judicature Society. Many improvements and much interchange of experience occurred during the administration of Henry Chandler, the first director. It seems likely that under Warren Olney III, the present director, and with the support of the Chief Justice and his colleagues, as well as the judiciary as a whole, there will be further developments of great moment. The administrative office in New Jersey has been an effective adjunct to its modern court structure. Centralized administration has been introduced in New York through the creation of a Judicial Conference upon the recommendation of the Temporary Commission on the Courts. Centralized administration is pushing forward elsewhere. One of the effective agencies aiding this movement is the Institute of Judicial Administration at New York University, created under the inspiration of Arthur Vanderbilt and now efficiently directed by Shelden Elliott. Columbia, through Professor Maurice Rosenberg and others, has contributed important studies in this general field.

Along with proposals for the improvement of court organization and administration have come proposals for the improvement of procedure. The federal rules, both civil and criminal, were prepared by distinguished committees with the cooperation of the organized bar, and have paved the way for procedural simplification and reform elsewhere. Procedure in some of the state systems has also been simplified. In New York a complete overhaul of the unduly complicated Civil Practice Act was begun under the aegis of the Temporary Commission on the Courts with the aid of Professor Jack Weinstein of the Columbia Law School and an outstanding Advisory Committee. It is now being carried on as an independent project under the continued supervision of Professor Weinstein and others. The federal rules have taught that simplification of procedure and broadened discovery increase the opportunity for pretrial disposition of cases and shortened trials. While the legal profession does not universally accept these developments and there is some nostalgia for the good old days when lawsuits were more like games of skill, substantial leadership for reform has always come from the organized bar. Judicial Councils in many of the states make substantial contributions to procedural and other reforms and the movement for such councils stemmed from the efforts of the organized bar.

The movement for uniform state laws on a variety of subjects has also been fostered by the organized bar. Here the American Bar Association has made an outstanding contribution in the field of substantive law revision. Its work in this area dates back to the appointment of an Association Committee in 1889. This Committee's work led directly to the creation of the Conference of Commissioners on Uniform State Laws. Thereafter, the Association partially financed the work of the Conference. The tangible accomplishments of the Commissioners are reflected in the presence on the statute books of most states of a substantial number of uniform acts, many dealing with vital subjects. Today the work continues, and through the Commissioners and support for their work the organized bar is facilitating changes and improvements in new areas of substantive law.

Concurrently with the activities of the Commissioners on uniform state laws has progressed the enormously fruitful work of the American Law Institute, created in 1923 as a device to bring together the skills of judges, lawyers, and law teachers in restating important parts of the law. The Institute continues as a vast cooperative effort which is now channeling its energies into such new fields as the restatement of foreign relations law and tax law. The character of the Institute's debates and discussions and the scholarly contributions of its many participants amply demonstrate the kind of constructive lawmaking which the profession can produce when its best minds work together.

In various states, like New York, the need for continued study of additional areas for reform of the substantive law has given rise to the creation of such organizations as the Law Revision Commission. Here, generally on a part-time basis, leading scholars and lawyers keep the body of the law of the state under continuous scrutiny. Where there is an apparent anachronism or some ancient principle appears to have outlived its usefulness, a study is conducted and legislation recommended. In all such efforts, the organized bar has had a part in staffing the Commission, studying its work, and recommending the adoption of its proposals.

The organized bar has recognized that its responsibility for contributing to procedural reforms is by no means limited to the courts. Observing abuses in other areas of government, the bar has studied the need for reform and contributed to public education as to the desirability of improvement in a number of fields of governmental activity. The importance of fair procedure, of inclusion of the essential elements of due process in all operations of the three great branches of government is gospel with most lawyers and therefore with the organized bar.

Perhaps the bar's most notable single accomplishment in these other areas has been its contribution to reforms in the procedure employed by administrative agencies. With the expansion of governmental activities there has been a concurrent expansion of administrative bodies, both at the federal and at local levels. There are some who believe that these agencies should, in general, be left free of procedural restraints. A few zealous advocates even suggest that the administrative agencies cannot properly function unless they are left unfettered and administrators given the widest possible discretion as to all aspects of procedure. But it became evident at an early stage in this proliferation of administrative activity that the usual consequences of exercise of unfettered power by the new and vast bureaucracies were leading to abuses of the rights of many citizens. The absence of rules encouraged an absence of the basic elements of fair trial and due process. Recognizing that all of the rules applicable to courts might not apply to the conduct of administrative hearings, the bar nevertheless felt that many of them could be remolded to protect the new machinery from abuse. Accordingly, the Administrative Procedure Act was ultimately adopted as a result of the insistence of the organized bar, and improvements in administration have been the subject of steady consideration ever since.

The bar has, in recent years, become concerned with the absence of rules of fair procedure in congressional investigations. Recognizing the importance of the investigative power of Congress, the bar observed that some investigations bore little, if any, relationship to legislative objectives. In others, the rights of individuals were disregarded and congressional committees sometimes behaved as if they were also charged with the duties of grand juries and criminal courts. Following a preliminary study by the Association of the Bar, a Special Committee of the American Bar Association, in a comprehensive study of congressional investigations since the foundation of the republic, recommended the adoption of a code of fair procedure for all congressional committees. This would have assimilated the procedure of the many committees which have functioned with fairness with that of the comparatively few which have not, and would have added some improvements, such as effective right to counsel, which are dear to lawyers' hearts. The recommendation was made at about the same time that a general revulsion of feeling against the worst abuses of such committees took place. While no general code has been adopted, particular committees have adopted rules and the general tenor of procedure has improved.

Widespread criticism of the operation of the government's loyalty and security programs led to a careful study of that subject by a Special Committee of The Association of the Bar, headed by its present President, Dudley B. Bonsal. The report of that Committee, although not yet acted upon by the Executive Branch of the government, was recognized as a thoughtful and valuable contribution to this difficult subject. Very recently another special committee has been studying the passport problem, and its report represents another valuable contribution by the organized bar to the puzzling problem of government administration and the balance of the needs of liberty and security.

While the foregoing constitutes a fair sampling of the major areas of what may be loosely considered lawmaking in which the organized bar plays an important role, a full treatment would require a listing of the actual committees of many active bar associations. Taking The Association of the Bar as an example, such a listing would show that the organized bar concerns itself with consideration and education as to the need for improvement of the law in almost every major field. Thus, committees on admiralty, aeronautics, arbitration, Bill of Rights, various courts, copyright, criminal law, domestic relations, federal and state legislation, insurance, international law, labor and social security legislation, medical jurisprudence, municipal affairs, patents, real property, surrogates' courts, taxation, trade regulations, and trademarks show a catholicity of interest which is not only remarkable but also productive.

Any such summary would be inadequate if it did not mention the growing concern of the organized bar with the concept of the "rule of law" in all areas of the relationship between citizens and government and among governments. This concept, vague though it is, is steadily becoming the rallying point for American lawyers and indeed for lawyers of the free world. A chair on the subject has just been established at the law school of Duke University. It is devotion to this concept which has led American lawyers to advocate the limitation of possible arbitrary action by various branches of our government through the adoption of identifiable rules in such areas as administrative law, congressional investigations, and so forth. And there is also a growing feeling that the principle is the key to appraising the conduct of other governments and their dealings with their own people and with other states.

One of the great developments of the last few years has been the creation and activity of the International Commission of Jurists. Formed originally in Berlin under Dr. Friedenau, the Commission is now functioning at The Hague as an international body concerned with the rule of law everywhere. The bar of the United States has been interested in this organization from the beginning. It has participated in meetings and in support of the work of the Commission. The Commission has reviewed activities in occupied countries which have violated the municipal law of those countries. It has instituted an examination of the meaning of the "rule of law" in all countries of the free world. A committee of the American Bar Association, under the chairmanship of Ernest Angell, has conducted a most fruitful study of that question in the United States. Similar analyses have been prepared in other countries. Out of this should come a general agreement on the meaning of the "rule of law" by which the conduct of governments may be judged. The entire matter is to be reviewed at a conference in Delhi in January, 1959, conducted under the aegis of the Commission.

Recent presidents of the American Bar Association have repeatedly emphasized the importance of the "rule of law" in international affairs. The treatment of that subject by Grenville Clark and Professor Sohn in *World Peace Through World Law* constitutes a major contribution to the discussion. This whole matter is a challenge to the organized bar, not only of this country but of the entire free world. If lawmaking is to continue over any long period of time, it is evident that assurance of general adherence to the "rule of law" will be essential to the survival of the agencies that further the process.

Comment

BY HARRY W. JONES

CARDOZO PROFESSOR OF JURISPRUDENCE, COLUMBIA UNIVERSITY
SCHOOL OF LAW

The range of ideas in Mr. Seymour's fine paper suggests to me that this discussion, on the role of the bar, is a kind of meeting place for the three that have preceded it. There is, indeed, an element of truth in the old gibe that our American tradition guarantees "a government of lawyers and not of men"; this, first and foremost, because the bar is the main source from which the state recruits its official power-holders: three fourths of its elected legislators, the lion's share of its top administrators, all of its judges. These are figures to which we lawyers point with pride, but there are sobering overtones for the law schools and for the organized bar. Lawyers, to be sure, are the dominant occupational group in Congress and the state legislatures, but are they, by and large, the lawyers we would think of as the better lawyers, the stars of our profession? To be local about it, how many Whitney Seymours, Louis Loebs, and Harry Tweeds do you find in the typical state legislature? And what can the organized bar do to get some of them there? With the candor appropriate to a serious discussion, I ask the same question about our judges. Our Traynors, Fulds, Breitels, and Schaefers would be stars in any league, but how many such genuinely superior men are there on appellate courts and trial courts of general jurisdiction, and what can we do to see that the bar offers not of its average but of its best—and that the offer is taken up by those in political power?

My comments, however, are not directed chiefly to the work of lawyers who have become official lawmakers, and not even to the matter, so admirably treated by Mr. Seymour, of the lawmaking influences of the organized bar. I will address myself instead to lawyers participating in the processes of lawmaking as representatives of private clients. Some of my ground is familiar and builds on earlier discussions presented in this Conference. In this country, we have an adversary system of adjudication, and we follow, within workable limits, a policy of stare decisis. These two institutions, taken together, make the practicing lawyer a full participant in lawmaking. The effectiveness and fairness of the lawyer's adversary argument affects not only the outcome of the particular case but also the future of the law's development. Justice Breitel's analysis of judicial lawmaking made clear the extent of a court's dependence on counsel for the presentation and adversary testing of juridical hypotheses. Mr. Gardner's paper underlined the same element in the administrative decisional process, and Professor Newman gave us an impressive reminder that lawyers, as spokesmen for clients, might contribute far more to the wise formulation of legislative policy than they have heretofore. To the layman it is a paradox to say that the lawyer, as a professional partisan, makes an indispensable contribution to equal and impartial justice. Those of us who believe, as I do, in the adversary system see the matter differently and regret the decline of the art of advocacy, the bar's widespread neglect of opportunities for effective professional representation before legislative committees, and the siphoning off of much of the bar's best talent from litigation to various other professional functions.

But, in a larger view of things, the shift in the bar's center of gravity from courtroom work to law office work represents no net decline in the lawmaking influence of the bar. For we cannot appraise the role of the bar as lawmaker without taking full account of the work lawyers do, in their offices, in devising institutional structures and arrangements for private enterprises and associations. This, I am convinced, is the most important work performed by lawyers in our society today, and we must not lose sight of it.

Our American system makes no effort to extend the enacted law to every phase of industrial, business, and cultural life. Wide latitude is left for autonomous development through agreement, trade practice, and private regulation. The lawyer is the person who must, as Lon Fuller puts it, "design the framework of voluntary collaborative effort." This is the area of private lawmaking, where the office lawyer is legislator. Trust receipts and letters of credit, pension trusts and executive incentive plans—even the power structure of today's corporation and trade union—are all constructions of the lawyer's art.

In this aspect of its work as lawmaker, the bar encounters moral problems of which few of its leaders are sufficiently conscious. My concern here reflects my service, for several years now, on the Joint Conference on Professional Responsibility of the American Bar Association and the Association of American Law Schools. The lawyer drafting a standard "take-it-or-leave-it" contract clause, or preparing the constitutional documents for a great enterprise, is inclined by tradition to think in terms of the interests of the clients who retained him. But these arrangements will have the effect of law—for most practical purposes—on the vital interests of many persons not then present in the lawyer's office. These "outsiders" are not themselves represented, as they would be in courts or in legislative committee hearings. In his *ex parte* work as office lawmaker, the lawyer must rise above the pressures that urge him toward complete identification with his client's view of things. For he will be judged, in the long run of it, less by his success as a client caretaker than by the durability and essential fairness of the institutional arrangements which are his contribution to law in society.

Mr. Seymour, in his closing paragraphs, says some important and challenging things about the organized bar and the rule of law. I have lately been privileged, in Chicago and Warsaw, to discuss the rule of law with lawyers and judges from every country of Western Europe and every principality on the Eastern side of the Iron Curtain. This much I have learned. The rule of law, government under law, is not a common man's concept. Lawyers are its only accredited custodians. But we are uncomfortably aware that our professional brothers have not always been faithful to their trust. The German bench and bar were the very first bastion to fall, surrendered *nolo contendere*, in Hitler's revolution against the idea of law. Everywhere on the other side of the Curtain, save only for a few in Poland and Yugoslavia, the legal profession, more than any other, reflects the ideology of the governing class. On this great issue of our time, we American lawyers are doubtless more dedicated to the rule of law than any other group in our society, but not remotely so dedicated as we ought to be.

A lawyer—a real lawyer—should react to unfairness, inequality, or abuse of procedure as a bishop reacts to heresy or a painter to a meretricious composition. What our bar needs is a capacity for indignation—indignation against congested dockets and unregulated contingent fees that threaten substantial justice in half of the civil cases filed in our courts; indignation against universities, including the best ones, that take the lawyer's role in society so lightly that they train doctors in clinical groups of two or three but support legal education only on a low-cost, mass production basis; indignation against political deals that put third-rate lawyers on first-grade courts and tempt bar associations to stamp "qualified" on judicial candidates who are, at best, "pretty good" but not really good enough.

If we are to have a living rule of law in which the world's new countries can find inspiration, the organized bar must combine the physicists' dedication to objective inquiry with the single-minded zeal of the old Anti-Saloon League. The task of the bar is greater than we think. Our bar associations need less part-time committee work and more reforming passion. For, when we talk seriously today about the rule of law, "We stand at Armageddon, and we battle for the Lord."

Comment

BY ROBERT B. TROUTMAN
SPALDING, SIBLEY, TROUTMAN, MEADOW & SMITH, ATLANTA

No one in the United States is better qualified than Mr. Seymour to discuss his subject. For long years he has devoted his great talent to the work of the organized bar. His labors include the efforts of the bar associations in his home city of New York, as well as the nation-wide activities of the American Bar Association and its work in foreign climes. He has brought to these organizations vast study and broad courtroom experience. Thus he knows at firsthand something of the workings of the courts of the land. He appreciates that most of our cherished "rights" were won by men who hammered them out case by case in the courtroom—by lawyers, clients, and judges who had the courage to resist tyranny of the monarch or the mob.

In his paper Mr. Seymour traces the history of the organized bar in the United States and describes many of its activities in the process of lawmaking, defining "lawmaking" in the broadest of terms to include not only statutes, but judicial decisions, administrative regulations, and the customs and conditions which become a part of institutions. He gives credit to the organized bar—rather than to the effort of the individual lawyer—for the main contribution which lawyers have made to lawmaking. Truly, he has made a strong case for the "efforts" of the organized bar to improve our system of law. On the record, the bar is entitled to "E" for effort.

There have been activities in the organized bar in every hamlet and county in the land. Mr. Seymour points out that in his City of New York a member of the bar who feels "some obligation to participate" in the organized bar should belong to: the American Bar Association; to at least three local associations; to The American Judicature Society; and probably to several other professional societies. In my small city there are four local bar organizations, with a meeting of some sort at least every week, not to mention the committee work.

If there ever was an "organized" profession—ours is it. It has some organized activity in which any lawyer who has the slightest interest in "lawmaking" may find an opportunity to use his talents. Yet after seventy-five years the American Bar Association has been able to persuade only about one third of the lawyers of the country to join its ranks. Not more than 40 percent of the 30,000 lawyers in Manhattan, the Bronx, and Brooklyn belong to the local bar associations. The great metropolis of New York is the financial center of our country, if not of the world. More students are being trained for the law in the environs of New York than in any other place. The great Columbia Law School has poured thousands of its graduates into this system of law men, and by far the larger percentage has remained in New York.

Since the school was established, people have moved from the farms to the huge cities like New York. Here they are congregated seeking a better way of life. The lawyers have followed them here. More than 30 percent of the American lawyers are located in eight cities. In these communities the courts are having their greatest difficulty in disposing of their cases. The dockets are congested and the wheels of justice are grinding slowly, at an ever-mounting cost.

According to the reports from leaders of the organized bar in New York, the delay in getting court cases decided shocks the conscience of all who feel any responsibility in the field of law-making. And the delay is not confined to New York alone. It exists in many other communities where the bar is also well organized. Columbia alumni attribute the failure of the Temporary Commission on the Courts of the State of New York to attain a much-needed reform to indifference of the bar and the "massive inertia of the public generally and the bar in particular."

As we review seventy-five years of organized effort and one hundred years of preadmission training in such great law schools as Columbia, well may we ask what is the underlying cause of this indifference on the part of lawyers? The apathy of the voting public is even more noticeable. Mr. Seymour states that only an infinitesimal number of voters in a New York State survey knew the names of any of the judicial candidates for whom they were voting and that only about 1 percent knew the name of the highest judicial officer in the state. One can comprehend opposition to a change in the court system or to policies advocated by the majority of the organized bar. There can be honest differences of opinion. But indifference and apathy on such issues are indeed difficult to understand.

Mr. Seymour touches upon the age-old criticism of political considerations in the selection of judges, whether elected or appointed. In the main, lawyers hold the keys to this problem.

I will cite but one example. At every American Bar Association meeting I have attended the Attorney General of the United States has made an address. The recommendation for the appointment of federal judges is in his hands. In the last seventy years more than 93 percent of these appointments were members of the political party to which the Attorney General and the President belonged. Can the public be blamed for taking into account political considerations in the popular selection of judges, when for seventy-five years the organized bar of the country has made but feeble effort to change the federal system where the method of selection is by appointment?

At almost every bar association meeting—whether in New York or London or Atlanta or Seattle—our leaders from home and abroad, who occupy the highest positions on our courts and at the bar, address us on the "rule of law" and the common law and its unifying effect upon the people who live under its system. They remind us that "ours is the government of laws and not of men." Nevertheless, these laws must be administered by men. Justice is rendered by the men to whose hands the people have entrusted their courts. In the 1930s, Mr. Seymour states, one of the great contributions of the organized bar was to defeat the "court-packing" measure. The "rule of law" was not under attack. The men on the Supreme Court bench who were declaring the law were being assailed. The effort to enlarge the Court failed, but time brought a change in the men who were declaring the law, without a word in the basic law being changed. The same words received at the hands of different men have different meaning. And we have witnessed a great social and economic revolution accompanied by an expansion of the powers of the federal government undreamed of by our fathers, with no change whatever in the language of the law. There has simply been a change in the judges who declare it.

Our most treasured rights and freedoms were established by men—clients, lawyers, judges, and jurors in the courtroom. And today they are being preserved by men in the same forum. They can be preserved only so long as men are dedicated to their preservation.

The rendition of justice to the citizen is indeed the supreme duty of government. In America the people have retained the ultimate power of government. When the people threw off the yoke of kings upon whose "grace" all justice depended, they took upon themselves the duty of seeing that justice be done. They have set apart a special class of citizens to do the job, viz., the lawyers, and granted to them a special license. The machinery of justice is in the hands of these lawyers, whether on or off the bench. Thus the supreme duty of government becomes the first duty of the lawyer. Surely, it should be his first interest. Is it so regarded by the leaders of the bar throughout the nation?

Can we realistically say that the administration of justice in our courts is the prime concern of all our teaching—preadmission and postadmission? To what end are we training law students? What are the "bread-and-butter" courses in our seminars and institutes held under the auspices of the organized bar? Are they aimed at the more efficient and economical operation of our court systems? Or is the emphasis upon making the lawyer a keener competitor in the commercial world as a staff member to big labor, big business, or big government? Is the aim to whet the wits and increase the knowledge that the lawyer may attain a higher standard of living in a society committed to material ends?

Our economic system, in all its phases, must have counsel and legal guidance. Lawyers must supply it. The task of the organized bar of America is to find the means of supplying that need, without in the process destroying the interest of its members in their primary responsibility for the rendition of justice in our courts. The people have a right to expect from their lawyers and judges a system of courts which will operate with a degree of efficiency and economy, suitable to a society which has become accustomed to more efficient methods. They have the right to know whether their selected representatives in the courts—lawyers and judges—are truly concerned about the operation of the courts. And they have a right to know, at firsthand, if possible, just how the machinery of justice operates. Relatively few citizens come into direct contact with the courts. Most of their information is acquired secondhand. We have found no suitable way to acquaint the people with their courts in operation. Certainly the movies and the theaters give no accurate portrayal of actual court proceedings. From newspaper coverage the public learns only through the eyes and ears and pen of a reporter. It is asserted that radio and television broadcasts impair the dignity and decorum of the courts. The problem is now under study by a committee of which Mr. Seymour is the chairman. Our system is bottomed on the proposition that if the people are properly informed they will respond with a fair solution to any public problem. They have the ultimate responsibility and power.

How can they be expected to vote intelligently on either reforms in the system or the judges who preside therein without firsthand knowledge of their operations? We can only conclude from Mr. Seymour's discussion that our methods to date have failed to inform the public even as to the identity of the judges they have themselves elected.

Is this not the occasion to reexamine our definition of "success" at the bar? By what standards do we measure it? Can our profession be a "success" if its members are indifferent to the operation of our system of justice? Is it too much to ask that we rededicate ourselves and our associations to a love for justice as the primary interest of the individual, lawyer and layman alike?

We lawyers must day by day walk the roadway of life with the people of this nation. We and they are subject to all the human frailties. The road is sometimes dusty and sometimes muddy. Someone has described the lawyer who treads it as a "mud-spattered sinner and a star-dusted saint." Although his feet are in the muddy road of life, he must keep his eyes upon the stars. Only by so doing will he meet his full responsibility to see that justice be done though the heavens fall.

The Future of International Lawmaking

BY PHILIP C. JESSUP

HAMILTON FISH PROFESSOR OF INTERNATIONAL LAW AND DIPLOMACY
COLUMBIA UNIVERSITY SCHOOL OF LAW

The Centennial of the Columbia Law School affords an appropriate opportunity for retrospective and prospective glances at the evolution of international law. Given the accelerated pace of developments in science and technology and, as a consequence, in all human affairs, it is reasonable to anticipate that the advances in international law within the next century will be more extensive and more far-reaching than those which have occurred since the middle of the nineteenth century. Lawyers may expect to see international institutions playing a much larger role than they do today. They may well find that the sacrosanct area of "matters which are essentially within the domestic jurisdiction," so carefully excluded in 1945 from the competence of the United Nations, has dwindled to nothing, or at least nothing of consequence.

It was within the period immediately following the founding of the Columbia Law School that a number of lawmaking milestones were placed along the road of the law of nations. In 1861-62 Francis Lieber was giving a course at Columbia on the laws and usages of war; in 1863 his pioneering contribution to the codification of those laws and usages was issued as General Orders 100 for the Government of the Armies of the United

States in the Field. This was the beginning of international legislation through treaty on the laws of war. The Geneva Convention for the Protection of the Wounded followed in 1864 and
the latest Geneva conventions were signed in 1949. At The
Hague in 1899 and 1907 the nations drew up the treaties which
are named for that city and which technically remain in force
today even though many of their provisions now have lost touch
with reality. In 1865 the first of the great international public
unions, the Universal Telegraph Union, was formed, followed
nine years later by what is now the Universal Postal Union.
These were the progenitors of modern international organization, although the earlier river organizations of the Rhine and
Danube also contributed importantly to the development of the
concept and the practice.[1] There were dreamers and architects
of universal peace plans then and earlier, but in the 1860s and
1870s few anticipated the development of international organization which is the reality of the United Nations today.

Through this same period one finds some of the great cases
in international arbitration, understood as a judicial process. The
Alabama Claims arbitration between the United States and Great
Britain followed the Civil War and later came the arbitrations
of the cases of the *Behring Sea Fur Seals* and of the *North Atlantic Coast Fisheries.* Numerous Mixed Claims Commissions
settled thousands of claims cases, most often between a great
and a small power but also between such relative equals as the
United States and Great Britain. Of more significance in the
historical picture, however, is the final achievement of the
establishment of a permanent international court with a fixed
bench of judges. The effort to solve the key problem of finding
an equitable system for the selection of judges failed at the
Second Hague Peace Conference of 1907 but was solved in 1920
and the Permanent Court of International Justice came into

[1] A pioneer in the study and teaching of international organization was Professor
Joseph P. Chamberlain of the Columbia law faculty.

being as part of the League of Nations. Through its successor, that court continues to exist today under the name of the International Court of Justice, the "principal judicial organ of the United Nations."

Throughout the period, international law also underwent its customary process of development through the practice of states, revealed not only in diplomatic correspondence but also in legislative and administrative acts and in the decisions of national courts. Just recently more evidence has been published to show the extent to which governments have acted on legal advice when questions of international law were raised in the conduct of foreign policy. Lord McNair has published the three volumes of his annotated edition of "International Law Opinions," being representative samples of the advice given the Crown by its Law Officers over the span of some four centuries. The opinions of the Legal Adviser (formerly the Solicitor) of the United States Department of State have never been published, although one finds traces of them in the works of Moore, Hackworth, and Hyde. Recently, Professor David Deener has produced an interesting analysis of "The United States Attorneys General and International Law" (1957), which gives some inkling of the extent to which the legal factor has guided government practice on international questions throughout our history. We may anticipate during the years to come more publications in which the archives will be opened by legal research, and volumes comparable to the digests of Moore and Hackworth will reveal the practice of other countries. Such projects are reported to be now underway in Great Britain, France, and Switzerland.

In so far as the decisions of national courts have portrayed or controlled state practice on matters of international law, ready availability and the precedent-seeking habits of common law lawyers, as well as inherent merit, have made the decisions of English and American courts familiar to international lawyers everywhere. In the century past, due in part to the traditional civil law view, the jurisprudence of other countries made less impact. In 1929 Lauterpacht began to solve the problem of availability through the publication of *"International Law Reports,"* which first appeared under the title *"Annual Digest of Public International Law Cases"*; one hundred and fifty-one cases from twenty-eight different national jurisdictions were reported in the 1950 volume reviewed last year in the *Columbia Law Review*.[2] Meanwhile the statute and practice of the World Courts had stressed the importance of judicial precedent.

One interesting type of national court which contributed significantly to the development of international law in the past, but which is unlikely to reappear, was the prize court. As early as the sixteenth century in the countries of Europe prize courts functioned regularly during the numerous wars and judged with remarkable impartiality and according to the law of nations the rights of shipowners, cargo owners, and other maritime interests. The decisions of the federal courts of the United States sitting in prize during and after the Civil War are among the notable contributions from this country, although Story and Marshall had already left their impress on prize law much earlier, following in the footsteps of the great Lord Stowell. Prize law has largely fallen victim to modern methods of warmaking, although scattered cases are to be found in recent wars both large and small. The Judicial Committee of the Privy Council reviewed the nature and extent of prize jurisdiction as lately as 1953.[3]

In the United States the Court of Claims has from time to time been assigned by Congress specific tasks in international law, such as to decide the French Spoilation Claims (over six thousand of them). At times it has sat in a role which it considered to be indistinguishable from that of an international arbitral tribunal.[4]

2Jessup, Book Review, 57 COLUM. L. REV. 305 (1957).
3Schiffahrt-Treyhand v. H. M. Procurator-General, [1953] A.C. 232.
4Royal Holland Lloyd v. United States, 73 Ct. Cl. 722 (1931).

The interests of law and justice would be well served in the decades ahead if the courts of the United States would resume their leading role in pronouncing upon questions of international law. State courts and the lower federal courts are still inclined to do so, but the Supreme Court seems to have developed something of an allergy to international law. The great leading judgments of a Marshall and the international outlook of a Hughes or a Jackson seem scarcely to be found on the bench today. Only in the field of maritime law can one still expect to find the Court deciding international legal problems with the directness and the expertise which is characteristic of the current judgments and opinions of the International Court of Justice. In the absence of any statutory bar in the United States to the application of international law, only the current fashion of jurisprudential theory prevents the Supreme Court from applying international law as it is applied in those countries whose constitutions expressly incorporate it into municipal law, or as it is applied by the International Court of Justice.

Part of the trouble lies with the Department of State and the Department of Justice, which do not seem to have made any special effort to disabuse the Supreme Court of the wholly unreal notions which it harbors about the relation of its decisions to the conduct of the diplomatic relations of the United States. If the Court would look into this problem, it would see that its invocations of the separation of powers and its assertions that certain matters are entrusted under our constitutional system to the political branches of the government are rooted neither in precedent nor in political reality nor in good sound judicial statesmanship. The subject is a familiar one among international lawyers and need not be labored here. Whether the judicial custom and habit in the matter will change is hard to say.[5]

[5]The subject has been more fully developed by the writer in THE USE OF INTERNATIONAL LAW (Thomas M. Cooley Lectures, 8th ser., 1958, University of Michigan

If maritime law still offers full play to the Supreme Court in dealing with a legal subject in which one relies on ancient international custom, that same law of the sea still needs common international action to give it precision and predictability, as through the conclusion of international treaties. Arnold W. Knauth's two volumes of *"Collected Maritime Conventions"*[6] published in 1958, are the latest testimony to this process. But contemporaneously also, the Geneva Conference on the Law of the Sea has demonstrated that the process is still vigorous and that the International Law Commission of the United Nations may well continue to have a function which was not wholly anticipated by Professor Julius Stone writing in the *Columbia Law Review* two years ago.[7] The methods utilized in preparation for this Conference and those at it were a great improvement on those of the League's codification conference of 1930.[8] It is quite possible that hereafter the United Nations General Assembly in adopting resolutions for the guidance of the Commission will have in mind that its most useful function will be to prepare the bases of discussion for international conferences where the legal precedent may be tempered by the practical economic or political necessity, just as it is in the lawmaking process in a national legislature or parliament. One may recall here what Charles Cheney Hyde, lately Hamilton Fish Professor of International Law and Diplomacy at Columbia, wrote in 1945:

The assembling of representatives of all interested States in conferences committed to the task of codification of the law serves to reveal the under-

---

Law School, 1959). See also SECOND SUMMER CONFERENCE ON INTERNATIONAL LAW PROCEEDINGS (Cornell Law School, 1958).

[6] 6 & 6A KNAUTH, BENEDICT ON ADMIRALTY (7th ed. 1958).

[7] Stone, *On the Vocation of the International Law Commission*, 57 COLUM. L. REV. 16 (1957).

[8] Jessup, Editorial, 52 AM. J. INT'L L. No. 4 (Oct. 1958); Jessup, *The United Nations Conference on the Law of the Sea*, 59 COLUM. L. REV. 234 (1959).

standings of the participants concerning what the existing law prescribes.
The relevations indicate the extent of differences of opinion as well as
possible bases of accord, and so illuminate the pathway towards progress.
Political barriers are seen in their true proportions, and the extent of their
influence duly weighed. The value of proposals is ascertained by means
of practical tests indicating whether a general approval, or one far short
of it, or even widespread opposition is to be anticipated. The conclusions
of such assemblages are thus likely to reflect the consensus of governmental
opinion touching the desirability of suggested changes. Through such
bodies the efficacy of the legislative function of the international society is
realized. They afford opportunity to sound the opinion of its membership
as to the sufficiency of the existing law and as to the significance of demands for restatement or modification. Because of the method by which
it is welded together the constructive product of such conferences is likely
to enjoy great and possibly lasting respect. If they convene at regular and
not too infrequent intervals they breed a continuity of intelligent effort
put forth in, and drafted from, every quarter for the loftiest purpose. For
these reasons it is not improbable that through the exercise of the legislative function the international society may at times endeavor to mold
and recast the form of the law that is to obtain among its members.
Whether the effect thereof is to be more potent than that resulting from
enunciations of international tribunals, and in particular from those of the
Permanent Court of International Justice, must depend upon a variety of
considerations the relative influence of which remains to be seen. The
decisive factor will be the degree of success which attends the effort of the
one agency rather than the other to make such delicate and reasonable
adjustments between the interests of the individual State and those of the
community of nations as will unceasingly appeal to civilization as truly
responsive to the requirements of international justice.[9]

No doubt the international lawyers of many generations have
felt the challenge of their times. The first dozen years of this century, with their emphasis on treaties of arbitration and conciliation
and peace pacts, so much deplored by George Kennan, saw a
flowering of international law. The League of Nations era at the

---

[9]HYDE, 1 INTERNATIONAL LAW CHIEFLY AS INTERPRETED AND APPLIED BY THE
UNITED STATES 9 (2d rev. ed. 1945).

end of the First World War was again a time when international law seemed on the verge of overcoming the greatest obstacle to its development, namely the lack of procedural and institutional aids. The reaction at the end of the Second World War was more restrained, perhaps because many still nourished memories of past disillusionment and perhaps because those younger persons who experienced the war looked at the problems with grim determination rather than with stars in their eyes.

Today it may be an illusion, but new challenges, and therefore new opportunities, seem to be carried on the breath of prevalent lawlessness. These new challenges must be examined, but before doing so one must restate the perpetual challenges to the profession of international law.

The perpetual challenge to the international lawyer is greater than that to the lawyer in the national field of law because the international lawyer is always struggling with the problem of the establishment of peaceful and orderly relations among nations. In other words, he is still attempting to solve the riddle of how man can achieve international peace. It may be said that the lawyer in the national field is equally striving always to reach the goal of justice and that this goal is still elusive to the grasp. This may be true, but justice is only one element in the search for international peace and the international lawyer must go still further on his quest.

It is also true that people are inclined to say that the international law of today does not touch the great issues of war and peace. It is a fact that international law does not have behind it the sanctions which would make possible, for example, control of the rivalry between the United States and the Soviet Union. Years ago John Bassett Moore, the first holder of the Hamilton Fish Chair of International Law and Diplomacy at Columbia University, pointed out that national law has not succeeded in eliminating civil war from the world, and until civil wars can be eliminated there is still less prospect of eliminating international wars.

Nevertheless it is a mistake to underestimate the importance of the matters which are dealt with by our international law. As any reader of the daily press in mid-1958 could appreciate, the fishery question is a great and vital issue for Iceland. The solution of the fishery question depends upon the rules of international law governing the extent of territorial waters and the freedom of the seas. The conflict between the United Kingdom and Iceland has been essentially a dispute about the existing law. Like many other legal disputes it has behind it great economic interests. Similarly the question of the diversion of waters of international streams is a great and vital issue for countries like Pakistan and the Sudan. According to the statements of their foreign offices, even though the basic reasons are not quite so apparent, sovereignty over small sections of Antarctica is a great and compelling problem for Chile and Argentina. In a national society it is important that the daily routine of life is subject to law. The routine contacts of states in the international society actually are conformed to international law. This actuality is in itself important.

In meeting the perpetual challenge of the skeptical common law lawyer, the international lawyer seeks for an explanation of the reasons why the members of the bar have not yet accepted international law as a genuine part of the national legal system. This is more true in the United States than in most of the other countries of the world. Generally in the European university system of education and in universities in other countries which have been influenced by the European system, international law is a regular part of the curriculum of all persons planning to go into law. This is not so in the United States. A European lawyer could hardly begin his legal career without having been exposed to some contact with international law and without having had international law included among the subjects upon which he was examined. In the United States, on the other hand, the great majority of the young men and women graduated from our law schools have never been exposed even to a single lecture on international law. The United Kingdom, within a year's time, has taken the step of including international law in the examinations set for the bar, but no state of the United States has as yet taken this step. International law is not thought to meet the pragmatic test to which law school curricula and bar examinations are usually subjected.

Nevertheless in the United States there are signs of change, and we may see very significant developments in this respect during the decades ahead. An interesting example is afforded by the latest meeting of the American Bar Association. Under the leadership of Past President Charles Rhyne, much of the discussion turned on problems of international law and a new committee under the leadership of former Governor Thomas E. Dewey, appointed especially by President Rhyne to examine international law, lent added authority to the consideration of this subject. The Attorney General of the United States, in addressing the meeting in New York of the International Law Association in September, 1958, argued for a greater use of the International Court of Justice, and both he and the Legal Adviser of the Department of State have raised the question whether we should not abandon the old hampering reservations which we attached to our acceptance of the compulsory jurisdiction of that highest international tribunal. It is discouraging to compare these fine words with the actual pleadings of the United States before that Court in the *Interhandel* case (*Switzerland* v. *United States*) where one does not find any great eagerness to submit an actual controversy to international adjudication.

All the same, there does seem to be progress and there is a greater consciousness among members of the bar which may well be reflected in action. Part of the process is to be found in the current work of the American Law Institute in preparing its restatement of the "Foreign Relations Law of the United States." The circumlocution in the title is evidence of the past reluctance of the bar to enter upon the disdained field of international law.

Perhaps all of this new understanding of international law is an aspect of the widening international responsibilities of the United States and the widening impact of international affairs on all phases of American life. Perhaps devotion to international law is a badge of national maturity in this twentieth century. Although in the eighteenth century the infant United States was a leader in the development and practice of international law, today it is not to be expected that a wholehearted acceptance of international law will be found in the societies in revolutionary flux as they emerge into national independence. International law belongs with an international outlook and does not blossom in the rank young growth of nationalism or in a virgin forest of isolationism.

Among the perpetual challenges to the international lawyer, especially in the United States, are the challenges by the political realists. It is unnecessary to recall this controversy in detail, but everyone is familiar with the general attitude of the student of international affairs who concentrates on the power element and dismisses international law as unworthy of an important place in any consideration of the forces which affect international affairs. In a study of intellectual attitudes, it is tempting to suggest a parallel between the attitude of these political realists toward the international lawyers of today and the earlier attitude of the positivists in international law as they looked with some disdain upon the school of natural law.

These are among the old challenges which still confront us and will continue to confront us. But there are other challenges which are new.

First among the new challenges is that of the natural scientist. The natural scientist in challenging the international lawyer is not incredulous or contemptuous, but anxious, questing, demanding. The scientists have opened new areas and new problems and they demand that the international lawyer—and the political scientist as well—shall find the solutions for these new aspects of life which confront humanity.

The scientists have demonstrated that their technical studies are an important part of the political process in international affairs. For example, in August, 1958, in Geneva the scientists from the Soviet Union and its allies and from the United States and other NATO powers completed their studies on the problem of determining whether the testing of nuclear weapons could be detected by some scheme of international checks. They made a common report setting forth their agreed conclusions, which should set at rest the arguments back and forth which have clouded this issue for some time. The way may well be paved—perhaps after some propaganda skirmishes—for a political agreement to abolish nuclear testing.

Next, it has now been agreed that similar technical studies may investigate the question of measures to prevent surprise attacks, once more as a prologue to political agreement. A still further subject in the whole disarmament field which may lend itself to this approach is the examination of possible means of supervising the production of fissionable material.

These technical scientific studies are not only possible prologues to political agreement but they immediately pose tasks of legal engineering, if the conclusions are to be embodied in legal agreements or, that is, treaties. It must be realized that studies in law and government may be just as technical as those in nuclear physics or in meteorology or seismology or other branches of the natural sciences. The recent Conference on the Law of the Sea at Geneva illustrated very well how technical scientific studies as well as legal and political studies entered into the solution of an international problem as a prelude to the agreements sought.

Science also has opened or is opening new areas on the earth's surface. The most striking example is that of Antarctica, which is becoming more accessible and better known as a result of scientific exploration. In that vast continent there are old claims to sovereignty based on the traditional international law which are advanced by Argentina, Australia, Chile, France, New Zealand, Norway, the Union of South Africa, and the United Kingdom. The United States has never made such a claim, and does not admit that any other claim is well founded. The law governing the acquisition of sovereignty over territory previously *terra nullius*, as well as the maintenance of such sovereign rights, well illustrates the flexibility of international law. The Permanent Court of International Justice brought this out clearly in the case of *Eastern Greenland*, where it was prepared to stretch the traditional rule of effective occupation in a realistic way to fit areas where there was practically no native population and where human habitation was difficult. The traditional law still finds application in such disputes as that between France and England over the islands in the English Channel which both countries claimed. They submitted the issue to the International Court of Justice. In searching the title the Court was forced to go all the way back as far as the Norman conquest, but it had no difficulty in finding the law applicable to the settlement of the dispute.

In the Antarctic during 1958 we saw demonstrated the cooperation which was bred by the International Geophysical Year. The International Geophysical Year arose out of private discussion among scientists of various countries. It was organized by the International Council of Scientific Unions (ICSU), which established a special international committee called the Comité Spéciale de l'Année Géophysique Internationale. The common designation is now IGY. The plans were elaborated as early as 1952, when invitations were sent to all nations to form national committees. Actually some sixty-seven countries participated. The participation of the United States was arranged, not through the Department of State, but through the National Academy of Sciences, which is the adhering body to ICSU for the United States. The National Academy of Sciences organized the special American national committee for the IGY and had the support of the National Science Foundation, which aided in securing a special appropriation of $13,000,000 from Congress. This amount was later supplemented by further congressional appropriations. Many private organizations participated in the American effort, and there were various types of governmental support and cooperation. In the polar regions and particularly in the Antarctic, the United States Government cooperated fully, largely through the Navy Department. At Moscow in the summer of 1958 a further large IGY nongovernmental conference planned for the continuation of international scientific cooperation along many lines.

Under the IGY the nations claiming sovereignty in Antarctica, plus Belgium, Japan, the United States, and the Soviet Union, worked together happily and without friction in the region, the scientists again ignoring whatever political frictions have been surrounding them. As a consequence, the United States in May, 1958, proposed a continuation of the cooperative scientific effort in the Antarctic. The general purport of the proposal was to suggest that since the IGY was drawing to a close it was desirable in the interest of mankind, of the preservation of peace, and of the purposes of the United Nations that all of the nations principally concerned should agree to continue scientific exploration in the Antarctic, without involving political claims or other similar territorial considerations. All eleven countries including the USSR have agreed in principle to the proposal of the United States, but no actual plan has been sanctioned. However, it would seem likely that there will be a continuation of international cooperation in Antarctica. Nevertheless, it must be recognized that this is only a temporary solution. In 1956 the Indian government took steps to place the problem of Antarctica on the agenda of the General Assembly of the United Nations, but this action was not ultimately carried through. Among the various claimants of sovereignty, the Chilean and Argentine governments have perhaps been the most vigorous in the assertion of their claims and in the refusal to submit the rightfulness of their claims to international decision. Both of these governments declined the proposal of the United Kingdom to submit the controversy to the International Court of Justice.

Antarctica is a vast empty continent, almost as large as Europe and the United States combined. It has no inhabitants, and therefore the problem of dealing with a native population, which has historically arisen in connection with the development of other continents, does not arise in this case. Owing to the climatic conditions and the fact that scientific explorations have not yet been completed, no definite source of mineral wealth in the area has as yet been identified. There are, however, reports that such wealth exists. There are also reports that certain areas could conveniently be utilized as airfields. Suggestions have appeared in the press that parts of the continent might be used as stations for testing atomic bombs. It may be true that the polar regions offer special advantages for the launching of manned missiles into outer space.

It seems credible that with the progress of scientific development, and with perhaps new discoveries as a result of the international cooperative explorations, very great importance may be attached to various operations in this area of the world. Before any such development which might intensify international conflict concerning national claims to the area takes place, it has been thought by some that a more permanent international solution should be found.

In 1948 the United States suggested formally to other Antarctic powers, which did not at that time include the Soviet Union, that the solution of the problem of conflicting claims might be reached through agreement upon "some form of internationalization." In 1950 the Soviet government put all claimant states on notice that it considered the future of Antarctica a matter for international agreement. United Nations administration has been urged by a leading Japanese newspaper, and Prime Minister Macmillan discussed internationalization during his visit to Australia and New Zealand in February, 1958.

Although there are many problems to be solved before a successful United Nations administration could be developed even for a vacant area like that of Antarctica, this South Polar region does offer the most likely opportunity for an experiment in international administration. It is fantastic to think that the world will allow this now-empty area to become some new battleground, some new source of contest and conflict. Lessons learned in carrying out an international plan in this area before national rivalries become more intense, might be turned to good advantage in other situations, particularly in connection with the still future, but rapidly developing, problem of outer space.

There is no reason why international lawyers and students of government should not be working out now the detailed plans for some kind of international administration of Antarctica. Such work indeed is underway and may again eventually form the prologue to political agreement.

Science has opened up to man contact with outer space. This is not the place to discuss the scientific probabilities of space travel, of access to the other planets, and other developments which so recently seemed fantastic but which now more and more confront the statesmen and other persons who are realistically looking at the world as it is going to be.

The problem of outer space can be considered in a number of different ways. Some of the current discussions approach the matter from the point of view of armaments, noting that intercontinental ballistic missiles or other projectiles launched from the ground may traverse outer space before returning to a terrestrial target. Viewed from the launching spot or the target area, outer space is involved in the general issue of disarmament. It was so treated in a recent exchange of documents between the United States, the United Kingdom, and France on one side and the Soviet Union on the other on agenda proposals for summit talks.

If one considers the question of satellites launched from the earth but then placed in orbit, one again may find certain military significance and may consider the regulation of satellites in orbit a problem connected with disarmament. At the present stage, the further and perhaps much more distant questions of interplanetary travel or sending rockets to the moon seem as yet not to be fully identified with military problems, although these issues can not be excluded. The latter category of situations, however, seems at present to lie more within the range of scientific cooperation than elsewhere.

A very large number of legal and scientific associations have addressed themselves to a study of the space problem, and there is already an abundant literature on the "law of space"; a recent bibliography lists over two hundred and fifty items. The Legal Committee of the Consultative Assembly of the Council of Europe is one of the many bodies which has the subject under study. There are technical discussions concerning the dividing line between the air space, which is already subject to international convention and regulation, and the space above or beyond the air space. It seems unnecessary in this paper to detail the technicalities involved in these discussions. It is clear that an international issue of eventually very grave significance is posed by scientific developments in the exploration of outer space. The exact solutions may have to wait upon further knowledge. However, it may be pointed out that in current discussions there are various positions which are not wholly reconcilable. There are suggestions that the sovereignty of the state should extend indefinitely into outer space or at least as far as the security interests of the state might dictate. At the other extreme is the suggestion that outer space should be considered *res communis* and that all exclusive national use should be precluded. There are also suggestions that when man is able to reach the moon or other planets it should be understood that there will be no acquisitions in a national interest but only in an international interest.

Some forty years ago international law was able to respond adequately to the development of air travel and a considerable body of international air law has developed during the last four decades. With the enhanced speed of life in general there is no reason why development of space law should not occur even more rapidly. The subject is to be discussed in the 1958-59 session of the United Nations General Assembly, and it is likely that a study commission will be set up as proposed by the United States. Once again we find here a field in which the natural scientist and the lawyer must work closely together and where the lawyer must take account of the developments in the natural sciences.

Coming back to earth we find the scientists opening up another set of possibilities. There are frequent reports of the progress which is being made with the experiments in the development of an inexpensive process for taking salt out of sea water. This goes hand in hand with progress in the experiments with the control of thermonuclear reactions which might usher in an era of cheap power throughout the world. This may be long in coming but we are talking of the situation two or three decades from now. If there is cheap power and a cheap process for desalting ocean waters, there is no reason why vast desert areas such as those of the Sahara should not be turned into fruitful districts capable of absorbing the excess populations of many of the crowded surrounding states. Why should not legal engineering anticipate the problems which will arise at that point, and why should not a vast desert area like the Sahara be treated as a great international region instead of being cut up by the national frontier lines which now disappear in its sandy wastes? The cooperation of Egypt, Lybia, the Sudan, Algeria, Tunis, Morocco, France, and others might well be sought in a new venture under United Nations auspices, which would be truly revolutionary. And the Sahara is merely one example.

The second great challenge to which we must look forward is the challenge of institutional identity and action. By this I mean the evolution of international organization. It includes the whole concept of an entity composed of many states which has a separate personality and separate rights and duties. The parallel is by no means exact but just as the concept of the corporation was a revolutionary notion in our private law, so the concept of the international organization as an entity separate and apart from its members can play a revolutionary part in the evolution of international law.

At the very outset this concept challenges much of the theory of international law which has been conceived of as a law between and among states. Much of the traditional thinking and the theory of the basis and development of international law are in need of modification once one accepts the notion that an international organization is itself a subject of international law. The advisory opinions of the International Court of Justice in the case of *Reparations for Injuries Suffered in the Service of the United Nations* (*Bernadotte* case) and in the *UNESCO* case already show how far we have moved in the direction of accepting the international organization as equivalent to a state in many legal respects.

There are of course constitutional problems aud problems of administrative law arising from the existence and operation of international organizations. Many of these have already been explored in the literature, notably by Wilfred Jenks. The jurisdictional problems have been examined, as, for example, in Jean Lalive's lectures at The Hague Academy of International Law. The relation of the international organization to the national state, in terms of their respective interests in the individual employee or official, is again a subject of very considerable interest on which one finds useful writing such as that by Maxwell Cohen, Crosswell, and King. Then there is the field of what can be called international parliamentary law, which properly belongs in any consideration of law broadly conceived.[10]

Parenthetically, perhaps the new reaches of international law are suggested by the multiplicity of terms which are beginning to make their appearance in the literature. In addition to international parliamentary law, one finds discussions of international constitutional or international administrative law. Much has been written about international economic law, international financial law, and international monetary law; a special "school" has developed along these lines under Professor Schwarzenberger in London. There are the abundant devotees to the field of international penal law or international criminal law. International air law and international space law go along with international maritime law which has a much older history. One finds also in modern writings discussion of the establishment of a branch known as international uniform law. It has also been proposed as somewhat of a countermeasure but nevertheless also as indicative of the new scope of international law, that all of these fields as well as the traditional divisions between public and private international law should be subsumed under some such label as "transnational law."[11]

Parallel with this evolving recognition of institutional identity one finds an increase in the emphasis upon the individual as a

[10]The writer has explored some aspects of this subject in his lectures on "Parliamentary Diplomacy" at The Hague Academy of International Law, 89 RECUEIL DES COURS 185 (1956).

[11]JESSUP, TRANSNATIONAL LAW (1956).

subject of international law with all the disturbing and difficult problems which that raises, especially for the theorist. Linking this with the development of international organization, one should note that on September 4, 1958, with the deposit of the ratifications of Iceland and of Austria, the International Court of Human Rights for Europe under the Rome Convention was made legally possible and will now be brought into existence. Here as in the Coal and Steel Community, in the Common Market, and in Euratom, Europe is perhaps blazing new trails which the rest of the world may desire to follow.

Third among the new challenges confronting the international lawyer is the challenge of the need for a secure peace. It was suggested at the outset of this paper that this is part of the perpetual challenge, but the newness of degree may well here be regarded as a newness of kind. The development of the new thermonuclear weapons and of the means of their delivery, especially as all of these are perfected in the years to come, creates for us a kind of problem which challenges the old concepts of national sovereignty and calls with an insistent voice for imaginative legal thinking as a prologue to political agreement.

Lawyers and scholars have already begun to pave the way. One must note Clark and Sohn's significant work published under the title *World Peace Through World Law* after some dozen years of cooperative effort and the publication of drafts which have received comments from around the world. It is their thesis, well documented, that the acceptance of world law (about which the politicians always prate) involves complete national disarmament and the acceptance of a world peace force of military character. Their great contribution lies in the detailed examination they have made of the problems which are involved in such a transition. Similarly one finds the studies of Henkin and Melman published at Columbia University in 1958 also constituting pioneering examinations of the detailed problems confronting law and government as we move to the next essential stages of the life of nations and of man.[12]

All of these studies help to dispel the illusion that we have reached the end of the road to a secure peace by accepting some one of the little steps along the way, such as supervision of nuclear tests or some inspection scheme. Inevitably one must go on to the whole panoply of supranational institutions if one is to meet the challenge of the need for secure peace in the nuclear age. It matters not if one thinks in terms of twenty years or fifty years or of a century. It matters little whether one thinks that this will not be accomplished save by the tortured and deformed remnants of the human race who may survive the great holocaust of another and nuclear war. One may agree that the time is not yet ripe, in the sense that the thinking of mankind has not yet moved to the stage of action. This does not mean that the time is not ripe for the preparatory studies, for the work of the international lawyer which must be prologue to the eventual agreements of politicians and governments.

Looking at the question of the calendar, it is a matter of some difficulty to determine what is sensible and what is merely ideal. As a traditional gradualist I have been inclined to think that progress in these matters must come by slow and halting steps one after the other, each one advancing us only a minute distance along the road. Perhaps this is not true. Perhaps with these new elements with which science confronts mankind the change on the international level will be revolutionary, as great changes have historically taken place on the national level. We may leap from one point to another, not now but sooner than we think.

It would be a great mistake for the international lawyer confronted with the vast tasks which open up in the future perspectives to ignore the needs of the moment. No matter how rapidly

[12]HENKIN, ARMS CONTROL AND INSPECTION IN AMERICAN LAW (1958); MELMAN (ed.), INSPECTION FOR DISARMAMENT (1958).

supranational institutions may develop, there will still be need for regulation of the practical affairs of groups of peoples. The present corpus of international law regulates these detailed relationships and is in constant need of being built up and strengthened. If the gradualist interpretation be the sound appreciation of the future course of history, then it is of special importance that the rule of law in all transnational situations be developed progressively in the interest of creating a habit of law among peoples and governments.

It is not necessary to wait for unanimity in the adoption of a greater devotion to the rule of law and to the acceptance of more legal controls of international conduct. It is quite possible for the United States and for like-minded states to form a "law bloc" which will be composed of those states ready to apply in their own interrelations not only the substantive rules of law but the procedures necessary to give them reality. This would be an open-ended bloc in which the membership of every nation and people would be welcomed but which could operate even while some maverick nations remained outside or while some new peoples were schooling themselves in an understanding of the utility of law in their national life.

The future of international law thus holds opportunities never before equalled for international lawyers as they seek to grapple with the problems of their profession. The responsibility for imaginative leadership will rest with the universities, with the faculties of law and political science. As they turn out more and more graduates who are conscious of the international problems, we will find more and more persons in positions of governmental responsibility who will share the conviction that progress must be made along these lines of endeavor so that the international rule of law will be not merely a political slogan but a reality.

Comment

BY JAMES N. HYDE
NEW YORK CITY

The inability of the international sector of law to regulate the most vital questions of peace or war and the use of force represents one perpetual challenge which Professor Jessup has described. Yet on less vital matters, principles of law regulating the practice of states are generally observed. In considering the future of international lawmaking, it is therefore appropriate to reflect on the role of law in matters of war or peace.

Largely formalistic prohibitions, usually labeled principles of international law, have been postulated on the existence of an international community. This community is seen as ordering the existence of subordinate states. It has been described as that group constituting the civilized nations. Although ten years ago Lauterpacht used that concept, in his most recent edition of Oppenheim he defines "community" as the body of a number of individuals or individual states.[13] The test is not whether or not they are "civilized." "Community" derives from their being more or less bound together through such common interests as create a constant and manifold intercourse between them. From the existence of such a community, his definition of international law follows, as the body of customary and treaty rules which are considered legally binding by states in their intercourse with each other.

If one turns to Soviet lawyers, Vyshinsky[14] saw law generally as having two elements: rules of conduct expressing the will of the dominant class, and rules of community life sanctioned by

13 1 OPPENHEIM, INTERNATIONAL LAW 4 (6th ed., Lauterpacht, 1947); 11 (8th ed. 1955).
14 VYSHINSKY, THE LAW OF THE SOVIET STATE 50 (1948).

state authority. Soviet lawyers see the world divided into the socialist and capitalist camps with opposed policies or, as some would say, opposed law.[15] Therefore, the rule of law in the relations of the two camps can be no broader than the principles on which there is common consent of all states.[16] From this has followed the Soviet assertion of the principle of state sovereignty in its widest form, "formal impenetrability." Thus one Soviet lawyer called sovereignty "a judicial banner in the struggle of freedom-loving peoples for their independence."[17]

Manfred Lachs, of the University of Warsaw and a diplomat as well, has accepted this absence of shared concepts between East and West. He has suggested that the principles on which there is common consent between the two camps be studied as what he calls the legal problems of peaceful coexistence between capitalism and socialism.[18]

Another approach was suggested by Alejandro Alvarez of Chile. He saw law developing on the basis of social interdependence. Therefore, he argued, the concept of the absolute sovereignty of states must end. In a dissenting opinion written shortly before the end of his term on the International Court he said:

It is also necessary to bear in mind the fact that certain fundamental legal conceptions have changed and that certain institutions and certain problems are not everywhere understood in the same way: democracy is differently understood in Europe and in America, and in the countries of the Eastern group and those of the Western group.

At another point he observed:

15W. W. Kulski, *Soviet Comments on International Law and International Relations*, 47 AM. J. INT'L. L. 125, 133 (1953).

16J. STONE, LEGAL CONTROLS OF INTERNATIONAL CONFLICT 61 (1954).

17O. Bogdanov, Book Review (unpublished in the United States) of 1 C. C. HYDE, INTERNATIONAL LAW, Publishing House for Foreign Literature, Moscow, 1950.

18Lachs, "Le Problème Juridique des Nationalisations et des Enterprises d'Etat ou Collectivisées," paper prepared for International Association of Legal Science, Rome, 1957.

From the middle of the 19th century, as the result of the appearance of important factors which had not previously existed, the traditional *individualistic* regime of the absolute sovereignty of States began to give place to a new regime, that of *interdependence,* which gave rise, as I have said, to the *law of social interdependence.*[19]

India's Constitution provides (Article 51) that the state shall endeavor to maintain just and honorable relations between nations, and foster respect for international law and treaty obligations *in the dealings of organized peoples with one another.*[20] Here one notices the notion of organized peoples and by inference a community of them. Yet in its eleven years as an independent state the Indian government has stood firmly on the principle of determining for itself what matters are within its own jurisdiction in the controversy with Pakistan over Kashmir.

One younger Egyptian lawyer, Ezzeldin Foda, in sketching a possible Arab Court of Justice with regional jurisdiction, emphasized the need of the Arab states to see themselves as one nation. He feels that the Western secular norms of sovereignty as an absolute and unlimited right of the state, although they have permeated the relations of the Arab states in the past, cannot endure. They lack solid ground, because the Arabs are one nation, and the Arabs and the Moslem world one territory.[21]

Even this brief sampling shows that one cannot today deduce the existence of a single international order, with generally accepted and binding norms covering such fundamentals as the legal and illegal use of force, as well as collective measures to meet armed or subversive attack. On the other hand, one should be slow to accept the Soviet thesis of two legal orders with a breakdown of juristic communication between them.

Solidarity, which is the basis for any domestic system, is relatively undeveloped. We have properly been reminded of John

[19]Anglo-Iranian Oil Co. Case (jurisdiction), [1952] I.C.J. Rep. 93, 127, 128.
[20]BASU, COMMENTARY ON THE CONSTITUTION OF INDIA 238 (2d ed. 1952).
[21]E. FODA, THE PROJECTED ARAB COURT OF JUSTICE 122 (1957).

Bassett Moore's observation that national law has not eliminated civil war. We are living today with problems of the application of principles of American constitutional law to questions of civil rights. In short, within an international community, law can develop. Law cannot create the community. Nation-states still retain a wide area of discretion to determine for themselves which are their domestic matters, or the extent of their own sovereignty.

The lawyer need not apologize for straying, as I have, into international politics because the reality of law in matters of war or peace must come from contact with these formidable political realities. The dynamics of international politics are themselves a major resistance point to the organization of an international community, and hence to the development of law. Here, then, is the setting in which the lawyer, perhaps as a government official, perhaps as a teacher or as a practitioner, will function.

One of the new challenges which Professor Jessup has discussed is the creation of a wider international community, with greater order, thus capable of affecting more directly matters of war or peace. There is no immediate prospect for world government along the lines of the Clark-Sohn plan, because that plan is postulated on a highly developed community of interest between East and West. Therefore, let us turn to what Professor Jessup calls the evolution of international organization.

Considering first the regional organization of states, an identity of community interests has developed in the Americas to the point that such minor political disputes as have arisen have been settled by the Organization of American States. When the Charter of the Organization provides[22] that every American state has the duty to respect the rights enjoyed by every other state in accordance with international law, that article has certain practical results leading toward the treatment of these political disputes as legal controversies to be approached with legal techniques.

[22]CHARTER OF THE ORGANIZATION OF AMERICAN STATES, April 30, 1948, ch. III, art. 7., Pan American Union, Law and Treaty Series, No. 23, p. 26.

The new European Economic Community, creating the European Common Market, is a delegation by member states to a central authority of the power to make binding decisions. The six members include former enemies during the Second World War. Relations of the member states with one another and with the central authority are governed by the constitutional law of the Community as interpreted by its court.[23] These are thus no longer clearly matters of public international law.

A further significance of the regional pattern may lie in the fast rate of fragmentation of the world into an increasing number of small states, some hardly able to survive. We are seeing this pattern evolve especially in Africa today. There are already eighty-one members of the United Nations, whereas there were fifty-one in 1945. It is a possibility that this fragmentation could modify the power pattern of two superpowers, so that regional groupings would be of primary political importance. The existence of endless small political entities might dilute the concept of absolute sovereignty. As a result, regional organizations could develop as power centers, and regional economic arrangements assume greater importance. The assumption that political units are bound to be incorporated into larger groups may be open to question.[24] The larger organization may be looser rather than stronger, and still provide the basis for one system of law.

The United Nations system is closest to a universal organization. The United States, the Soviet Union, and the other members have found it necessary to discuss the great issues of war or peace in the Security Council and the General Assembly. They have thus used the forum and procedure which the United Nations offers, and have discussed the issues in terms of Charter principles.

[23]Treaty establishing the European Economic Community and connected documents, Rome, March 25, 1957, published by the Secretariat of the Interim Committee for the Common Market and Euratom, Brussels.

[24]DeVisscher, Theory and Reality in Public International Law 107 (Corbett transl. 1957); see also note 21 supra.

I have touched on that wide area of reserved powers called domestic jurisdiction. There is also a power of United Nations members to initiate the discussion of any question within the scope of the Charter. For better or for worse, this makes it possible to bring controversies before a United Nations body for discussion, and that body will decide for itself whether such discussion invades the domestic jurisdiction of the member states concerned. This is directly contrary to the concept of absolute state sovereignty.

The shrinking of the world owing to the speed of communications and the increasing interdependence of areas in economic terms have provided a field in which the United Nations system has filled immediate needs—the need to regulate air and electronic communications, maritime practices, and now even the discussion of primary commodity prices. Some see in these technical and economic developments a functional approach which avoids a frontal attack on the principle of sovereignty and reserved powers.[25]

As to the United Nations system as a whole, I do not suggest that discussion and references in speeches to Charter principles settle power conflicts. Probably there is now no settlement for some of them. I do suggest that the United Nations forum and procedure, with its experience in the economic and technical fields, provides in some fields the international community of interest on which law is based. It is a possible hypothesis that this gap between regulated and unregulated conduct will narrow. Secretary General Hammarskjold feels that the United Nations has become a bridge over a period of transition to world community.[26]

[25]Mitrany, *The International Technical Assistance Program*, 1953 ACAD. POL. SCI. PROC. 145-46; see remarks of Eugene R. Black, President, International Bank for Reconstruction and Development at Annual Meeting: "Economic growth is at once the best hope and probably the only real hope for mankind today." I.B.R.D. SUMMARY PROCEEDINGS 10, 15 (1958).

[26]Address by Dag Hammarskjold, *The Vital Role of the United Nations in a Diplomacy of Reconciliation*, Houses of Parliament, April 2, 1958, 4 U.N. REV. 6-10 (May 1958).

Lauterpacht has put it more strongly. He feels that the economic and technical activities are common interests which represent a powerful unifying factor.[27] These, he observes, are the realities of national intercourse between states, and political intolerance and economic nationalism must be regarded as temporary. He concludes that one international community is, at least in the long run, a reality. Perhaps less affirmatively DeVisscher sees the plan of the United Nations as a potential order in the minds of men. He concludes that it provides a meeting place for those who seek the peaceful settlement of disputes. This is enough to justify its existence, he adds, but too little to warrant any expectation of security.[28]

Finally, let us look at the role of the lawyer working in a community which is at best only partially organized. I have mentioned the conflicting theories of Lauterpacht, Vyshinsky, of Lachs, Alvarez, Foda, Hammarskjold, and DeVisscher. These men come from different countries, but they have at least two things in common. They were trained in the law and their work and principal occupation for substantial periods has been international organization, in all but one case the United Nations system. After his years on the International Court of Justice, DeVisscher wrote: "And it is primarily to legal policy that the vast enterprise of international organization belongs—a decidedly creative task."[29]

Perhaps it is the lawyer's role to participate in the negotiation or mediation of a controversy between states which they do not consider suitable for judicial settlement. Working with politics and law, he it is who can supply the legal ingredient important not only to a lasting settlement, but as a precedent. Perhaps it is his role to work on some technical economic matter involving rules quite separate from those concerning the relations of states. Even

[27] 1 OPPENHEIM (8th ed., Lauterpacht), *op. cit. supra* note 13, at 12-13.
[28] DEVISSCHER, *op cit. supra* note 24, at 115.
[29] *Id.* at 363.

in the more familiar atmosphere of the International Court on the question of applicable law, his main guidance may be what the Statute of the Court describes as "the general principles of law recognized by civilized nations."[30] In each of these situations, if he is an American, he will be presenting his point of view to a group in which Anglo-American lawyers are in the minority. He will therefore need to be able to communicate with decision makers of differing cultural backgrounds.

The lawyer concerned with the international sector of law will continue to be a pioneer. Command of languages and breadth of scholarship are taken for granted, as well as his familiarity with the principal institutions, rules, and practices which we often call positive international law. Yet the importance of technical excellence of craftsmanship is more than a matter of personal professional pride. It has, as Wilfred Jenks has put it, "a vital bearing on the extent to which law can fulfill effectively its part in the life of society and meet the claims which an emerging world community is entitled to make upon it."[31]

In other words, the lawyer must be not only a pioneer but a professional. It is he who must see clearly the difference between formulations of hopes or goals as principles of law, and their reality as applied to collective security. He must be able to analyze and counsel on the danger of paper solutions which could not survive the realities of an existing power pattern.

[30] Stat. Int'l Ct. Just. art. 38, para. 1c.
[31] Jenks, *Craftsmanship in International Law*, 50 Am. J. Int'l L. 32, 33 (1956).

Comment

BY EUSTACE SELIGMAN
SULLIVAN & CROMWELL, NEW YORK CITY

Can the World Court become a substitute for war to remedy injustices? Professor Jessup in his comprehensive and stimulating paper expresses his approval of current efforts to induce the United States to abandon its existing hampering reservation to the acceptance of the compulsory jurisdiction of the International Court of Justice. He favors the proposal as a step toward developing a world rule of law.

A leader in these efforts is former President Charles Rhyne of the American Bar Association who, in his annual address, said:

To pull the world out of its present drift toward destruction, and to set it on the path of progress toward peace, a dramatic new approach to peace is essential. Settlement of international disputes through law in the courts is such a plan. We American lawyers have a tremendous duty and responsibility. We of all groups appreciate that law used in a world judiciary is the key to world peace.

Our instinctive reaction as American lawyers devoted to the cause of peace is to favor the proposal. Nevertheless there are weighty objections to it. I should like to outline these objections and also to make an alternative suggestion.

We are apt to consider that the creation of the United Nations was a step forward in promoting the world rule of law. To what extent is this the case? It is true that under the Charter nations have renounced the use of force except in self-defense. But if there is to be a world rule of law, is it not essential that a nation which has renounced force to obtain its rights should be able to obtain such rights by peaceful means?

Under private law, an individual cannot resort to force to collect a debt or to enforce some other right, but as a necessary corollary he can go into court and obtain his rights. A similar need exists in the case of nations if we are to have a world rule of law. As Secretary Dulles wrote in *War or Peace*:

There can never, in the long run, be real peace unless there is justice and law. Peace is a coin which has two sides. One side is the renunciation of force, the other side is the according of justice.

The Charter, however, provides no method for a nation to enforce its rights if they are violated by another nation. The Suez incident is an illustration of this; Britain and France claimed a violation of treaty rights by Egypt but they were unable to appeal to any tribunal which would pass on the validity of their claim, and enforce it if valid. Accordingly, they contended that they must be entitled to use force notwithstanding the apparent Charter prohibition.

One alternative to resorting to force in such a situation would be to create machinery to bring about the world rule of law which is now nonexistent. This would require two basic changes in the Charter. The first would be that all members should be compelled to accept the compulsory jurisdiction of the Court; the second, the creation of a means for enforcing decisions of the Court. At present there is only Article 94 of the Charter, which provides that if a party fails to comply with a judgment of the Court, the other party may appeal to the Security Council, which may, but is not required to, decide upon measures to be taken to give effect to the judgment. This article would have to be changed so as to require the Council to enforce all judgments of the Court by any means which were necessary. This change, to be effective, would also have to be accompanied by a giving up of the right to veto such enforcement measures.

Unless these changes were effected, mere acceptance by the United States of the compulsory jurisdiction of the Court would not bring about a world rule of law. However, even if these changes in the Charter could be adopted—which politically seems most improbable—a further and more fundamental question arises as to the desirability of adopting them, and of bringing about a world rule of law similar to that of private law.

Merely to suggest this doubt will appear to many as regrettable. However, there is a question which must be faced. The issue which is raised is whether law and justice are necessarily always synonymous, or whether law is not frequently a rule deemed generally desirable, but which may work injustice in individual cases.

An example from private law which illustrates this is the question as to whether a bona fide purchaser of stolen property should be required to give the property up to the original owner. The general rule is that the original owner recovers, but the opposite rule applies in the case of goods bought in market overt or in the case of negotiable instruments. Can both rules be characterized as just?

Or take the case recently in the New York courts. Is it just to require a reporter to divulge the source of his information, or should the exception of confidential communications be expanded to include a statement to a reporter?

Furthermore, the conflict between law and justice becomes accentuated when conditions change so as to require a change in the existing rule of law. In the field of private law, the need for such change has always been recognized, and it has been accomplished in part by courts more or less frankly reversing themselves and in part by legislative action.

In the international field, the need of change is equally well recognized. To quote again from Secretary Dulles:

Change is the law of life. New conditions are constantly arising which call for change lest there be injustice. Such injustices tend ultimately to lead to resort to force unless other means of change exist. Peace must be a condition where international changes can be made peacfully.

Can any legal mechanism be provided for making changes in existing rules of international law necessary to effect justice? In the absence of a world legislature, there is the alternative of giving the power to the Court. Is this feasible? Or is not the growth of the common law an inapplicable analogy in the field of international law?

In our own country we have seen the serious consequences of the Supreme Court's reversal, in the interests of what it and a majority of us believe to be justice, of its prior decision on the segregation issue—even though the reversal was unanimous. It will prove difficult enough, in a comparatively homogeneous community united as one nation, to obtain acceptance of the decision in the South, which passionately proclaims its injustice; surely the reversal by the World Court of an existing rule of law on a similarly vital issue would not be accepted by a nation against which the judgment was rendered.

As long as separate nations continue to exist with different languages, cultures, and institutions, and until we have a world federation—which is a far-distant goal—is it not inevitable that neither the United States nor any other country will be willing to give a tribunal of men, however wise and impartial they may be, the final power, by majority or even unanimous vote, to change an existing rule of law on matters affecting their vital interests? On the other hand, is it not equally impossible to expect them to continue to be bound by a rule of law which is no longer fair, in view of changed conditions?

Finally, the question as to what is justice, in most international disputes of importance, is a political and not a legal question. Such matters as the construction of treaties are of course proper issues to leave to the Court, and we should, in all treaties we enter into, agree to do this. However, it is wishful thinking to believe that there is an easy road to peace by going further and submitting all international disputes to the World Court for decision on legal grounds. In the case of Kashmir, for example, as a matter of law it unquestionably belongs to India, since the ruler of the country exercised the option given to him by Britain to accede to India. However, if justice is to govern, should not the wishes of the inhabitants be considered in deciding the question? If so, they would undoubtedly favor joining Pakistan. Again, former Governor Thomas E. Dewey has proposed that we seek to have the question of the legal title to the islands of Quemoy and Matsu submitted to the World Court for decision, presumably welcoming an adverse decision as a face saving device permitting Chiang Kai-Shek to withdraw. But would the United States be willing to submit to the Court the similar question of the legal title to Formosa, where the decision conceivably might be adverse to us if based on legal principles and if all other considerations, such as the wishes of the inhabitants or perhaps the defensive needs of the Philippines, were to be ignored? Quite certainly the answer to such a proposal would be no, and properly so.

If there are thus valid objections to attempting to create an enforceable world rule of law similar to that of private law, is our only alternative to give the Charter the construction which the British and French gave to it as one of the justifications for their action at the time of the Suez intervention—namely that the basic covenant in Article 2 of the Charter to refrain from the use of force has no application to a nation having no aggressive intent but merely seeking to enforce the continuation of its unrestricted use of the canal?

The obvious difficulty with this construction is that it emasculates the Charter. If every nation can unilaterally determine whether or not the use of force is permissible, the entire machinery to prevent aggression becomes inoperative. No nation—not even Hitlerian Germany or North Korea—ever admitted to starting an aggressive war or one without just cause.

However, there is a third choice that might be considered —intermediate between attempting to create a world rule of law and giving up all efforts to restrain aggression. It would be to amend Article 2 so as to provide that resort to force by one nation against another should not be prohibited if the second nation had refused to satisfy a complaint of the first nation, which a majority of the Assembly had found to be justified.

Such an amendment would accomplish two things. First, the complaint would be presented to a political institution, the Assembly, and not to a court of law. Second, a nation whose complaint had been found justified would be permitted to resort to force if necessary in order to get the relief it was entitled to. To this extent it admittedly would narrow the existing prohibition against the use of force. This may appear a step backward in our efforts to eliminate war, but that would not necessarily be the case. Furthermore, it would have the virtue of avoiding entering into agreements which we do not honestly intend to carry out under all conditions.

Whether the suggested amendment to the Charter could obtain the necessary votes is a practical question which cannot be answered in advance other than to say it would appear to be a possibility. If not, substantially the same result might be achieved by the adoption by the Assembly of a resolution, comparable to, but the reverse of, the Uniting for Peace Resolution, which would provide for a vote by the Assembly as to whether a threatened use of force was, in the light of existing circumstances, consistent with the purposes of the United Nations and therefore not in violation of Article 2. The two resolutions would together then constitute a mechanism for the submission to the Assembly of the question of whether the actual or threatened use of force in a particular situation would or would not be justified. If the decision were that it was unjustified, resistance by collective security measures would then be recommended. However, if the decision were to the contrary, the unilateral use of force would thereby be acquiesced in as justified. The effect of this would be to change the present basic Charter concept of a prohibition upon all acts of aggression to a narrower one of a prohibition only upon unjustified resort to force. If this change were made without Charter amendments, a conflict between the Security Council and the General Assembly would be possible, which could, however, be avoided by a helpful use of the veto.

Such an amendment or resolution would not necessarily increase the resort to war; rather the threat of war might lead to the according of justice by the nation adjudged to be in the wrong. Had it been in effect, the Suez dispute might have been resolved without war. If a decision had been rendered against Nasser, and Britain and France had then threatened to use force, he would probably have complied with the decision, unless, perhaps, Russia intervened. On the other hand, if the decision had been in Nasser's favor, Britain and France in all probability would have given up any attempt to go against it by resort to force.

Let us apply it to a case such as Formosa. If, for example, the question were submitted by us to the Assembly as to whether a just solution of the existing threat to the peace would be to give the inhabitants of that island the right to vote to join mainland China or to be independent, a decision by the Assembly in favor of this solution would establish that Communist China would be guilty of the unjustified use of force if it thereafter attacked Formosa.

On the other hand, suppose that the Assembly should decide that Formosa ought to be handed over to Communist China irrespective of the wishes of the inhabitants. This would be extremely unlikely today. However, there is no assurance that the decision of a majority of the Assembly will always be a just one according to our view of justice. Although up to the present time the United States has had little difficulty in getting a majority vote in the Assembly on all issues in accordance with our views as to what is fair and just, with the continuous addition of new members this may not go on indefinitely. If that time should come, would we be willing to accept such a vote as an expression of world opinion and obey it?

In such an event, it is suggested that a legitimate distinction could be made between defensive and offensive use of force. Assuming that the inhabitants of Formosa should refuse to accept the decision of the Assembly, and an attack on it should be made by Communist China, then we could still, if we decided, defend Chiang on Formosa. Presumably we would go through a soul-searching process before deciding not to accept the Assembly's decision, and we would no doubt be influenced by the size of the majority against us, how many European nations it included, the extent to which it may have been brought about by fear of reprisals from the Communist countries, and so forth.

If we finally did so decide, we would not thereby be committing an act in violation of the Charter, even though the Communist attack had been recognized as justified by the Assembly. The Charter restraints would be inapplicable to such a case, and both parties would be free to act as if there were no Charter. Defensive action is clearly recognized as lawful under the present Charter, and would continue to be so even if the suggested change were to be effected and if offensive action were to be sanctioned by the Assembly in a particular case.

However, let us assume the case where offensive rather than defensive action would be necessary to enforce a claim we believed to be just, but where the Assembly had voted that our claim was unjust and that resort to force would be wrongful.

An example of such a case, involving not the United States but another country, would be an attempt by Pakistan to force India to withdraw from Kashmir in order to permit the holding of a United Nations-conducted plebiscite in that country, notwithstanding a vote by the Assembly that resort to force was not justified.

This kind of a case would be basically different from the defense of Formosa. Pakistan, or the United States in a similar position, would not be acting defensively but would be seeking to change the status quo for a reason which we were unable to convince a majority of the Assembly was a just one. Here, I submit, we should be willing to give up the use of offensive force to enforce our claim even though we considered a vital national interest to be involved, and should limit ourselves to other means of trying to attain our objectives.

To accept this restriction on our right to use force would appear to be a concession we should make to the cause of peace. It would be a more limited restriction than the one we have already agreed to—perhaps unwittingly and certainly unwisely—in the present Charter. It would be still more limited than what would result from accepting the compulsory jurisdiction of the World Court. Realistically, however, it is the maximum restriction which we can expect the United States or any other great power to live up to at the present stage of world development. It is a reasonable compromise position between those who object to any limitation on our sovereignty and those who would agree to obey all decisions of the World Court.

To close on this note would give an incomplete and unduly pessimistic picture of the future prospects for peaceful settlements of disputes between nations. There is of course the very important conciliatory machinery of the United Nations which has been effective in a steadily increasing number of situations in inducing antagonistic nations to come to agreement. And if the suggestion made above were to be adopted, it should not be assumed that the Assembly would lightly give the go-ahead signal to starting a war. On the contrary, we can be sure that efforts would be intensified to make use of every other possible alternative to solve the dispute, including, if necessary, resort to collective economic measures.

In addition, there is another approach of great importance which Professor Jessup's paper emphasizes, namely the entering into of multilateral or bilateral agreements or treaties between nations, dealing with both legal and political issues. A recent example was the conference on the law of the sea, held under the auspices of the United Nations in Geneva. Four different conventions were agreed to at this Conference. On one issue only, namely the change in the traditional three-mile limit, the necessary two-thirds agreement could not be obtained. This is not a ground for undue pessimism either, because the compromise proposed by the United States, which preferred the existing rule but was willing to yield to the views of others, was successful to the extent of receiving the approval of a majority of the nations.

It is therefore to be hoped that possible sources of conflict between nations can increasingly be avoided by the machinery of voluntary agreements which seems to have greater chance for effectiveness than the imposition of a settlement from without. Only if we recognize that mutual concessions must be made to the viewpoint of other countries as to what is justice, will we be able to attain that elusive but much desired goal of peace on earth between nations.

Legal Institutions in England Today and Tomorrow

BY ALFRED THOMPSON DENNING, P.C.
LORD OF APPEAL IN ORDINARY

In the Introduction to this Centennial volume, it is said that "in England, two wars within a generation accompanied by profound social and economic changes, have presented a much sharper challenge to the institutions of law than in the United States."

Indeed, our British legal institutions—by which I mean our Parliament and our courts of law—have been presented with a challenge, and to meet the challenge, they have changed much. I will describe some of these changes, but before I do so I would set forth a reminder of the purpose of legal institutions. Their purpose—their task—varies according to the kind of society in which one lives. If it is a communist society—where there are multitudes of people who have been long oppressed—the purpose of legal institutions is to ensure that everyone conforms to the rules which the party in power has laid down in the interests of the working people and to protect them from exploitation. If it is a Western society, whose people have been brought up to believe in the supreme value of the individual personality, the purpose of legal institutions is to protect the individual from arbitrary power whether exercised by the government or anyone else.

England today stands midway between these two extremes. We are a welfare state, a planned state, a socialist state—call it what you will—whose philosophy is summed up in slogans such as "fair shares for all," "equal opportunity for all," and the like. Go back a hundred years in England and the philosophy of that day was "each one for himself, and the devil take the hindmost." The philosophy is today more like the Christian philosophy: "Do as you would be done by," but there is a rider added to it: "Do as you would be done by, but if you don't, the State will see that you do." The state takes a hand in everything. Many great industries are nationalized, and there is talk of more nationalization for industry to come. Many of the social services are nationalized, others subsidized by the state. There is a comprehensive national insurance policy whereby the state insures everyone against sickness, disablement, and unemployment. And so on.

These great social and economic changes have had their impact on our legal institutions. These too have changed. In all this we have followed out our usual practice, which was summarized by Lord Macaulay in these words: "The history of England is emphatically the history of progress. It is the history of a constant movement of the public mind, of a constant change in the constitution of a great society."

Let me then set forth the changes that have come over our legal institutions in recent times and also of the challenge which the future holds for them.

First of all, Trial by Jury, which, said Sir William Blackstone "ever has been, and I trust ever will be, looked upon as the glory of the English law."[1] This great bulwark of our liberties was secured to Englishmen by the Great Charter—Magna Carta—signed by King John at Runnymede, where the American Bar Association in 1957 erected a memorial. Sir William Blackstone urged upon us that it was the "duty which every man owes to his country, his friends, his posterity and himself, to maintain to the utmost of his power this valuable constitution in all its rights."

[1]BLACKSTONE, COMMENTARIES 379-81 (1768).

He said this of civil cases as well as criminal. "Every new tribunal," he went on, "erected for the decision of facts, without the intervention of a jury, is a step towards establishing autocracy, the most absolute form of government."

Yet this trial by jury has now virtually disappeared in England in the great majority of civil cases, though it remains intact for criminal cases. The change, of course, was easily made. It was done by a simple act of Parliament. We have no written constitution in England. If Parliament chooses to abolish the right to trial by jury, no court can say it nay. And so Parliament abolished it and no one regrets it. In a few cases such as libel and slander, malicious prosecution and false imprisonment, there is a right to trial by jury, but in all other civil cases the court has discretion in whether to order a jury or not. Yet very few people ask for a jury; and in the ordinary run of cases—injuries on the roads, accidents in factories, and the like—if they do ask for a jury, it is refused. The reasons are obvious. If all these cases were to be tried by juries, there would not only be a strain on the manpower of the country (already strained to the utmost in these days of full employment) but there would be great delays in the hearing of cases. And there is no reason to suppose that a judge will not deal with the case just as well as a jury. Indeed better. People know where they stand with a judge. He gives his reasons, and, if he is wrong, he can be put right by the Court of Appeal; whereas a jury are often quite unpredictable.

But in criminal cases every man charged with an indictable offense is entitled to trial by jury. Summary offenses (such as minor motoring cases) are tried by lay magistrates. Many an indictable offense is also dealt with by them, if the accused asks for them to deal with it. But every man still has his undoubted right to claim trial by jury: and it is still the law that, once he is acquitted by a jury, there is no power in anyone in the land to gainsay it. This great institution remains in England

and will, I trust, always remain. The importance of it has recently been stressed by my friend and colleague Justice Devlin, who used these eloquent words: "The first object of any tyrant in Whitehall would be to make Parliament utterly subservient to his will: and the next to overthrow trial by jury, for no tyrant could afford to leave a subject's freedom in the hands of twelve of his countrymen. Trial by jury is more than an instrument of justice and more than one wheel of the constitution: it is the lamp which shows that freedom lives."

Next, take the bar of England—an institution evolved over the centuries—almost as old as juries themselves. It is rather different from the American bar. The bar of England are advocates, whose work is to plead in court by word of mouth—both in courts of trial and in appeal courts—and not by written briefs. It is their long tradition that they will defend any man, and put his case before judge and jury, fearless of any consequences to themselves. This tradition was never more clearly stated than by Erskine in his *Defence of Tom Paine:*

I will forever, at all hazards, assert the dignity, independence and integrity of the English Bar, without which impartial justice, the most valuable part of the English constitution, can have no existence. From the moment that any advocate can be permitted to say that he will, or will not, stand between the Crown and the subject in the court where he daily sits to practice—from that moment the liberties of England are at an end.

The courage and independence of the English bar is as high as it ever was: but there is a very present danger to this great institution. The danger comes from something with which American attorneys may not be acquainted—the decline of litigation. The criminal courts are as busy as they have ever been, but the civil courts are slack. There is a maxim which has come down to us from Roman days: "Interest reipublicae ut sit finis litium." It is in the interest of the state that there should be an end to litigation. True, too much litigation is an evil, but too little also has its drawbacks, because it means that the bar will not attract the best men into it. Young men, who see the large rewards offered by science and industry, will hesitate to join a calling which is not only precarious but in which the financial rewards are small.

What is the cause of this decline? Is it permanent or only temporary? The causes are manifold. One of the principal causes is the great extent to which people cover themselves by insurance against their liabilities. All motorists in England are bound to insure themselves against third-party risks. All employers insure themselves against liability to their workmen and also to the public at large. Householders insure themselves by comprehensive policies against liabilities of all kinds. The result is that when a person is injured in an accident, his claim is in effect—though not in form—against an insurance company. And the insurance companies are able to predicate with reasonable accuracy what the result of the claim will be if it is taken to the courts. They have been much helped in this task because the law has been simplified in recent years. In nearly all accident cases, the question now is simply: "Whose fault was it?" There is no doctrine of common employment. There is no distinction between invitees and licensees. There is no doctrine of last clear chance. There is no doctrine of contributory negligence. If both are to blame, the damages are borne proportionately according to the share of responsibility. The result is that insurance companies are able to assess their liability with fair accuracy and settle the claims long before they come to court. In the doubtful cases they often pay up rather than spend time and money in litigation. They only fight the cases they think they will win.

Another reason for the decline in litigation is the formation of giant combines and nationalized industries. In earlier times when small separate concerns were in dispute, the courts had to resolve it. Now when they are all part of a larger entity, the dispute is solved by the board of directors or by interdepartmental decision.

Yet another reason lies in the business field. The cost of litigation, its formality, and the public exposure to cross-examination make businessmen prefer to settle their disputes by arbitration. They prefer to go to arbitrators to whom, as one of them put it recently, "we do not have to explain everything."

Finally, and perhaps most important, solicitors do not advise their clients to litigate. They make no profit out of it. It is too poorly paid. They point out to the client the risk of losing the case. So more and more cases are settled. But it is no good suggesting that the costs should be increased. Every layman thinks they are high enough as it is.

What is to be the result of it all? One result will be, I think, an easier interchange between the two branches of the profession, if not an actual fusion of them. Solicitors will be able to become barristers, and barristers, solicitors with little difficulty. Barristers will tend to become, not so much advocates, but rather consultants; and the clear-cut division of the profession, which has lasted so long, will become blurred. I would myself deplore this, because this very special institution—the bar of England—has been responsible, more than any other, for ensuring the good administration of justice in England. It is the training ground of judges. It is the repository of the traditions of courage, fairness, and frankness. Above all it instills in all its members the cardinal virtue of independence. These men have shown themselves throughout the centuries fearless of speech, ready to condemn wrongdoing wherever it is seen, and to resist oppression in any form and from any quarter. It will be a sad day for England if the pressure of events leads to their disappearance or decay.

Now for our judges. Their reputation stands as high as ever it did. The people have great confidence in their independence and impartiality. But they have had to face a challenge as great as any in our history—the challenge of new tribunals and statutory inquiries. When Parliament embarked on the creation of the

Welfare State, it created a great new set of rights and duties of a kind unknown before—rights and duties for the most part between man and the state—and it entrusted the adjudication on these rights and duties, not to the courts or to the judges, but to new tribunals. Claims to insurance benefits, claims to pensions, claims to compensation, and a host of others all went to new tribunals. The reason was because the ordinary courts were thought not to be suited to the task. Some of the disputes are so numerous that the courts would not have sufficient judges to cope with them. Other disputes involve so much specialized knowledge that they need specialized judges to deal with them. And, more often than not, expedition and economy are essential factors which, it was thought, the courts did not possess. So Parliament set up new tribunals with the qualities demanded in the new age: speed, cheapness, informality, expert knowledge. Often there was no appeal to the courts from these tribunals. It looked as if a new legal institution had emerged over which the judges had no control.

This challenge has been met and overcome. The courts themselves led the way by a series of decisions in which they held that if a tribunal went wrong in point of law, and its error appeared on the face of the record—so that it was a "speaking order"—the courts could interfere by certiorari and quash the order that was erroneous.[2] Then last year a great advance was made by a strong committee presided over by Sir Oliver Franks—once Ambassador to the United States—who laid it down that "tribunals should properly be considered as machinery provided by Parliament for adjudication rather than as part of the machinery of administration." The recommendations of that committee have recently been passed into law. In a new act passed on August 1, 1958, Parliament has required all these tribunals to give their reasons for their decisions, and has given an appeal to the courts from their

[2]See Rex v. Northumberland Compensation Appeal Tribunal, [1952] 1 K.B. 338 (C.A.); Gibson's case, Regina v. Medical Appeal Tribunal, [1957] 1 A.B. 574 (C.A.).

decisions on points of law. This brings these tribunals fairly and squarely under the rule of law. It is necessary, of course, that the courts should give a liberal interpretation to what is a "point of law"; but there is good guidance by the House of Lords on this matter. If a finding of fact is unsupported by the evidence, or is a finding to which no reasonable man could come, then it is erroneous in point of law and can be reversed.[3]

In this new act Parliament has made another great innovation. It has set up a new legal institution in the shape of a Council on Tribunals. This council will make rules of procedure for all tribunals and will keep under review the constitution and working of these tribunals. The result of this will be to bring the tribunals more and more within the judicial system. They will be in effect special courts dealing with specialized subject matters. Their procedure will not be so formal and expensive as the ordinary courts but it will be fair and expeditious. The normal constitution of these courts will be a legal chairman and two laymen specially qualified for the task. They will be part of the hierarchy of courts just as much as the magistrates courts and the county courts are.

But the new act does not deal with tribunals. It also deals with another legal institution, which I may call statutory inquiries. Let me give an instance of what I mean. When the owner of land in England desires to develop it in any way—to build on it, or to change the use he makes of it—he has to get permission from the planning authorities. If the authorities refuse it, he can appeal to the Minister. There are thousands of these appeals, so much so that the Minister is overwhelmed by them. The Minister sends down an inspector to hold an inquiry and, after receiving his report, the Minister gives his decision. Similar inquiries take place when it is proposed to take land compulsorily. There used to be many complaints about these inquiries. Decisions were made without any reasons being given; and a man might find his property

---

[3]Bracegirdle v. Oxley, [1947] K.B. 349; Edwards v. Bairstow, [1956] A.C. 14.

taken from him, or be prevented from developing it, by the *ipse dixit* of a Minister without any redress whatever. But they have now been put on a proper footing. The inspector's report has to be published or, at any rate, sent to the person concerned; and the Minister has to give his reasons for his decisions. These form part of the record of the proceedings, with the result that if he goes wrong on a point of law, his decision can be reviewed by the courts of law. And if there is any special matter for concern about the way these inquiries operate, it can be brought before the Council on Tribunal. They, too, are being brought out of the administrative system and into the judicial system.

Now I come to our greatest English legal institution of all—the supremacy of Parliament. In legal theory Parliament is still sovereign, but in point of fact the government of the day is sovereign. At the general election people vote for one party or other, the leaders of the winning party form a government, and that government rules the country for the next four or five years. The individual members of Parliament exercise a good deal of influence still—especially by means of questions to Parliament—but they do not count for so much nowadays as they used to do. Much more influence is exercised by the organized interests outside Parliament—"pressure groups," as they are called in the United States—and it is these I would consider. In England there are thousands of organizations of this kind. The workers form themselves into trade unions; and the trade unions form themselves into a Trade Union Congress. The farmers form themselves into the National Farmers Union. Many industries have their own trade associations, and these form themselves into the Federation of British Industries. The local authorities form themselves into associations. And so forth. These associations raise money by subscriptions of their members, they employ secretaries to promote their ends, hold conferences to expound their views, and so forth. These associations all seek to exert influence in matters which concern them— by doing all they can to influence public opinion in their favor, by seeking to get the support of members of Parliament, by publicity in the newspapers, and so forth—for they know that in the long run it is public opinion that counts.

What is the influence of these associations on the government of the country? It is, I believe, an immense influence—more than most people realize. Take the National Farmers Union. Each year the Government Department and the Union together undertake a review of prices for all the principal agricultural commodities. These prices are guaranteed prices and are binding on all concerned. Take the decisions of the government on affairs relating to industry. The Government Departments have not the full information available on which to make a decision. They get it from the Federation of British Industries. When the government contemplated the reform of local government, they consulted the various associations concerned in it. The truth is that on the one hand all these associations have something to offer to the Government Departments—information, advice, and a convenient means of communication—and on the other hand no government can afford to ignore them, because each association in its way represents a considerable section of the public. If any of these pressure groups should become too strong—so that they could influence the decision in favor of their own sectional interests in a way contrary to the national interest—it would be a great danger to our democracy. It would be a more serious challenge to our legal institutions than any we have known. But at present these pressure groups are, I believe, no more than a useful corrective to the great powers of the government. They form a channel—or rather many converging channels—whereby the mass of the people can influence the government at the most vital point, the point where decisions are made; and by so doing they play a valuable part in our constitution.

Thus far I have considered challenges to our English institutions which have been met and are in the way of being overcome.

Now I turn to challenges which are still with us and to which we have not yet found the answers.

The first challenge lies in the power and influence of the great industrial combines and corporations. This has all taken place over the last hundred years. The first of the acts which created limited liability companies was passed in 1856. Now the company system has so developed that it covers nearly every business of substantial size in the country. And the running of these businesses is not in the hands of the shareholders. It is in the hands of the directors and managers; and these, in effect, appoint their successors. They are a self-perpetuating oligarchy. In point of law the duty of directors is to act in the best interests of the company—that is to say, in the interests of the shareholders—but in point of fact they go much further. They dip their hands into the company's coffers and give large sums of money to universities and colleges, and to good causes of all kinds. Nominally they do it in the interests of the company—so as to increase its good will. But this seems rather farfetched. Take an instance. When the Lord Mayor of London opens a fund for the relief of distress, large donations will be made by many companies—that is, by the directors applying the companies' monies—without consulting the shareholders at all. Many other instances could be given. They all show that when directors give away these monies they do it, not in the interests of the company, but of charity; and as often as not they do it, as good works should be, unobtrusively and without proclaiming it from the housetops. The practice has been carried so far that the directors of these companies are today the patrons of the sciences and the arts, of learning and of education—and they do it all with other people's money.

If such be the position of the great companies, what about the position of the great foundations? One of the most remarkable features of the last twenty or thirty years, both in England and in the United States, has been the formation by rich industrialists of charitable foundations. They transfer to these foundations large blocks of shares in companies. The foundations, being charities, are exempt from tax on the dividends; and in England, at least, they can reclaim the tax that has already been paid on them. This means that the income of the foundations from dividends is nearly doubled by a subvention from the general body of taxpayers; and it is administered by the trustees and directors of the foundations in whatever way they think best. They subsidize thousands of institutions—legal, scientific, and artistic. They subsidize individuals by making travel grants and fellowships. They use their resources to promote the dissemination of opinion and views which seem to them to be worthy of encouragement.

I do not say this is wrong. On the contrary, when I see the most valuable contributions which these foundations have made to our civilization, I say it is a very good thing. But I would draw attention to the great power which is thus entrusted to the foundations and the correspondingly great responsibilities which fall on the trustees and directors of them.

What is the future of these powerful institutions? So long as they are run with a due sense of responsibility, as they are now, all well and good. But if they should lose it—if the directors and trustees should ever succumb to the temptations which are said always to attend the exercise of power—there will be a call for their dissolution or at any rate for public control of them. Remember the monasteries. They too were the patrons of learning and of the arts and the sciences, they too were the dispensers of charity, but they had to be dissolved. Let not our modern equivalent go the same way.

The next challenge lies in the power and influence of the trade unions. They are nowadays one of the greatest powers in the state. They have come into being under the cover of one of our essential freedoms—that men should be able freely to associate together in a just cause. One hundred years ago this freedom was not recognized. Trade unions were illegal associations. But in 1871 Parliament began to set things right and then, by a series of acts, not only took away any taint of illegality from trade unions, but enabled them to achieve their ends without fear of actions at law. Responsible officials—or even irresponsible agitators—can induce men to come out on strike at a moment's notice, in breach of their contracts, without being liable to an action for damages, so long as it is done in contemplation or furtherance of a trade dispute. If the officers or servants do any wrongful act on behalf of the trade union, if they commit any violence or do any damage in the course of a strike, the union is not liable in damages. Trade unions are above the law.

What is the future of these legal institutions? Are they likely to be made subject to the law? At present the responsibility of the leaders and the members depends on the rules of the union. When a man joins a union, he is bound by the rules. The rules are said to be a contract between the men themselves and between them and the union. But they are in no sense a contract freely negotiated. A man must accept them or go without employment. They are nothing more nor less than a legislative code laid down by some members of the union to be imposed on all members of the union. If the union or its members happen to break the rules, the man can get redress to some extent in the courts, but so long as the union and its officers keep within the rules, he has no redress. These rules often contain strict requirements: a man must pay his subscriptions, must obey the instructions of the counsel, and must come out on strike if the union directs him to do so, and he is liable to expulsion if he does not comply with the rules. If he is expelled, he may be put out of work altogether, because the union enforces a "closed shop."

It must be plain to all that this power of expulsion imposes a great responsibility on those who exercise it: and it was well emphasized by a distinguished judge, Justice Harman, who said recently in a case:

It was boasted on behalf of the defendants that 95% of the engineering works are closed shops. This means that expulsion from the union makes it almost impossible to earn a living at the trade in the district. It is not for English lawyers to dislike or distrust the principle of the closed shop, for they are all members of a society which itself lives and thrives on this principle. No man, unless he has served his time and received his union card—that is to say, his call to the Bar—may (save in his own cause) address the Supreme Court of England. Such monopolies are only justified if they are so regulated as to promote the public interest. Moreover, the weapon of expulsion from such a society is a step of the most extreme gravity, only to be entered on after very careful inquiry and in the case of the very gravest offence.

This last sentence of the Judge should be written over the doors of every society which exercises a monopoly over a calling in which men earn their living. It should be embodied in the rules. A man's right to work is just as important to him, indeed more important, than his rights of property. If his rights of property are invaded, the courts have well-known causes of action to protect him. His house, his furniture, and his investments are all well safeguarded by the law. His right to work should also be safeguarded against any unjust invasion of it.

Turn now to the responsibility of the unions to the public at large. When men originally combined to improve their conditions, the right to strike was a weapon which they used against their employer. If the men did not work, the employer would suffer—he would not make profits—so in his own interest he was compelled to improve their conditions. But the outlook changes altogether when the employer is not an individual or a company which is making profits but is a nationalized industry which is making losses. It changes, too, when the dispute is not between the employer and the workmen but between one union and another union or between a group of men and the union to which

they belong. When strikes occur over these disputes, many innocent persons are injured. Many lose work and wages without any
fault on their part. Others are put to great hardship and incon-
venience. This is a state of affairs which should not exist in a
civilized community.

So long as these unions are run with a due sense of responsibility—with a true regard to the national interest as well as to
their own members—there will be no call for a change. But if
they should abuse their great powers—and sacrifice the national
interest to their own—there would inevitably be a demand that
they should be brought under the rule of law.

In the last resort all these matters fall to be resolved by the
force of public opinion. But what is public opinion? And how is
it to be ascertained? Is it the opinion of the majority of the people?
I doubt it, for it exists without a referendum to ascertain it. Is it
the opinion of the best informed people? I doubt this too, for they
often differ among themselves. Public opinion is, I think the
opinion of those individuals who are sufficiently concerned to form
a judgment on the issue and to express their views upon it—and
who are also, by their upbringing and outlook, fairly representative of the majority of the people. These represent, so to speak,
the inner consciousness—the inner feeling—of the people as a
whole. Their opinion, more often than not, is based not on reason
but on what is felt to be for the best in a given situation. Their
opinion is influenced by many imperceptible forces acting at innumerable points—newspapers, broadcasts, telecasts, conversa-
tions with others, and so forth—and yet it builds up into the one
irresistible force, the force of public opinion.

It is at this point that each of us comes face to face with his own
personal responsibility. Each of us has some part to play, something to put into the balance toward the formation of public
opinion, whether positively by thinking and doing something
about it, or even negatively by thinking nothing and doing noth-

ing. In such a great university as Columbia are those who should think and do—those who should lead public opinion. Let us see to it that we fulfill our responsibilities to our fellow men. Draw on our great heritage of freedom—which is given to us, not to waste, but to use for the good of all. Pray God to grant us a right judgment in all things. Live out our lives in the spirit which William Wordsworth so well expressed:

> We must be free or die, who speak the tongue
> That Shakespeare spake: the faith and morals hold
> That Milton held: In everything we are sprung
> Of earth's first blood, have titles manifold.

Comment

BY DEREK W. BOWETT

LEGAL OFFICER, UNITED NATIONS

One of the developments brought out by Lord Denning of especial interest is the decline in the use of the jury, particularly in civil cases. This development is of interest because it raises a rather more general question of the participation of the layman in the legal system. Lord Denning has said of the jury that they are "often quite unpredictable." What I want to consider is how far some analogy might be drawn with another aspect of lay participation in the legal system, namely the institution of a lay magistracy.

The Magistrates Courts are a fourteenth-century institution and they now include some 25,000 magistrates appointed by the Lord Chancellor, who acts on the recommendation of the Lord Lieutenant of the County, who in turn acts on the recommendation of an Advisory Committee.

The qualifications for appointment include residence within an area of fifteen miles, an age limit of seventy-five years (sixty-five for juvenile courts), but not a legal training. It is perhaps worthy of note that the Justice of the Peace Act of 1949 provides for the establishment of courses of instruction for magistrates to be arranged through Magistrates Courts Committees. The people from whom magistrates are chosen are local government officials, retired businessmen, labor union officials, shopkeepers and the like. They are not now dominated by the upper-middle class, epitomized by the country squire or the local mill owner.

The importance of this institution can readily be seen when we realize that these courts deal, at one stage or another, with over 90 percent of the cases that come before the courts. They have a considerable criminal jurisdiction: they issue warrants for arrest, grant bail or commit to prison pending trial, actually try those cases which are triable summarily or in which, being triable summarily or upon indictment, the accused elects to be tried summarily. In many cases dealing with more serious crimes, they act as examining magistrates before committing the case for trial by a higher court. Of course their decisions are open to appeal to Quarter Sessions and thence to the High Court, or by way of case stated to the High Court.

These courts also have a certain civil jurisdiction over minor matters of civil debt, over affiliation orders and certain domestic proceedings, although, be it noted, they have no powers to grant divorce.

The upshot of this considerable institution is that for the average person who comes into contact with the legal system in operation through the courts, the Magistrates Courts are that point of contact. The impression of the legal system which he gains is very often the impression derived from experience in these courts. It is for this reason that the question of the effectiveness of the institution of a lay magistracy merits serious consideration.

I venture to suggest that, partly because of the increasing volume of statute law, the issues of law placed before these courts are of growing complexity. Of course the magistrates benefit from the legal advice of the Clerk of the Court, who is either a barrister or solicitor of five years standing. But the Clerk may not participate in the decision and the degree to which he influences the court even on matters of law is, in practice, very largely a matter of personalities.

Even if it be conceded that these courts are mainly concerned with questions of fact, does it necessarily follow that the layman is equally competent with the trained lawyer? I have considerable doubts on this score.

My own personal view is that the more frequent use of a legally qualified and paid chairman would improve the standing of these courts. The use of stipendiary magistrates in the major towns is increasing, and I do not see why a system could not be envisaged in which lay participation was combined with the use of qualified lawyers.

This possible development might have a further advantage in that it would alleviate the increasingly serious position in which members of the bar are placed because of the decline of litigation. I share fully Lord Denning's pride in the record of the bar and of the legal profession generally; I also share fully his concern over the future of the bar. Now the part-time employment of members of the legal profession as qualified members of the Magistrates Courts could do something toward remedying the present position.

Another development which would be, in my mind, a happy one, would be for members of the legal profession in England to widen the scope of their professional activities. My acquaintance with the practice of law in the United States is so slight as to make it an impertinence on my part to draw comparisons. However, I shall take that risk in suggesting that in the United States, especially in fields such as corporation and tax law, the activities of the lawyer range over fields into which the English lawyer rarely ventures. Though we have experts in income tax law in England, the bulk of advice on tax matters is given not by lawyers but by accountants. This is perhaps partly the result of a professional conservatism and also partly the result of the fact that neither our law faculties in the universities nor the Inns of Court offer instruction in tax law. This disregard of an increasingly important part of our law is not to my mind justified by the argument that tax law has no "educational" or "academic" value. I personally believe that we should be a little more realistic about these matters and make more effort to train lawyers for these newer spheres of law. The importance of developing these wider activities will increase, certainly for the solicitors in our legal profession, when the general introduction of registration of title does away with the remunerative work of conveyancing.

Now I am prompted by Lord Denning's extremely interesting comments on the "greatest English legal institution of all —the supremacy of Parliament" to say something about the increase in the power of pressure groups and about law reform.

I think the concern for the loss of the individual's right to work in the struggle between the unions and employers is a fairly general one. Similarly, I think there is general concern over the influence on our parliamentary system of the trade unions. However, at this stage I doubt whether legal remedies for these situations are really feasible. Lord Denning has defined, and I think well defined, what public opinion really is. He also says that "it is at this point that each of us comes face to face with his own personal responsibility." Now here is, in my own view, the real answer. I do not see any really effective solution in a democratic system other than that which could be arrived at when, by means of education and experience, the individual members of the unions recognize their own personal responsibility for the policy of the unions and, most important, recognize their responsibility toward society as a whole.

Lastly, I would say a brief word about the machinery available through Parliament for law reform. Society is developing very fast and our law must change so as to reflect adequately the values and balance of interests which are acceptable to society at a particular time. It is a trite observation to say that Parliament now has all too little time for its strictly legislative functions. But even apart from the question of time, there has long been felt some anxiety about the machinery by which law reform is executed. Of course, we have our Private Members Bills; the Defamation Act of 1952 is a recent example. But this rather odd institution cannot carry the main burden for law reform. At the moment responsibility for law reform is divided between the Offices of the Lord Chancellor and the Home Secretary, and, as is often the case with divided responsibility, much is lost in the division. I recall a statement by Professor Seaborne Davies on the BBC Third Programme on October 23, 1952, when he said: "Somewhere between the Home Office and the Office of the Lord Chancellor there is a large hole where projects for the reform of systems of the criminal law are deeply interred."

The *ad hoc* setting up of Lord Chancellor's committees is really not a substitute for a body with continuing responsibility in the field. Moreover, although some Government Departments have a limited sphere of responsibility—as is the case with the Board of Trade's responsibility over our Companies Acts—what is required is a more comprehensive and integrated planning. The movement for the creation of some kind of department or ministry of justice dates back to the early nineteenth century, and there are recurrent pleas for such an institution. In the absence of such an institution, anachronisms remain too long in our law: common employment lasted till 1948, the common law rules on contributory negligence, as mitigated by that curious "last opportunity rule," until 1945, and, despite Lord Denning's best endeavors, the doctrine of consideration is still with us. There may be many ways in which improvement of the legislative process could be brought about, but some unity and continuity of responsibility is clearly desirable, and I should hope that, in this respect, "tomorrow" will see some change in our legal institutions.

Comment

BY RONALD H. GRAVESON
DEAN OF THE FACULTY OF LAWS
KING'S COLLEGE, UNIVERSITY OF LONDON

Lord Denning has painted a vivid impressionist picture of England's legal institutions. My task, as I see it, is not to varnish the painting, but to try to fill some of the blank spaces on the canvas, of which I detect three in particular.

The first of my disjointed comments must deal with legal education. If we recall the seven centuries of history of the Inns of Court, that cradle of learning of the common law world, there need be no apology for mentioning the training of lawyers as one of our British legal institutions. Mr. Whitney North Seymour[4] has spoken eloquently in this Conference of the work of the American bar in developing legal education, and it is my good fortune to be having close and practical experience of the American system of legal training as I speak these lines.

Much has already been said and written about the relative merits of legal education in the United States and in England, and I would add only a word. One often hears that legal education in America is based on the case system, while in England it is based on the lecture system.[5] This summary comparison of two systems is a good deal less than a half-truth. It leaves much unsaid.

[4]*The Bar as Lawmaker*, pp. 174-97.
[5]See, for example, the articles on legal education, 43 Col. L. Rev. 423-85 (1943), reviewed by the writer in 25 J. Comp. Leg. & Int'l L. (3d ser.) 54 (1943).

I need not remind the audience of where the common law originated, or of the fact that it consists of cases. We are not yet
sufficiently advanced or sophisticated in England to have succeeded in teaching the common law without cases. In fact, since
Lord Denning's first appointment as a judge of the High Court,
we have been doing so more than ever before.

But looking to the future, there are valuable lessons for us in
England to learn from the experiments and experiences in
America, both in method and in subject matter. I think particularly
of the absence of any course in England devoted to legislation.
And there may be ideas on legal education in England which
might be found interesting in the United States. We should see
what each other is doing. We should be prepared to learn from
each other's experience, whether that experience be success or
failure.

My second comment concerns an institution which is really
an institutional attitude in England, and one of the greatest
importance. In its form of respect for the law, reflected in the
unarmed English policeman, for instance, it is part of our common
heritage of the rule of law. Another reflection, to which I would
like to draw attention, is the popular attitude toward our judges
in England. It is one of great respect, mingled with awe among
some of those who do not know them, and with friendship among
some of those who do. What are the practical consequences of
this respect that has traditionally been paid to the bench? There
is a long history of this attitude, going back to the beginnings of
the system of assizes in the thirteenth century, when itinerant
judges were the embodied representatives of the king in the country. But history apart, the points of interest for us today in this
genuine and widespread feeling of respect and confidence are two.
In the first place, it enabled us in England during the Second
World War to dispense with jury trials in civil actions, an important step to which Lord Denning has referred. In this way, while

the striking change was prompted by the need to save manpower in time of war, its success was possible only because society in general and the legal profession in particular were confident in the ability of the judges to be fair judges of fact. This change, however, effected not only a saving in manpower. It was retained after the war, modified in strictness,[6] because it also speeded litigation. As such, it was one of the important factors tending in these postwar years to place us in the position in which an action can be set down for hearing in the High Court of England, heard, and disposed of in about eight weeks from the commencement of proceedings. Partly, of course, this is also due to a traditional refusal on the part of judges to allow parties to exploit and abuse court procedure for their own purposes, such as by requests for successive adjournments on unsubstantial grounds.

The other consequence of this respect for law and its administrators is the relatively small number of appeals in England. It is not that the losing party feels any happier in an English trial than in one in the United States. It is simply the case that his counsel has good reason to advise him against making frivolous appeals where there is no genuine and substantial basis in fact or law.

Our problem for the future is the preservation, and if possible, the strengthening of this attitude of respect for the law. Shall we succeed in this by retaining the idea that law is a sacred mystery, or by making its life better known to more and more people? To me it seems clear that a wider general understanding among non-lawyers of the ways in which law is made and works would ensure, not simply more respect for law, but law more deserving of respect.

The last missing piece which I shall try to add to this painting is the name of the artist, for it would be most inappropriate if I were to omit to mention one of our most notable legal institutions.

[6]A jury trial may be allowed by the court chiefly in cases of defamation or special difficulty.

Lord Denning described himself briefly as an institution with both judicial and legislative functions. In fact, he represents that institution which in the thirteenth century bore the name of Hengham, in the seventeenth that of Nottingham, and in the eighteenth that of Mansfield. He shares our own age with Cardozo and, perhaps, Brandeis. These names characterize the judicial institution which runs, like Coke's thin golden thread, throughout the historical pattern of the common law. For our judicial system, in which the judge stands above the pressures of politics, money, or government, not only gives him the lawmaking power of precedent, but to those judges who can avail themselves of it, the liberty of independent thought for the progress of the law.

When, over half a century ago, Dean Roscoe Pound called for the progressive sociological interpretation of precedent,[7] he pointed a judicial path to legal progress which had already been trod by a few great figures in our past, but which needed to have the common as well as the uncommon judge tread it in this impatient age of expanding society. This message on the legal needs of our century, for long accepted as axiomatic in the United States, has been too little heeded in England, and it is in this context that the work of Lord Denning is important. It is in this context that many approve of his views, and that many disapprove of them; but none can ignore them, for the things he says have an uncanny way of coming true. Throughout his judicial career, he has been distinguished by a clear and deep appreciation of the legal needs of contemporary society and of the necessity of keeping law up-to-date in order to meet those needs.

Of the many instances of a fresh and vigorous approach to problems which can be found both in Lord Denning's judgments and in his well-known lectures and writings, I will mention just a few examples. The first, reminiscent of Lord Chancellor Nottingham, was his call a few years ago for a new equity, fashioned to the needs of our time and freed from the hardened arteries,

[7]Pound, *The Need of a Sociological Jurisprudence*, 19 GREEN BAG 607 (1907).

if not the *rigor mortis*, of the old, disillusioned equity with which we still deceived ourselves. Like his institutional predecessors, he has done much to unite the diverse dimensions of the law. In time, reminiscent of Chief Justice Hengham, he has given a contemporary and up-to-date interpretation[8] of the Mischief Rule, relating to the construction of statutes, to a sixteenth-century case,[9] though not without the frowns of his then judicial superiors.[10] In space, in the tradition of Mansfield, he has worked to unite in legal minds the understanding of English and international law through his chairmanship of the Society of Comparative Legislation and International Law. In the same field he has devoted himself with energy to the creation of a British Institute of International Law. In method and approach, like so many of his brother judges in the United States, he forms a bond of understanding and friendship between the practicing lawyer and those who teach. The House of Lords differs from the United States Supreme Court in several respects, one of which is that the British court considers itself bound by its own previous decisions.[11] There is little to commend this principle, but it remained for Lord Denning, as the most recently appointed Lord of Appeal in Ordinary, to express this view not long ago in these words: "It would, I think, be a great mistake to cling too closely to particular precedent at the expense of fundamental principle."[12] Are we in England then not right in thinking that we see here the working of a vitally progressive legal institution, one of tomorrow as well as of yesterday and today, and that we can feel here the pulse of the living body of our law?

[8]Magor & St. Mellons Rural Dist. Council v. Newport Corp., [1950] 2 All E.R. 1226.
[9]Heydon's Case, [1584] 3 Co. Rep. 7a.
[10]Magor & St. Mellons Rural Dist. Council v. Newport Corp., [1952] A.C. 189.
[11]London St. Tramways Co. v. London County Council, [1898] A.C. 375.
[12]London Transport Executive v. Betts, [1958] 3 Weekly L.R. 239.

Legal Institutions in America

BY WILLIAM O. DOUGLAS

ASSOCIATE JUSTICE OF THE SUPREME COURT OF THE UNITED STATES

To mark the Centennial of the Columbia Law School, we have engaged in the anxious and treacherous task of looking down the corridors of the oncoming century in an effort to discern what may be the evolution of our legal institutions. It is an anxious search, since nuclear fission has brought us to the point where man can wipe out from this planet not only civilization but life itself. It is a treacherous task because of the speed with which world communities are evolving. We can no longer think of law in narrow parochial terms. We must experience a greater awareness of a legal structure that extends beyond the boundaries of a single nation. This has been our point of departure. With that in view there are some highlights to touch as we examine the legal institutions which will serve as the vehicles for the operation of a society given to rule of law, both at home and abroad.

I

Today the administrative agency is supreme in state and federal governments. Its functions are manifold and varied. Some functions are adjudicatory, the kind that lawyers traditionally associate with the judiciary. Others are legislative in character, as, for example, the rule-making function. Some are executive in nature. And still others combine in various degrees all three. Today there is hardly a citizen who is not affected in a substantial manner with the operations of these agencies whether it be the authority that grants or revokes his driver's license, the body to which he submits his income tax return, or the agency that determines the fares he pays when he ships his produce or travels himself. The agency is supreme because of its pervasive influence in American affairs. It is also supreme because, once launched into its orbit, there is often no real effective control over it, as Warner W. Gardner emphasizes, whether we think in terms of congressional action, executive supervision, or judicial review.

The administrative agency fulfills an essential role in a government that promises to be no less dependent on it in the future than in the past. The national and world problems will certainly not get less complex in the years ahead. Those who constitute the governing authority will lean more and more on these agencies to do the daily work of government. The administrative agencies will continue to be important referees in the clash of private versus public interests. They will continue to be the repositories of a vast discretion which it is necessary to lodge somewhere.

The chief problem that lies ahead concerns the coming of age of this agency. We have, I think, gone far in developing professional standards for those who sit in the administrative seats. Those standards do not yet measure up to the ones we demand of the judiciary. But they have been progressing in that direction. The legislative has written into some acts the requirement for disinterestedness on the part of the agency heads. The Administrative Procedure Act[1] and allied legislation have set ground rules for these agencies that are designed to produce fair procedures. By and large provisions have been made for judicial review. These are all healthy measures. Each seeks to impress on the officials in question a realization that the enormous powers they exercise are powers in trust, not to be capriciously or selfishly employed.

[1] 60 Stat. 237 (1946), 5 U.S.C. § 1001 (1952).

In the years to come other rules will doubtless be added to those that now protect the administrative procedure against abuse. A few specific improvements might be mentioned. One is a requirement that the reasons for every adjudicatory decision be stated. This requirement, imposed in England by the Tribunals & Inquiries Act of 1958, should be made universal. When an officer (or a board) has to state precisely why he acts he will tend to take more sober, more considered action. That requirement will also make judicial review more meaningful. A second step forward would be a requirement that where an agency sets up rules to govern the conduct of its business, it be held rigorously to compliance with them. That is the philosophy of *United States ex rel. Accardi v. Shaughnessy*[2] and *Service v. Dulles*,[3] and it should also be a universal requirement. It is, moreover, shocking that a person can lose not only his job but his reputation and professional standing on the basis of the statements of some faceless informer. Certainly we have the inventive genius to develop procedures more sane, more protective of human rights, more just than those employed in the loyalty proceedings.

We have witnessed in recent years the use of outside pressures to influence administrative decisions. At times it has seemed that some agency decisions were for sale. Public opinion has promptly reacted to those abuses and will add more safeguards to the exercise of agency discretion. The means are certainly as important as the end itself. Even high-minded men need reminders that all power is subject to abuse and that submission to known rules is essential if justice, not caprice, is to prevail. Yet important as strict procedural safeguards are they will not be the sole solution of the problem. The ultimate solution will come not alone from the standards written into law but from the mores of the community.

We will have the kind of government that the prevailing morality demands. When I was in the Executive Branch administering

[2] 347 U.S. 260 (1954).   [3] 354 U.S. 363 (1957).

the large affairs of one agency, there were those in Congress who did not hesitate to pound my desk demanding that a decision be made in a particular way for a constituent. Other members of Congress—and I think the great majority—had a keener sense of the proprieties and stayed aloof. But as long as some of those in power feel free to intrude, as long as they try to impose their will on agency heads, the agency as an institution of government will not have reached full maturity.

Full maturity comes with public recognition that these agencies are as sacrosanct as the courts. When the prevailing morality demands that no one tamper with them, they will have reached a zone of effective protection which rules of law cannot easily compel.

Full maturity comes also from influences within the agencies. We have all known in our experience administrators who belonged to a true priesthood. They were conscious of their trusteeship, and meticulous in their conduct. They were meticulous in enforcing the law as distinguished from their own predilections. They also shaped their lives so that no base influence could reach them in the performance of their official duties. There are more men and women of this kind in government than one can know about by reading the headlines. We have, I think, gone a substantial distance in developing high professional standards for our administrative agencies. We have a distance still to go. We will cover the remaining ground as we develop deep-rooted traditions respecting government.

Laws will play a part. But the greater influences will come from the law teacher, the pulpit, and the editorial page. This is a matter of education. The public must be educated as to the requirements of good government. Men and women must be educated to give their best lives to government, seeking their compensation from the exhilaration of living on a higher plane than the market place offers and from the inner satisfaction of following the path of law

and justice so difficult at times to discern in the welter of conflicting claims.

When the administrative agencies have reached the full
maturity of which I speak, governments can come and go, leaving hardly a ripple in the administrative domain. The ideal
is a fairly permanent administrative staff of experts whose pronouncements on the law they enforce gain prestige and weight
by their professional standards. Those standards reflect not only
an aloofness from politics but a high degree of competence.
If we make the administrative agency the repository for the
incompetent or for those who cannot quite make the race in
their own professions, we will suffer the evils of mediocrity.
The professionalism of which I speak has high intellectual as
well as ethical standards. We must see to it that much of the
cream of the oncoming generations is attracted to these government posts. At present we have more to fear from mediocrity
than from corruption.

There was a time when the intelligentsia flocked to Washington to man the bastions. Those days may come again. At
present the bulk of our elite are turning elsewhere for adven-
ture and livelihood. Washington, D.C., and the state capitals
get few of the new recruits. This is commonly attributed to
the high financial returns in other lines of endeavor. That plays
a part, but in my view only a minor one. The real reasons involve intangibles. One is the severe scourge given to the public
service in recent years from those who, marching under the
banner of Americanism, have hunted down the nonconformist
as well as the subversive. There are numerous other reasons why
the climate in the nation's capital that prevailed, for example, in
the 1930s has never quite been restored. One chief task ahead
is to re-create the conditions that make a career with government
an exciting life.

Other groups or blocs—labor unions and industrial oligarchies alike—also have powers that are truly powers in trust. They can be used wisely by conscientious men or brazenly by evil men. They often affect the citizen as basically as an official government agency. There is going to be an insistence that the exercise of these powers be fairly employed, whether it be the management of funds, the expulsion of union members, or the investigation by employers of the "loyalty" of employees. In this area we stand, I think, on the verge of controls—controls imposed from within and from without.

The need of the investigative power which Congress and the state legislatures enjoy will continue to be great. Investigation is one essential of the lawmaking function. The right of any legislator to ask a single searching question is fundamental to our scheme of things. Yet we all know that an investigation can be subtly transformed from a legislative function to a trial. The line is difficult to mark. But the transgression can be real and devastating to the citizen. Moreover, we need to remember, when we are flush with excitement, that while Congress has its own unique way of punishing for contempt, the whole array of the Bill of Rights comes into play when the federal courts are asked to punish a recalcitrant witness as a criminal.[4]

Here, too, I think we are on the verge of controls—controls imposed from within. There is a lively sense of the need for some restraint in congressional circles. The proposals have been numerous over the years; and they will evolve into safeguards imposed by Congress itself—procedures that will prevent the excesses which we have sometimes witnessed in recent years.[5]

The courts have gone far this century in improving their stand-

[4]Watkins v. United States, 354 U.S. 178 (1957); cf. Sweezy v. New Hampshire, 354 U.S. 234 (1957).

[5]Among the many recent proposals in Congress to enact procedural safeguards for witnesses appearing before congressional committees, those offered by Senators Wayne Morse and Herbert Lehman are the most pervasive. (See S. Con. Res. 64, 83d Cong., 2d sess. (1954). The Senators proposed that witnesses be permitted counsel at all hearings, who could object to questions and procedure and argue to the committee; that witnesses be given advance notice of the subjects on which they

ards. The New Jersey system of court organization has made for greater efficiency. That idea will spread. The Federal Rules of Civil Procedure and the Federal Rules of Criminal Procedure— which, it should be remembered, were the result of judicial and legislative collaboration—have been, contrary to the expectation of some, singularly successful. The Civil Rules have made a particularly profound impact in their provisions for discovery and for pretrial orders. More and more states will follow their example. We will in the years ahead make a trial less a sporting chance, more a sober search for truth.

The future needs of litigation will put increasing loads on the experts who make our system work. First are the lawyers who in every trial represent a bit of the public interest as well as a particular client. Their role as officers of the court will doubtless receive new emphasis as time goes by, as Whitney North Seymour has stated. New Jersey is one state that is doing a remarkable job in seeing to it that every defendant in a criminal case—both felonies and misdemeanors—is represented by a lawyer. The bar and bench have worked out administratively a smoothly operating program for the designation of lawyers to represent criminal defendants.[6] The system works well; and members of the New Jersey bar show in their eyes the pride they have in the system. It is shocking to find cases in an appellate court where laymen

---

will be interrogated; that witnesses be entitled to invoke evidentiary privileges; that they be permitted to explain answers and enter statements in the record; that their counsel be allowed to cross-examine adverse witnesses; that hearings be had only when a majority of the committee is present. Representative Hugh Scott also proposed a reform of investigating procedures, which, *inter alia*, would permit witnesses to object to radio or television broadcasting of their testimony, and to demand that adverse testimony be taken in executive session. See H. Res. 61, 84th Cong., 1st sess. (1955).

On the general subject of improvement of procedure for committee investigations see Fortas, *Legislative Investigation: Methods of Committees Investigating Subversion*, 29 NOTRE DAME LAW. 192 (1954); Chase, *Improving Congressional Investigations: A No-Progress Report*, 30 TEMP. L.Q. 126 (1957); ABA SPECIAL COMM. ON INDIVIDUAL RIGHTS AS AFFECTED BY NATIONAL SECURITY, REPORT ON CONGRESSIONAL INVESTIGATIONS (1954).

[6]See Trebach, *The Indigent Defendant*, 11 RUTGERS L. REV. 625, 636 (1957).

were convicted of major offenses and, in spite of their requests for a lawyer to represent them, stood trial alone. The climate of judicial opinion has been such that the requirement for counsel has not been read into the constitutional standards of due process of law. I hope that judicial climate changes. If it does not, the reform must follow other channels. One is to adopt the practical expedient of following New Jersey's custom of designating lawyers in every criminal case where the need is felt. Even misdemeanors often present complex issues of fact and law which require a lawyer to unravel.

One alternative to the New Jersey system is the public defender. Some nine states—notably California—have had broad experience with the public defender. And for more than two decades bills have been introduced in Congress for the establishment of the public defender system in the federal courts. That proposal has received the support of the Judicial Conference, the American Bar Association, and the Department of Justice. As recently stated by the Senate Committee on the Judiciary, "In the eyes of the law, all human beings are to be treated equally, and in criminal cases the poor should have the same opportunity to defend their actions as those more financially able to afford counsel."[7]

Nearly two hundred legal aid societies also service the indigents across the land. The foremost society is the one in New York City. But here again New Jersey has taken the lead. Its State Bar Association and the bench have organized in every county of the state, but one, legal aid societies that are supported on a community chest basis. They service civil cases primarily. At the post-conviction stage, the New Jersey junior bar has organized habeas corpus advisory committees from which assignments of counsel are made.[8]

[7]S. Rep. No. 1829, 85th Cong., 2d Sess. 4 (1958).
[8]See Rossmore & Koenigsberg, *Habeas Corpus and the Indigent Prisoner*, 11 Rutgers L. Rev. 611 (1957).

In America the history of legal aid societies has been hitched to private philanthropy. England stepped over the line in 1949 and by the Legal Aid and Advice Act placed the cost on the public treasury, while keeping administrative control in the hands of the Law Society.

There is no reason why our bench and bar working through the panel system or through legal aid societies cannot take the burden of supplying counsel to all indigents in all criminal cases of any consequence. That is the preferable course. Then the bar retains its independence. There is something not quite congenial to our institutions when the government pays lawyers on both sides of a criminal case—as happens in the case of the public defender. What of cases with a political cast? Can we expect the government to service well each side of those prosecutions? Yet the demand for representation of the indigent defendant is strong, as indicated by the recent report of the Commission on Legal Aid of the Bar Association of the District of Columbia. The demand is so strong and the need so great that unless bar and bench produce a cooperative program, the movement for public defenders will be inevitable. A nation which makes a proud boast of equality can no more allow poverty to be the basis of discrimination than race, creed, or color.

Another group greatly to be affected by the evolution in our law is the psychiatrists. Our attitude toward crime and punishment is undergoing a radical change. The movement is slow and careful, yet its direction is plainly marked.

When Delaware in 1958 abolished the death penalty it became the seventh state to adopt a more humane, a more civilized attitude toward the criminal. Seven out of forty-nine states is not a high percentage. But the trend is significant when we look down the vistas of a century.

There were germs of a more civilized attitude toward criminals in our earliest history. Article XVIII of the New Hampshire Constitution of 1783 stated that "a multitude of sanguinary laws is both impolitic and unjust. The true design of all punishment being to reform, not to exterminate mankind." We are slowly passing from an age where crime was thought of in terms of sinful men who should be punished to an age when crime is conceived of as conduct of sick or diseased men who should be treated—and treated not as a class but on an individual basis. We are far from accepting the latter philosophy with all its implications; and we will not do so overnight. Yet that is the direction of our thinking.

The *M'Naghten* case,[9] decided in 1843, viewed in perspective, was an ameliorating influence. In the early days insanity was no defense. The evolution of that plea culminating in the *M'Naghten* rule was in mitigation of a harsh primitive system. Yet a century of experience has shown that the *M'Naghten* rule has little relation to realities. Just thirty years ago Mr. Justice Cardozo wrote, "Everyone concedes that the present definition of insanity has little relation to the truths of mental life." Much scholarship has gone into a study of new definitions. The pronouncements made in the *Jones* case[10] in 1871, and in the *Durham* case[11] in 1954 were historic. They conceived of insanity in terms of "mental disease."

That definition, once accepted, unites the lawyers and psychiatrists in exciting projects. They must first learn each other's language in order to communicate and explore ways of finding vocabularies that will do service for all the vexing problems that arise. If crime is thought of in terms of disease, the need for psychiatrists both at the trial stage and at the postcommitment stage will be enormous. Once we start thinking as a society in terms of treatment of criminals rather than revenge, our needs are greatly changed. The psychiatrist becomes the center of our concern. The truth is, however, that there are very few prisons where any real psychiatric rehabilitation program is seriously

[9]10 Cl. & F. 200, 8 Eng. Rep. 631 (H.L. 1843).
[10]State v. Jones, 50 N.H. 369.
[11]Durham v. United States, 214 F.2d 862 (D.C. Cir.).

undertaken. Where there is the will, there is not the personnel. The kind of work being done at Menlo State Park, New Jersey, is rare indeed. I think we can say that neither society nor psychiatry is ready for a quick overnight change from the conventional approaches. But the handwriting is on the wall; and the future trend is clear.

Meanwhile important intermediate steps are being taken which allow psychiatrists to help in evaluating the actual psychodynamics of individual defendants and convicts. The *Wells* case from California[12] gives the psychiatrist good credentials as an expert witness in testifying as to the ingredients of the "intent" with which the crime was committed. And the indeterminate sentence, so successfully used in a number of states, affords psychiatrists an opportunity to play significant roles in rehabilitation. The introduction of the Adult Authority and the Youth Correction Authority along lines pioneered by California, marks the changing emphasis from punishment of criminals to treatment of them as sick people. This new approach has brought the psychiatrists, as well as the sociologists, to the forefront. These new responsibilities will require them to tighten their disciplines and broaden their horizons to new professional requirements.

II

Acute calendar congestion is making conventional litigation almost archaic in some areas. Congestion is currently so great in the Eastern District of New York that it takes almost four years to bring a civil case to trial. Federal courts can improve their statistical records by drastically reducing or abolishing diversity jurisdiction. But the total federal-state load is not affected; and some state courts even now proceed under staggering loads. The flight to arbitration may accelerate. The introduction of pretrial techniques, so successfully used by Utah's state courts, may be

[12]People v. Wells, 33 Cal. 2d 330, 202 P.2d 53, *cert. denied,* 338 U.S. 836 (1949).

another device used to cut down the irksome delays. The use of compensation statutes to supplant conventional tort suits is almost certain to expand in the decades ahead. Administrative procedures will more and more encroach on what historically was judicial ground.

In spite of these likely trends the case load in the courts will continue heavy. England, as Lord Denning told us, has helped solve the problem of delay in *civil* cases by abolishing trial by jury except for rather narrow categories. American lawyers will be loath to give up that right. They know too well that judges, no matter how high-minded, develop callouses in their minds from the constant repetition of cases of a kind. They become stubborn in their failure to see a fact question whether for the one side or for the other. Lawyers find the fresh view of a jury a heritage too precious to give up in either civil or criminal cases.

Courts as an institution are too deeply fixed in our society to take a back seat. There is, I think, no sturdier element in the democratic system than an independent judiciary. It reflects the need on the part of the lowliest for belief that justice is administered once the center of things is reached. Faith that in spite of delays, costs, and shenanigans justice is not for sale, justice is impartial, and justice can be had by the common man is an essential keystone in the arch of the system that sustains us. The winds of passion can play, mobs can march, riots can take place; but there is long-run stability once the judiciary is viewed as the great rock that is unmoved by the storms that break over it.

The storms that break by reason of constitutional decisions are sometimes so great as to lead to constitutional amendments or attempts at nullification. Yet the judicial check on executive and legislative action is not something that is becoming archaic. Quite the contrary, Article 56 of the new French Constitution establishes the Constitutional Council to pass on the constitutionality of laws. The Turkish Constitution provides for the

Council of State to pass on the constitutionality of administrative actions of the government. India, Burma, and Pakistan provide for judicial review of the constitutionality of acts of the legislature. That power has been assumed by the Supreme Court of Canada and the Supreme Court of Australia. Despots dislike an independent judiciary. Once there is a written constitution it is but a short step to the assertion of the power of judicial review—provided the society has democratic values. Then there is abiding force in the statement of Marshall in *Marbury v. Madison*[13] that "the framers of the Constitution contemplated that instrument as a rule for the government of courts, as well as of the legislature. Why otherwise does it direct the judges to take an oath to support it?"

Judicial review of the constitutionality of the actions of the several States making up a federal system may not be essential to the preservation of federalism. But some federal referee is necessary if States, which often have had parochial views, are not to distort the constitutional scheme. What Madison wrote in 1831 needs repeating today:

A supremacy of the Constitution & Laws of the Union, without a supremacy in the exposition & execution of them, would be as much a mockery as a scabbard put into the hand of a Soldier without a sword in it. I have never been able to see, that without such a view of the subject the Constitution itself could be the supreme law of the land; or that the *uniformity* of the Federal Authority throughout the parties to it could be preserved; or that without this *uniformity*, anarchy & disunion could be prevented.

The major work of courts—federal and state—deals not with the Constitution but with the common law and with statutes. Statutes are the mainstay of litigation in the federal courts. In cases coming to the Supreme Court there are few which do not involve a federal statute, obliquely if not directly. There was a time when statutes were thought of as intruders; and the

13 U.S. (1 Cranch) 137, 179-80 (1801).

narrowest possible construction was given them. Sutherland in the first edition of *Statutes and Statutory Construction* (1891) deplored "legislative interference" in lawmaking. But those days are gone. Statutes are now hospitably received. The days when the judiciary was the paramount policy maker are over. The fact that a transaction does not fall squarely within the statutory prohibition is no longer a barrier to judicial action. The attitude of the civil law toward statutes[14] is more and more followed by other courts. An examination of current decisions in civil law jurisdictions[15] indicates that their approach to statutory construction is not today basically different from the one federal judges employ in construing acts of Congress.

Courts seldom refrain from the difficult task of construction. When they do so it is usually out of deference to an administrative agency whose expertise gives it the first say.[16]

We have no federal common law in the criminal field. Most of our civil litigation in the federal system also turns on statutory construction. Since *Erie R.R. Co. v. Tompkins*,[17] our federal courts have ceased fashioning a federal common law in diversity cases. Now the architects of the governing substantive law in diversity litigation are the state courts. There still is some room in other types of cases for federal courts to fashion a federal common law governing some commercial transactions.[18] At times Congress has provided sanctions for enforcement of certain types of agreements, leaving to federal courts the fashioning of the federal substantive law to be applied.[19] That is in the great common law tradition. Of course a court deals with policy matters

[14]See Pound, *The Theory of Judicial Decision*, 36 HARV. L. REV. 641, 647 (1923).

[15]See Galloway v. Wyatt Metal & Boiler Works, 189 La. 837, 181 So. 187 (1938); State *ex rel.* Thompson v. Dep't of City Civil Serv., 214 La. 683, 38 So. 2d 385 (1948).

[16]Armour & Co. v. Alton R.R., 312 U.S. 195 (1941).

[17]304 U.S. 64 (1932).

[18]Clearfield Trust Co. v. United States, 318 U.S. 363 (1943).

[19]Textile Workers Union v. Lincoln Mills, 353 U.S. 448 (1957).

not only when it fashions substantive common law but when it determines rules of evidence, as, for example, the propriety of a wife's testifying for or against her husband.[20] Federal courts are well-known policy makers in other procedural matters touching the working of the federal court system.[21] The same is true when principles of liability are stated and restated in the admiralty field.[22] When the Court performs that function, it does not take a very great step from the role it fills in construing a rather vague statutory term such as restraint of trade.[23]

Of course, courts, when construing statutes, necessarily engage in a species of lawmaking. It is what Gray called "legislating to fill up *casus omissi*."[24] The legislature often does no more than provide a general standard. Much debate and nice speculations take place concerning the application of the law to a specific case. There is sometimes little light gained from canvassing legislative purpose. Congress may have spoken in harsh, mandatory terms, using "shall" instead of "may." Yet did it leave no room for the play of discretion?

Sometimes the law has evolved through a welter of enactments. To find through the maze the trail that marks the policy involves a profound search.

The main thrust of the legislative purpose may be clear; it is the case in the penumbra that causes difficulty.

There may be gaps that break the symmetry of the law; and judicial embroidery may be necessary to complete the motif.

The policy may be clear. Would Congress have gone as far as the courts are asked to go if it had thought of the precise case? It is no help to ask what Congress intended. Exploration of the minds of those who voted for it would be fruitless even if possible. It would moreover be beside the point, which is to ascertain the

[20]Funk v. United States, 290 U.S. 371 (1933).
[21]McNabb v. United States, 318 U.S. 332 (1943).
[22]Pope & Talbot, Inc. v. Haun, 346 U.S. 406, 409 (1953).
[23]Standard Oil Co. v. United States, 221 U.S. 1 (1910).
[24]THE NATURE AND SOURCES OF LAW 173 (2d ed. 1921).

meaning of the words that were actually used. There are usually reliable records to show the purpose of the law. But these may be of little help. The full implications of what Congress did may never have been appreciated at the time. The application of the law may have brought about the first clear realization of its perplexities. Or the compromise which ambiguous language effected in Congress may have merely delayed a settlement of the issue. Where Congress has not clearly chosen the path it wants to follow which should the courts prefer?

These are mainly minuscule problems of policy, as Justice Charles D. Breitel points out. The Court in construing a statute is not free to choose the policy it would prefer as it does when it fashions a common law rule. Yet judges are human and every one of them is bound to see a problem through the windows of his own experience. One who once prosecuted under laws enforcing the commerce clause is apt to read the words "interstate commerce" more expansively than one who spent his years at the bar defending local interests. But that is the beginning not the end of the problem. A judge worthy of the tradition does not draw from the well of his prejudices in construing statutory words. It would be as much a subversion of the judicial function for him to read his predilections into a statute as it would be to use due process to put his own social philosophy into the Constitution. The problem is to stick with the legislative scheme and determine which construction is most consonant with it. Even when this is done, judges sharply divide, and will continue to do so. For these marginal questions in the law are so inherently provocative as to breed differences of opinion.

What may be the clear meaning of words to some creates ambiguities for others. The truth is that while we start with the words of the act, that is the beginning, not the end of the search. For words are inexact tools to say the least.

Most American judges look beyond the words to ascertain what occasioned the law and to learn what evil the enactment was designed to eradicate. There was a time when only the word of the spokesman for the measure or the committee report was considered.[25] Those are still the most authoritative pronouncements of legislative purpose. But the recent tendency in the federal system has been to ransack the entire legislative history for what light can be thrown on the problem of interpretation.[26] More and more does the search for the meaning of words take one through the morass of legislative history, looking for help from any competent source. This is a delicate task requiring much evaluation. Unless carefully performed it can lead to results that are treacherous. For some legislative history is artfully made to serve a selfish purpose. Judges, however, are aware of the problem.[27]

Some questions of statutory construction have constitutional overtones. I refer not only to strained constructions made to avoid constitutional adjudications. I include also those cases that pose the question whether the purpose of Congress in enacting the law was to displace state law. If so, the supremacy clause comes into play. That search often involves many imponderables. It is frequently an issue on which judges sharply divide.[28] Double regulation—both by state and federal laws—may be logically permissible but practically unsound. Dual regulation may be inherently so disruptive of the policy of the federal law that the purpose of Congress to foreclose state action may be what is implied.

In all cases of statutory construction—those that involve the supremacy clause as well as the others—the legislature has the

[25]United States v. St. Paul, M. & M. Ry., 247 U.S. 310, 318 (1918).

[26]Schwegmann Bros. v. Calvert Distillers Corp., 341 U.S. 384 (1951); Nashville Milk Co. v. Carnation Co., 355 U.S. 373 (1958); United States v. CIO, 335 U.S. 106, 113 (1948).

[27]United States v. American Trucking Ass'ns, 310 U.S. 534, 544 (1940).

[28]Hines v. Davidowitz, 312 U.S. 52 (1941); Rice v. Santa Fe Elevator Corp., 331 U.S. 218 (1947); Pennsylvania v. Nelson, 350 U.S. 497 (1956).

final word. If the congressional will is defied, the error can be corrected by an amendment of the law.

In the federal system there has been a healthy interplay between the courts and the Congress. One conspicuous example concerns the income tax where Committees of the Congress prepare a new law every two years. Moreover the Joint Committee on Internal Revenue Taxation and its highly efficient technical staff keep the judicial interpretations of the Internal Revenue Code under continuous scrutiny. Those decisions accordingly come up almost routinely for evaluation. The number that are prospectively changed or modified would add up to a healthy total over the period of a decade. A recent study indicates that apart from internal revenue cases, there were at least twenty-six instances between 1945 and 1957 where Congress by later enactment modified or changed the rule of law announced by the Supreme Court.[29] At times Congress may be expressing disagreement with a policy that an earlier Congress approved. Congress may be taking into account policy considerations which were inappropriate for the judiciary to consider. Congress with the benefit of hindsight may desire to limit the full thrust of an earlier law. The notion that the Court that made the ruling which Congress changed went contrary to a common understanding of what the law meant is nonsense. The questions of which I speak are close ones, on which judges divide. To be sure, some judicial construction has been so hostile to the statutory scheme as to change its character and greatly weaken it. Such was the history of the Federal Employer's Liability Act, all as related in H. R. Rep. No. 1222, 76th Cong., 1st Sess. Congress then restored the law as it was before the judges changed it. That history, which sometimes seems to repeat itself[30] is a lively influence in the close judicial scrutiny now given to FELA cases. But that illustration is a unique one. Judges, like

[29]Comment, 71 Harv. L. Rev. 1324 (1958).
[30]Tiller v. Atlantic Coast Line R.R., 318 U.S. 54 (1943).

other other people, have a difficult time in ridding themselves of habits of thought. But I do not know of a judiciary that is perverse. The truth is that the reach of a law may never be appreciated by the enacting body until it has been passed and put into practice. Congress is not omniscient; no matter how careful the draftsmen, all contingencies cannot possibly be foreseen; words are treacherous for the transmission of ideas. That is why constant legislative reappraisal of statutes as construed by the courts —such as we have in the case of the Internal Revenue Code—is a healthy practice.[31]

We are apt to think of judges when we think of human rights. But the courts have not always hewn to the line. During recent years there has been a sharp decline in respect for civil rights as the search for the subversive gained momentum. That decline was manifest in court decisions. It was conspicuous also in the administrative agency field. The whole loyalty program for government employees was indeed based on complicated and treacherous procedures before various agencies. Legislatures with their investigating committees also beat the drums of intolerance, also took shortcuts that were not in harmony with our principles.

Yet in the long view, legislatures and other conventions of the people deserve much credit for the fostering of civil rights. In the main the courts' record as guardian of those rights has been good. The genius of the judiciary in fashioning the writ of habeas corpus as a check on arbitrary power is one example. So are the decisions protecting civilians against military trials, the numerous rulings which outlaw devices to disenfranchise Negroes or to perpetuate racial discrimination, the banning of confessions obtained by coercion, the requirement of counsel, and so on.

---

[31]There are recent examples of speedy exercise of this power by Congress when the desire to change an announced rule was strong. Spiegel v. Commissioner, 335 U.S. 701 (1949), was changed nine months later by the Technical Changes Act of 1949, 63 Stat. 894; Anderson v. Mt. Clemens Pottery Co., 328 U.S. 680 (1946), was changed eleven months later by the Portal-to-Portal Act of 1947, 61 Stat. 84, 29 U.S.C. 251-62 (1952).

The list is long and striking. But when one looks down the long vista of Anglo-American history he learns that as many, if not more, victories for freedom were won in legislatures and conventions as in the courts. When it comes to human rights, we owe more than we commonly acknowledge to legislative law, as Professor Frank C. Newman has reminded us. Legislators have also been good guardians of liberty. They have curbed judges who at times have proved to be tryants, as the history of the law of contempt particularly shows. Their creative genius has designed many bills of rights for the common man.

Some modern democracies place the legislature in a dominant position. Such is the British system. But that system is not ours. The separation of powers is basic to our institutions. Thus the great office of the President, like the judiciary, must remain vigorously independent if it is to fulfill its historic missions.

There are periods in our history when we witness legislative encroachments. Woodrow Wilson in *Congressional Government* noted that trend. A cabal of congressmen sometimes brings a great executive department to heel, virtually dictating its policy. The power to investigate, that knows no restraint, can be powerful indeed. Coupled with the power over the purse strings it gives great leverage. Legislative power has sometimes been asserted to control what, in terms, seemed to be rights that had been placed by the Constitution beyond the reach of regulations. Two recent examples are First Amendment rights and rights of citizenship bestowed by the Fourteenth Amendment. In each instance Congress reached out to regulate those rights. These assertions of legislative power have in part been sustained by the judiciary.[32] But that kind of legislative invasion is not our main derangement. It illustrates the ebb and flow of power. It is not a major change in the concept of separation of powers. The stature of Congress

[32]Dennis v. United States, 341 U.S. 494 (1951); Perez v. Brownell, 356 U.S. 44 (1958).

like that of the presidency will depend on the character of the incumbents. It will also depend on the extent to which real power is transferred through numerous channels to the various cliques, groups, and blocs that make up "We The People."

Officials who do not echo public opinion may not be reelected. Officials who do no more than echo it may be paralyzed into inaction or propelled down false trails. On the great issues of foreign policy, international trade, war or peace, public opinion is often years behind. It is least versatile on those complex, impersonal issues. It may be so drugged on the emotionalism of some issues, such as foreign policy, as to be incapable of intelligent decision on problems that spell the difference between survival and destruction. A serious malady affects democratic societies when their leaders are led or propelled by mass opinion which is not informed or conditioned to existing facts. Equally fatal is the plight of those listening for the voice of the people and hearing such a babel that they only drift with the tides. This might be called the major derangement of the democracies in the twentieth century.[33] The fact that we may not even be aware that this phenomenon operates dangerously in our midst is evidence of the seriousness of the malady.

These are matters that go to the very vitals of our way of life. The remedy lies in a public attitude or philosophy. Are we to be a mature integrated people approaching problems in a civilized way? If so, then the press must be more than free in the constitutional sense. The press must use its freedom to be versatile and at home in the world of ideas and not serve merely as an instrument for propagating the prejudices of its owners. The family, the schools, and churches must prepare oncoming generations for a world of great diversity where one can live with intellectual excitement. We must as a people become more civilized in our attitudes, subduing the baser man for the common good and sub-

[33]See LIPPMANN, THE PUBLIC PHILOSOPHY (1955).

jecting ourselves to great discipline and our quarrels, big and small, to a rule of law.

We need to develop a climate of opinion that produces men capable of speaking for "the inner consciousness" of the people, as Lord Denning put it. Some nations have known rulers who adapted themselves to changing conditions and provided progressive leadership. We must find our aristocracy in men of learning and character who live and think above the requirements of precinct politics. This means a reversal of the leveling process we have experienced as we were more and more overwhelmed by conformity—the leveling process that has stifled criticism and discouraged outcroppings of genius and individuality.

III

We have heard much talk in recent decades about the need for a "rule of law" in international affairs. We have lawyers who with their new law on outer space seem to be seeking to reduce the entire universe to a legal problem. Seriously, the resolution of competing claims to outer space as well as to Antarctica and control over all instruments that use these areas, including intercontinental ballistic missiles, is fast becoming one of the great challenges of our day. Thus does international law evolve. Experts such as Dr. Philip C. Jessup remind us that we have healthy beginnings of international law in many fields and that its constant use will help build the needed mosaic more quickly than all the campaign oratory. Clark and Sohn in their scholarly work *World Peace Through World Law* have shown us an exact blueprint of what a true "rule of law" in international affairs would be like. Appreciation of the enormity of the disaster which atomic war would bring is stirring thoughtful men in all nations to bring their inventive genius into play. We may indeed be on the threshold of significant developments.

During the recent Suez crisis there was an interesting debate in the House of Lords. Lord McNair referred in particular to the Charter of the United Nations and showed how it took a long step toward the inauguration of a rule of law. Article 51 protects, of course, the right of a nation to repel by force "an armed attack." But Article 2 (3) provides that member nations agree to "settle their international disputes by peaceful means in such a manner that international peace and security and justice, are not endangered." And Article 2 (4) provides that member nations agree to "refrain in their international relations from the threat or use of force against the territorial integrity or political independence of any member state, or in any other manner inconsistent with the purposes of the United Nations."

Lord McNair maintained in the debate that "the legal position of armed force" has been "completely transformed."

It is no longer a discretionary instrument of policy but its use is regulated by law. That, I believe, is the view of the use and threat of armed force which is now held in the large group of countries with whom we normally co-operate and whose good opinion we cannot afford to forfeit. In all sincerity and humility, I would beg the Government to reflect upon my attempt to state the present rules governing the threat and the use of force, and to examine and to check it. If they come to the conclusion that I have stated those rules correctly, I think they are also bound to come to the conclusion which I have reached, which is as follows: that so far as the events in the present controversy up to date are known to us, I am unable to see the legal justification of the threat or the use of armed force by Great Britain against Egypt in order to impose a solution of this dispute.[34]

The development of the A-bomb and the H-bomb made the scientists who designed them powerful advocates for some system of law to contain them and control their use for destructive ends. The scientists turned to the bar with fervent pleas for the creation of legal and political institutions capable of dealing with the new

[34]199 H.L. Deb. (5th ser.) 662 (1956).

colossus. And many were bewildered when no ready solution was available.

Control of resort to force for a solution of problems has long been a goal of humanity. It is the ultimate problem with which law must deal. War as an instrument of policy is difficult to shed for it is caught up with high moral principles, deep feelings of security, and even survival itself. So we can hardly expect that force as an instrument of national policy can be utterly abolished overnight and law substituted instead.

But we can move toward that goal in several ways.

First, we can seek acceptance of the principle that all legal questions, *e.g.,* treaty rights, will be submitted to a tribunal for adjudication.

At present the requirements for compulsory submission are hedged in by many conditions. The final step in that direction would close an important gap. It would not be radical in nature. For, as stated by the Permanent Court of International Justice:

International law governs relations between independent States. The rules of law binding upon States therefore emanate from their own free will as expressed in conventions or by usages generally accepted as expressing principles of law and established in order to regulate the relations between these co-existing independent communities or with a view to the achievement of common aims. Restrictions upon the independence of States cannot therefore be presumed.[35]

Second, we should expand among like-minded nations the legal machinery for the settlement of disputes and controversies. By like-minded nations I mean, of course, those whose political traditions turn their faces toward law. Regional agreements have shown satisfactory developments. They can be greatly expanded.

Third, we should establish definite procedures for bringing the opposing camp—the Communist-dominated nations—to the settlement table. We need continuous consultation on problems that bristle with threats of war. We need—either within or without the

[35]Case of the S.S. "Lotus" P.C.I.J., Ser. A, No. 10 at 18 (1927).

United Nations—permanent committees or councils where continuous talk and consultation can be had. The roots of our international law start with procedural devices. We greatly need more and more vehicles for patient and unhurried talk—talk that is far from the summit, talk that is not recorded for television, talk that can quietly explore and reexplore all avenues to a peaceful solution.

Only then can diplomacy—which has suffered a great decline in the last generation—be restored to its former place of honor and utility.

We need to pick up at the point where Winston Churchill brought the problem in 1948.

I believe it right to say today that the best chance of avoiding war is, in accord with the other Western democracies, to bring matters to a head with the Soviet Government, and, by formal diplomatic processes, with all their privacy and gravity, to arrive at a lasting settlement. There is certainly enough for the interests of all if such a settlement could be reached. Even this method, I must say, however, would not guarantee that war would not come. But I believe it would give the best chance of preventing it, and that, if it came, we should have the best chance of coming out of it alive.[36]

Fourth, we must search for those problems, great or small, on which international unity can be achieved and bring them into some system of international control. Perhaps atomic energy will be the next to lend itself to a "rule of law."

These seem to me to be the dimensions of the problem. They indicate also the direction of our movement. The rate can be greatly accelerated if high-minded men from all continents unite in affirming that the rule of law points the way to peace and justice. That is the leadership the world sorely needs.

[36]446 H.C. Deb. (5th ser.) 561.

Comment

BY NOEL T. DOWLING

HARLAN FISKE STONE PROFESSOR EMERITUS OF CONSTITUTIONAL LAW
COLUMBIA UNIVERSITY SCHOOL OF LAW

My comments are, for one, to join in recognition and praise of the legislative process as a significant institution today and, for another, to suggest a subject matter on which that process can be most advantageously employed tomorrow.

To me, the most interesting feature of the proceedings of the Conference is the extent to which statute law has permeated the discussion. This is especially true of Justice Breitel's paper on "Courts and Lawmaking." To be sure, he does not go as far as Professor Newman on the line that legislatures "are better entrusted with lawmaking" than are courts and administrative agencies, though he does not say that "the institutional status of the legislature as the ultimate and paramount source of law must be unreservedly accepted." He puts less of a common law emphasis on the matter than did Justice Stone, for example, in his address in 1936, when he suggested that the common law had to reckon with a major problem of bringing about "the better organization of judge-made and statute law into a coordinated system." Justice Breitel is not so much concerned with what the judges can do on that job of organization as he is with what the statute law is doing to the judges—or, as he says, "the effect of the tremendous unprecedented growth of statute law on the judicial process." On the whole, he gives statutes a cordial welcome to the judicial sanctum.

As far as the law schools are concerned, legislation was relatively late in gaining recognition and welcome on the educational scene. Professor Newman has mentioned the pioneering work of the Columbia faculty. I can supply some firsthand testimony on the local progress; for it was as far back as 1912 —almost half the century past we are now celebrating—that Dean Stone himself set me off on the statutory road. One morning in the spring of that year he called me into his office (I was then a senior in the school), and this is the substance of what he said to me: "We are starting something new in the School. It has to do with statute law. Up to now we haven't paid much attention to it. But it is going to be important business in the future." He told me about the establishment, just the year before, of the Legislative Drafting Research Fund and said he wanted me to go talk with Chamberlain and Parkinson about its work. Then he added: "I think you will find it something in which you would like to have a part."

He was right. When I saw Chamberlain and Parkinson they made a fascinating story of the possibilities of (as Parkinson described it) "the legislative contribution to the development of the law." That was the beginning of my relationship with the Legislative Drafting Research Fund, a relationship which has lasted from that day till now and which has been marked by incomparable personal associations—from Stone and Chamberlain and Parkinson to Kernochan—and by memorable excursions into legislative enterprises. More to the point, it has given me the opportunity not only to see the expansion of the Fund's activities and influence but also to observe something of the mounting total of that legislative contribution of which Parkinson spoke. And it has created within me a confident belief in the adaptability and competence of the legislative process for the future development of the law.

It is from that background and with that belief that I come to the suggestion of a subject matter on which, as it seems to me, the legislative process can be most advantageously employed: the relationship between business and government. A short time ago "Management's Mission in a New Society" was the theme of a two-day conference in connection with the fiftieth anniversary of the Harvard School of Business. It was a suggestive theme and the discussion took a wide range. One speaker proposed a "new partnership" between business and the federal government as a means of promoting certain economic developments abroad. A further desirable addition to management's mission, having to do with the more immediate tasks of fostering and controlling the economy here at home, would be the adoption of a new attitude on the part of business toward government.

The new attitude should be one of less resistance to the legislative process—indeed, larger acceptance of it. In the course of my long association with the Legislative Drafting Research Fund I gained the clear impression that in the general area of legislation business has been largely preoccupied in resisting proposals put forth by others, or in winning short-term gains, and not much concerned with the creative task of devising long-time measures of its own. I have seen many examples of all-out, indiscriminate resistance but almost none of business on the affirmative side in taking its problems to a legislative body. Resistance, of course, has its proper place: there is plenty of room for it in our adversary system of getting at the truth; but it can be overdone. My own belief is that the legislative process offers much more promise to business and opens larger occasions for it to have a part in the wholesome development of the law than management commonly assumes.

There are signs that the concept of management's mission is being broadened. Something of a new attitude is reflected, for example, in the lectures on "Corporate Citizenship" by William T. Gossett at Washington and Lee University in 1956. With special reference to the role of the corporation counsel he remarked that "where once he functioned as an expert in the law, as it affected corporate behavior, he must now be a constant, sharpsighted student of the trends of society as a whole." In that capacity and in some circumstances he may have to "become an advocate of legislation." The insurance industry seems to me to present a situation where such advocacy would be in order. Fourteen years ago a decision by the Supreme Court brought the industry face to face with new questions hardly soluble without legislative intervention. The decision catapulted the business from the category of intrastate to interstate commerce and brought on a substantial problem concerning the effective operation of our federal system of government. I venture to say that the ultimate answers are going to be found in a coordinated program of state and national enactments, and I am altogether sure that the industry itself is in the best position to make the initial proposals of what that program should be. A recent example from a related field shows what can be done when management takes the initiative. In 1956-57 the atomic industry and insurers participated in a study of "Financial Protection Against Atomic Hazards." The study was carried on by the Legislative Drafting Research Fund and its results had a considerable impact on the content of legislation adopted shortly thereafter.

If business be disposed to take its problems to Congress, it can do so knowing that, for all practical purposes, the voice of Congress is final. Under the evolution of our constitutional scheme Congress has become the center of legislative power as it bears upon the economy of the country. It is reasonably clear that Congress can determine for itself how far into the states its commerce control shall run (the Court has even intimated that restraints must come from political rather than judicial sources), and clearer still that Congress can say to what part of commerce the powers of the states shall extend. "Judicial review of the constitutionality of the actions of the several states making up a federal system," Mr. Justice Douglas reminds us in his paper, "may not be essential to the preservation of the federalism." Umpiring that system may safely be left to the political departments. Also it has come to pass that the substantive limitation on the regulation of economic affairs once attributed to due process of law is near the vanishing point.

The sum of the matter seems to be that on the economic front, whatever may be true in other sectors, the Court is having less and less to do with the battle. And as I see it, this ebb in the tide of judicial review involves two consequences of present interest to us. For one, it tends to widen the base for the legislative opportunities of management to which I have referred, and for the other, it cannot but elevate and animate the legislative process by fixing full responsibility on Congress in the fashioning of its statutory products.

Comment

BY HERBERT WECHSLER
HARLAN FISKE STONE PROFESSOR OF CONSTITUTIONAL LAW
COLUMBIA UNIVERSITY SCHOOL OF LAW

No conference can be worth while, certainly not one marking a centennial, unless its theme is broad enough to guarantee that all the conferees will be exhausted long before they can exhaust the subject. This well-accepted principle, and this alone, sustains me in presuming to add further words to all that has been said since the beginning. But since no principle should be extended to the limit of its logic, I shall endeavor to be brief. In substance I propose three footnotes to the statement of conclusions Mr. Justice Douglas has presented. They represent my main reflections on the papers that are included in this Centennial Conference.

First—Though our summons was to think of legal institutions not only of today but of tomorrow, is it not a fair appraisal that our discourse on the whole has focused more upon the present than the future?

If this is so, it demonstrates more than the caution of our conferees; it bears important witness to the most abiding element in the entire human situation. We see the present only through a glass and darkly; our appraisals of the future rarely involve more than the projection of our hopes or fears. Prophecy is likely to be more informative about the prophet than about what will occur as time unfolds.

Nor is our vision stunted only in perception of the shape of things to come; it has a comparable limitation in the understanding of our past. Take any major element in our legal firmament and undertake to separate the casual and causal factors in its evolution —to borrow words John Buchan used in a delightful lecture about history.[37] How far can we proceed along that line? Suppose the courts by an insistence upon jury trial or on judicial fact-finding had stood intransigently against the administrative process in its early days. Would the development that all agree is here to stay have been averted, or would it have taken other forms and, if the latter, what forms would we have?

I do not mean by this, of course, to deny all predictive power in our field. Twenty-five years ago it could no doubt be said with reasonable confidence, as it was said by the most able of our number, that major governmental action in the realm of the economy was an inevitable prospect, the only open issues, what its form and its intensity would be. When Cardozo in 1921 wrote *The Nature of the Judicial Process*, it could perhaps have been thought with equal confidence that the conception of the common law as a closed legal system—which then had far more devotees than it is pleasant to remember—was a view not destined to survive.

[37]BUCHAN, THE CAUSAL AND THE CASUAL IN HISTORY (Rede Lecture, Cambridge, 1929).

How many points are there before us now respecting which even so general and marginal an affirmation can be made? How surely can we join with Mr. Justice Douglas in predicting that the path of law will carry greater safeguards for the individual, rather than submerge him further beneath the weight of government and other power aggregates, not to speak of the even greater weight of a mass culture wrought by mass communication? Who will be bold enough to say whether the judgment in the segregation cases will be judged fifty years from now to have advanced the cause of brotherhood or to have illustrated Bagehot's dictum that the "courage which strengthens an enemy, and which so loses, not only the present battle, but many after battles, is a heavy curse to men and nations."[38]

I do not emphasize these difficulties of prediction to introduce a note of gloom. My purpose rather is to vindicate the focus and the emphasis of our discussion. What we have done is, on the whole, as much as men can do in grappling with phenomena of this diversity and problems of this complexity. We have attempted to appraise and diagnose our situation in the major areas of lawmaking and law administration; the analyses that have been made have had both power and originality; they should assist in clarifying thought and point to possible improvement in our practice; they indicate some fruitful lines for work and cast some doubt upon the fruitfulness of others. This is, in my submission, all we can expect, even with all the talent and experience that is assembled here. We are agreed that there is much to strive for in improving our legal institutions. Let us agree to give our best to that great effort and to let tomorrow judge where we succeed and where we fail.

Second—When I ask myself if there is any single proposition on which our conferees have been united, I find it in their unwillingness to take the easy course of formulating easy generalities.

[38]BAGEHOT, THE ENGLISH CONSTITUTION 18 (rev. ed. 1914).

For Justice Breitel the problem of the role of the courts in relation to legislation is not a single problem but a multitude of different issues. It is not only a question of the clarity of legislative language—language which, as Mr. Justice Johnson said long years ago, "*is* essentially defective in precision; more so than those are aware of who are not in the habit of subjecting it to philological analysis."[39] There are statutes and statutes, reflecting different modes of legislative competence and affirmation. In suggesting that the interpretative process does and should adapt itself to these realities of legislation, I believe that an important contribution to an age-old problem has been made.

Where Justice Breitel insists upon distinctions in appraising the relationship of court and legislature—surely a fighting issue in our time—Mr. Gardner is no less insistent on distinctions between one administrative process and another. Not even the judicializing of administrative adjudications, which I should have believed a safe objective, is in his view a realistic or desirable goal, if put forth as a universal proposition.

As with the courts and the administrative organs, so with the processes of legislation. There are things that the legislative process should attempt; there are others that are well eschewed.

In all of this we may perceive, I think, a major and important change in climate of opinion within the last quarter of a century. The issues raised, for example, by Justice Stone in his address at the Harvard Tercentenary hardly now seem open; the lessons that he sought to teach with respect to judicial receptivity to legislation and administration have been well learned. But he addressed himself to the preliminary problems, made acute at that time by the rigidities and absolutes that interposed a barrier to change. Now that the absolutes and the rigidities have been dispelled, we face the harder problem of constructing theories that

[39]Martin v. Hunter's Lessee, 14 U.S. (1 Wheat.) 304, 374 (1816) (concurring opinion).

will take account of the distinctions that so evidently must be made. This is not the work of a day. It is the problem of a life-time of constructive effort for the ablest of the bench and bar and schools. Our contributors have said, in adaptation of Descartes, *Distinguo ergo sum.* They give us not the answer to our questions but a program for the rest of our years.

Third—Finally, I should observe that one point seems to me to be neglected in our treatment of the legislative process: an ap-praisal of its true potentialities for systematic renovation of the law. This is, in part, the point Professor Hays articulated in his comment on Professor Newman's paper.

It will be recalled that Justice Breitel, speaking from rich experi-ence, finds the political preoccupations of the legislature incon-sistent with any approach to "complete legislative management of the general law." I am not sure how large his emphasis is on the word "complete," but I submit that larger legislative management is necessary and desirable, that, indeed, there is no other way to prevent the anarchical proliferation of a system of case law. It may be that I speak from bias, which I recognize, as one engaged for many years in the attempt to reconstruct a single field of law.

I fully grant the obstacles to larger legislative management, not only in the political factor Justice Breitel has emphasized, but in the even larger question—how the work can possibly be done. Here I submit, as I have often argued elsewhere—and as I was glad to note that Justice Traynor urges—is a major opportunity for legal scholarship, a major challenge to the schools. For it is only by unhurried canvassing of all the issues in a field, the systematic rooting out of inconsistencies, the time-consuming search for in-formation that can shape and inform policy, that the entire corpus of a field of law can be evaluated and reframed.

This is not to say, of course, that larger legislative management implies necessarily—or even probably—less call upon the courts or on administrative agencies as creative organs in the application and development of law. I have some fear that such a false antithesis may have been thought to be implicit in some of our earlier discussion—especially the interchange between Justice Traynor and Professor Hart and Mr. Gossett and Mr. Gardner.

What is implied for me in larger legislative management is a considered disposition, at the only level that is even theoretically able to regard the legal system as a whole, of what it is desirable to attempt to settle by a legislative rule—of greater or of lesser specificity; what must be left to standards that will gain their largest content in the course of their interpretation and their application; what ought to be committed to the outright discretion of the courts or other organs of administration; and lastly but not least important, what should be left to "private ordering," to use a concept that Professor Hart has stressed, that is to the initiative and decision of individuals and groups sustained by law but not directed by it.

The difference between maturity and immaturity in any legal system inheres largely, I would urge, in how deliberately and carefully a judgment of this kind is made. It is a judgment that assuredly will vary as we move from one field to another in the legal order, though certain factors like the limitations of imagination, of analysis, and of language will be fairly constant and will always call in any field for much reliance on the agency that functions at the point of application—when any rule or standard meets the concrete case—the point which Professor Hart and Justice Breitel so rightly emphasize as one unique in challenging and testing power.

Perhaps it sums the thought up best to say that when I think of legislative management and renovation of the law, I have as much in mind the setting and the framework of decision as the actual decisions to be made. I should resist the thought that we can be content with less than sustained, systematic work upon the framework of decision that our law at its most fundamental level—which of course means the legislative level—prescribes or tolerates throughout its multitude of fields. And this is not a matter for *ad hoc* attention in relation to one or another narrow issue that has been presented in the course of litigation; it involves the entire corpus of the law—its positive content, its silences, its form, its gaps, the opportunities that have been missed that should be grasped.

Years of effort by the schools, supported as they will be by the bar, can set the stage for such an undertaking and, in my submission, bring it to fulfillment. We have seen it happen in commercial law and in procedure, to name but two examples. Mr. Justice Douglas went to Washington, if I remember rightly, after such an academic effort in finance. It is a work proceeding all the time on many different fronts, responsive to a challenge that endures.

Technical staffing by the legislature will assist and is progressing; I believe it can go further than it has. But in the end it is the confidence that legislators and legislative committees will repose in patient and disinterested effort by the bar and the judiciary and the schools that will surmount the obstacles that we perceive.

I can hope for nothing better for my school in the century that lies ahead than that it will be animated by this vision and will enlarge its contribution in this field.

The Living Law

BY STANLEY F. REED

ASSOCIATE JUSTICE OF THE SUPREME COURT OF THE UNITED STATES

Law, the governmentally enforceable rules controlling the relations of man with his fellows, necessarily changes with the evolution of society. Where law rules tranquillity dwells.

Throughout history legal institutions have developed to meet the new situations. Law is a vital, changing force. The bar, the courts, the administrative bodies, the legislative assemblies, and particularly the law schools face the necessity of conducting their activities with not only an understanding of the law of the present but also with an appreciation of the impending adjustments.

Changes in our law during the last half of the twentieth century will come, as they usually have in the past, more from our experiences with the practical effectiveness of existing law than from major alterations in our political or social institutions. How great are the differences that may evolve! How great may be their effect on our nation's life may be appreciated by recalling the rapid movement of the law since the first Roosevelt. Juristic changes have been as momentous as those in science and the arts. In those years we traversed a boundary of legal history, passing from where the functions of government were limited largely to the maintenance of order and the enforcement of contracts to where government had put upon it the far heavier burden of providing the means and opportunity for all its citizens to improve their condition materially and socially. For the foreseeable future, our legal institutions will adjust to this later concept of government, subject to the overriding necessities of national security.

In the fifty years from the Theodore Roosevelt to the Eisenhower administration we have enacted the Income Tax, the Federal Reserve System, the Agricultural Adjustment Acts, the Labor Relations Act, the Social Security Acts, cooperated with other nations in systematizing the law of aviation, patents, and copyrights, and ratified the Charter of the United Nations with the statute of the International Court of Justice.[1] Workmen's compensation has become a commonplace. National security has assumed predominant importance. The adoption of these legal institutions and interests has shifted the main course of legal development from a prohibition of evils to a positive support of human welfare. Would that some exceptionally talented jurist, neither judge nor advocate, but with extrasensory perception, could foreshadow accurately our likely future in legal problems. Such foreknowledge could enable us to support or attack the proposals. The recent changes remind us that their evolution will continue. The interpretations and the statutes of the last half of the twentieth century are obviously of major importance to our immediate future. My generation has learned that society, as we know it, can end. The present status of the law will not continue. Experience will compel modifications to meet new conditions. Changes will continue and our successors will find continued modifications necessary to meet the needs of society.

These changes in the law have followed equally important changes in the American economic and social culture. Growing scientific knowledge and a genius for business administration have multiplied production. Increasing urbanization and industrialization have brought concentrations of population and economic power. Transportation and communication have multiplied human contacts and the growing press has furthered interchange of ideas.

[1]S. Res. 196, 79th Cong., 2d Sess., 92 CONG. REC. 10706, (1946); 59 Stat. 1031 (1945).

Universal education has brought knowledge of problems and needs of groups or communities to all. Capital, management, and labor have struggled for a greater share of the results of American productivity, sometimes fairly, sometimes unfairly. Hard times have intensified clashes. Universal suffrage has given an opportunity for each to become an antagonist or proponent of the changes in the law that were expected to further that individual's interest, or that of a particular community, or that of the nation. First inquiry, then experiment, then experience, showed there were ways by which changes in the laws could improve conditions in general. Social changes brought the legislation and decisions that were needed to readjust the law to the new circumstances, not the reverse. These legal changes sprang from necessity. They were inevitable. Legislators and judges may have deferred or accelerated the pace of development, but conditions forced adjustments. The general acceptance of the shift of emphasis from prohibition of unlawful acts to welfare supports that statement.

A decision in the *Gold Clause Case*[2] that preexisting contracts for payment of gold coin were outside the broad power of Congress to regulate the currency would have threatened bankruptcy to debtors with gold obligations and legal tender income. If lack of constitutional power had barred settlement of industrial disputes through such measures as the National Labor Relations Act or the Taft-Hartley Act, our economy would probably not be as well adjusted as it is today.

When we observe the effect of these recent federal enactments on our federation, the increased exercise of power in the national government is plain, but is the power to legislate any greater now than when the great cases defined the supremacy clause and the necessary and proper clause of the Constitution?[3]

[2]Norman v. Baltimore & O.R.R., 294 U.S. 240 (1935).
[3]Marbury v. Madison, 5 U.S. (1 Cranch) 137 (1803); Cohens v. Virginia, 19 U.S. (6 Wheat.) 264 (1821); McCulloch v. Maryland, 17 U.S. (4 Wheat) 316 (1819).

I think not. As long as members of Congress hold state commissions, there will be no serious impairment of state sovereignty. It is not necessary for it to exercise all admitted constitutional legislative power.[4]

Congress has found need for legislation that does minimize the necessity of the exercise of state power in some fields. Authority for such legislation under the general welfare clause was established by the decision and opinion of the Supreme Court in the *Hoosac Mills* case.[5] This furnished a constitutional basis for the Social Security Acts.[6] The *Shreveport* case of 1913[7] upheld the power of Congress over intrastate matters affecting interstate commerce. This principle was the constitutional authority for the National Labor Relations Act, the Securities and Exchange Act, and the Wage and Hour Act. Thus it was possible to have the states and the nation cooperate in furthering opportunities for all as citizens of both sovereignties.

It is true that some of this legislation arose from interpretations of the Constitution that might not have commanded the approval of earlier generations under the conditions of their time. Ours is a written Constitution, adopted to lay down principles of government and to mark the limits of federal power. Foresight could not be so accurate or words so definitive as to assure no disagreement as to the application or construction of the Constitution. So there evolved our American doctrine of judicial determination of constitutionality, a doctrine that has commended itself to other nations with written constitutions. The most recent comparable instance is the Constitutional Council of Title VII of the new Constitution of the French Republic.

[4]E.g., the commerce clause: Kentucky Whip & Collar Co. v. Illinois Cent. R.R., 299 U.S. 334 (1937); United States v. South-Eastern Underwriters Ass'n, 322 U.S. 533 (1944); Prudential Ins. Co. v. Benjamin, 328 U.S. 408 (1945).

[5]United States v. Butler, 297 U.S. 1, 66 (1936).

[6]Steward Mach. Co. v. Davis, 301 U.S. 548, 587 (1937); Helvering v. Davis, 301 U.S. 619, 640 (1937).

[7]Houston, E. & W. Tex. Ry. v. United States, 234 U.S. 342, 353 (1914).

While the power to declare state and federal laws unconstitutional when violative of the Federal Constitution is nowhere expressly granted to the federal courts, the expressions in the Constitutional Convention, the explanations in the *Federalist,* the early and continuous line of decisions of men familiar with the purposes of the Founders, and the almost universal acceptance of the necessity for an arbiter have settled the question of judicial review for constitutional issues. The alternative is final determination of compliance with constitutional mandates by Congress or by the Executive. Since both of these arms of government have the power to initiate governmental action and to originate public measures in the heat of political conflicts and the height of popular discontent, the judiciary, which can only interpret and condemn after public hearing with reasoned decision, and which is without affirmative power to enact or administer, has been accepted as the arbiter of disputed issues of federal constitutional law.

While certainty as to the meaning of our Constitution is most desirable where grants of powers are in general terms, construction must continue as new situations arise. Chief Justice Hughes, in a memorable opinion for the Court in the 1933 Term, phrased it thus:

If by the statement that what the Constitution meant at the time of its adoption it means to-day, it is intended to say that the great clauses of the Constitution must be confined to the interpretation which the framers, with the conditions and outlook of their time, would have placed upon them, the statement carries its own refutation.[8]

Long ago Justice Holmes wrote, no "system of delusive exactness" can be extracted from the Fourteenth Amendment.[9] Justice Brandeis in 1931 and Justice Jackson in 1942 listed numerous cases in which the Supreme Court had overruled its earlier constitu-

---

[8]Home Bldg. & Loan Ass'n v. Blaisdell, 290 U.S. 398, 442-43 (1934).
[9]Louisville & N.R.R. v. Barber Asphalt Paving Co., 197 U.S. 430, 434 (1905).

tional decisions.[10] It would not be practicable to adopt a rule that a judicial interpretation of the Constitution by the Supreme Court could not be modified by a later decision, that such a change could come only by constitutional amendment. The power of the dead over the living would be too far extended. In the light of experience, changes in the application of the Constitution will continue by amendments, new statutes, and differentiating decisions.

While my discussion has drawn from federal law for illustrations, the deductions are applicable to state court decisions. The law of the state, except for the limited influence of the Napoleonic Code, is built on the same foundation, governed by the Federal Constitution, and administered by men trained in the same tradition. The duty to see that the law is kept abreast of conditions rests alike upon the courts, the bar, and the legislative bodies of our dual sovereignties.

These changes in our legal institutions, using the word as covering all phases of law as an "institution," pertain largely to that business of the courts which is usually classified as public. But even in the domain of private law—interpretation of instruments, marriage relations, criminal prosecutions, bankruptcy— there are innovations. Compare the *Williams* cases from North Carolina,[11] pertaining to the effect of a divorce decree in a state not the matrimonial domicile, and *Erie R. R. v. Tompkins*,[12] where the law of the courts of the state of trial, rather than federal law, was held to govern. As law is an integral part of our composite society, its changes affect all elements. Fortunately, our essential underlying principles are accepted by all. Law, no matter what changes occur, is directed at maintaining the separation of powers,

[10]Burnet v. Coronado Oil & Gas Co., 285 U.S. 393, 407 (1932) (dissent); Helvering v. Griffiths, 318 U.S. 371, 401 (1943). See Smith v. Allwright, 321 U.S. 649, 665 (1944).
[11]Williams v. North Carolina, 317 U.S. 287 (1942); Williams v. North Carolina, 325 U.S. 226 (1945).
[12]304 U.S. 64 (1938).

the sovereignty of the states, law and order, due process of law, equal protection and opportunity, freedom of speech, press and religion, national safety, and other such fundamentals of human relations, so that men may dwell quietly in their habitations. None contests the purpose of such changes, but many and divergent are the roads that are traveled in search of the goals.

Difficulties arise in applying these principles. Agencies for administration of government may go beyond the granted powers. Judicial review of such action is granted in some instances by legislative enactment.[13] In others judicial review is necessary or the citizen may be deprived of rights.[14] Even an Executive Order may be beyond the President's constitutional power.[15] Acts of sovereign states must meet all federal constitutional tests. In a great majority of cases, judicial review that fails to carry out legislative intention can be readily corrected by redrafting. Congress continuously does this so that the wishes of the legislative body prevail.[16] This power, except for unavoidable constitutional bars, added to the natural deference that the judiciary properly pays to the legislatures as the chief source of our modern legal codes, enables the various legislatures to attain their purposes.[17]

I have been reviewing the past. Other developments of the same character must be anticipated in planning for the future. While we may expect the elimination of pitfalls in procedural and substantive law and a continuation of our improved legislative draftsmanship, governmental regulations will necessarily be

[13]E.g., Administrative Procedure Act, 60 Stat. 243 (1946), 5 U.S.C. 1009 (1952).
[14]Compare Switchmen's Union v. National Mediation Bd., 320 U.S. 297 (1943), and Estep v. United States, 327 U.S. 114, 120 (1946), with Stark v. Wickard, 321 U.S. 288, 306 (1944).
[15]Steel Seizure Case, Youngstown Sheet & Tube Co. v. Sawyer, 343 U.S. 579 (1952).
[16]See Congressional Reversal of Supreme Court Decisions: 1945-1957, 71 HARV. L. REV. 1324 (1958).
[17]Compare United States v. Butler, 297 U.S. 1 (1936), with Mulford v. Smith, 307 U.S. 38, 48, and 52 (dissenting opinion). See SCHWARTZ, THE SUPREME COURT 368 (1957).

more rather than less complex. Legislation will grow. More people will be affected in more phases of their life. Lawyers must foresee and prepare for such changes.

The legislatures early realized that many fields of activity—e.g., carriers, communications, power atomic energy, labor management relations, securities—were each sui generis and could not be adequately regulated by ad hoc congressional enactments alone. Such activities became so enmeshed in the daily life of the nation that their starting or stopping, or other activities, could not be left as a matter of individual choice of the private owners. Wholly unregulated public utilities today would be anachronous.

This administrative law development will doubtless continue to expand. The states individually and the federal government in certain interstate commerce matters will probably be compelled to adopt some kind of accident compensation system to assure that the victims of accidental injuries, caused by private parties, with or without negligence, will receive fair payment for their loss of earning capacity. The experience of the United States with its Federal Tort Claims Act is a pioneer effort that may show whether payments should be such amounts as a jury may fix or whether a fair scale should be adopted. It is time for the hit or miss, delaying, litigation-breeding negligence laws of today to be revised. A more vigorous use of criminal penalties against careless tort-feasors will help, too.

We may well see soon in another field an extension of administrative law. A business under able management needs opportunity to expand both in its own interest and in that of the country. On the other hand, our nation is dedicated to free enterprise. That system has blocked socialism and socialism's reach for power in the state to determine the destinies of communities and individuals. We have long believed, and there is not the slightest tendency to depart from that conviction, that the foundation of such a desideratum as a free economy is open competition. It is crystal clear from our legislation and our convictions that competition is the authentic rule for American business. But business is often confronted with the problems of uniform industry prices, of action through trade associations on practices, of mergers, of consolidations, or of purchases of limited available sources of raw materials, such as bauxite, iron ore, or pulpwood. Enlightened self-interest, whatever may seem to be the temporary advantage of monopoly agreements, forces business to accept our laws against monopoly. But how can it be sure of what is the applicable rule of law. Mergers and horizontal or perpendicular expansion may be unlawful. The power of the Federal Trade Commission could be expanded or some other agency created that could determine such problems beforehand.

As far back as 1941, the TNEC recommended that the Federal Trade Commission be used to forbid mergers of competing corporations over a certain size, unless it was shown to the Commission that such merger was desirable.[18] As late as 1954 Congress adopted a similar plan for certain business licenses under the Atomic Energy Act of that year.[19] We have used prior determination of legality for consolidation of transportation facilities. Something approaching this suggestion emerges from the growing practice of consent decrees. When specific charges of violations of the antitrust laws come before the Department of Justice or evidences of unfair practices are uncovered by investigations of the Federal Trade Commission, consent decrees can be entered which eliminate objectionable practices or enjoin continuance of corporate structures that promote monopoly.[20] The adoption of the administrative process would offer opportunity for constructive effort to assist desirable business development.

[18]S. Doc. No. 35, 77th Cong., 1st Sess.
[19]Atomic Energy Act, 68 Stat. 938 (1954), 42 U.S.C. 2135(c) (Supp. V, 1958).
[20]United States v. New York Great Atl. & Pac. Tea Co., Civil No. 52-139, S.D.N.Y. (Feb. 19, 1954); 1956 ATT'Y GEN. ANN. REP. 190.

The challenge for imaginative change exists in every domain of the law. Lawyers have led in every phase of legal development, the executive, the legislative, the judicial, the private law field. To see that law keeps current with affairs is their duty. Equal Justice Under Law is their aim. To see that humanity profits from the law is given into their hands. Sometimes crime or oppression seems in the ascendency. Be not discouraged. Never dream "though right were worsted, wrong would triumph." We, the students of the Columbia Law School, may be justly proud of its past contributions and confident of the successful continuation of its efforts to promote the improvement of the administration of justice.

In Conclusion: The Duty of Responsible Criticism

BY WILLIAM C. WARREN

DEAN OF THE FACULTY OF LAW, COLUMBIA UNIVERSITY

As things go in the City of New York, where we are as ready to pull down as to build up, one hundred years of existence is something notable. It is so notable that we of the Columbia Law School, in celebration of its Centennial, are constrained to obey the command of the psalmist, "Sing aloud with joy." Indeed, a moment of joy is needed after two days and a night of viewing with alarm and trying to peer into the murky future. There is reason enough for unease over the prospect ahead. For what philosophic comfort there may be in looking back, remember the world of 1858—"Bleeding Kansas," the Lincoln-Douglas debates, John Brown plotting in New York to raid Virginia. There was no hint of all this at the opening exercises of our school in November 1, 1858. I take it that our present immense concern with the world about us is a vivid indicator of the great change in the stature of the law school and in the conception of the role it should play.

There are other things, too, which have changed at the Columbia Law School—whether for better or for worse it is not for me to judge. Theodore Dwight, our founder in 1858, who was soon to be named Warden of the School, had a superhuman capacity for work. He preferred to do all the teaching, rather than suffer additions to his faculty. His life was, therefore, not complicated with the unceasing diplomatic exertions which would have consumed his days had he assembled about him a group of highly charged individualists. The mimeograph machine had not yet been invented, nor that instrument of the fiend, the telephone.

Since so much of Dwight's time was his students', he was venerated. Veneration is something that cannot be generated today. We—dean and faculty—are only the objects of criticism—and not very constructive criticism at that. Yet this is one of the fortunate changes that has overtaken us, for it is a sign of a healthy teacher-student relationship. This critical pose began, I suspect, with the introduction of the case method under William Albert Keener, who succeeded Dwight. After all, you cannot resort to the procedures of Torquemada and be venerated. Fortunately the hand of time has a way of healing scars left by rack and screw in the classroom. An affection, sometimes a little grudging, is born. There are stories exchanged of Kirchwey, of Abbott, of Terry, of Ralph Gifford, of Jervey, of Michael, and of many others. They are told warmly, and not with bated breath as if the faculty were so many icons in so many niches. It is better so—we and our alumni should maintain a sort of husband-wife relationship of tolerant and critical affection.

During the Centennial Conference I forbore speaking of the future of our legal institutions; yet there is one about which I am impelled to say a word here. That is an institution more venerable than our own—one represented at the Conference both by a retired member and by an active member—the Supreme Court of the United States.

Judicial power to determine the constitutionality of actions of the other branches of government has been a major contribution of American experience to the science of government. The seeds for this development were sown in Colonial days when the English Privy Council was our supreme judicial tribunal. Judicial review was, moreover, a thing to which our forefathers were not blindly moved; for the power was much discussed at the time of the adoption of the Federal Constitution. There was, indeed, a New York pamphleteer who foretold results as dire as anything now predicted by our contemporary prophets of doom.

Mr. Justice Douglas has reminded us that this power of review continues to commend itself to other nations in the refashioning of governmental structures. And the events of the last three or four years have once again demonstrated that emotion-charged controversy is often generated in a system in which constitutional courts must decide far-reaching questions of governmental action as questions of law.

Vehement and impassioned reactions to Supreme Court decisions are, of course, not new. They have been encountered recurrently since the stormy days of John Marshall. The Columbia Law School was founded when the din over the Dred Scott decision had not yet abated. We were less than ten years old when an angry Congress overrode the veto of the Habeas Corpus Act designed to prevent judicial testing of its Reconstruction policy. In 1885 the press was again at the heels of the Court, and within a decade a great political party devoted a hostile plank to the sins of the federal judiciary. Some who are hearing these remarks were in law school when the Progressives came up with the sovereign nostrum of judicial recall. All will remember the attack of 1937.

But despite these violent attacks the Supreme Court has survived. It has kept pace with the expanding role of the federal government in the affairs of our country. The reassurance of history must not, however, make us unduly complacent about the recent attacks on the Court. History has an unpleasant way of not repeating itself. The nature of some of the recent criticism of Supreme Court decisions—particularly in the areas of internal security and segregation—gives cause for profound concern. When the legislature of one of our sovereign states issues a sweeping demand for impeachment of six Justices of the Supreme Court of the United States; when Congress is induced to give serious consideration to crippling restrictions on the appellate jurisdiction of the Court, and to virtual elimination of the doctrine of federal pre-emption because of disagreement with particular applications of established principles; when challenges to judicial integrity and cries of "judicial legislation" fill the air, the legal profession surely has a special cause for disquiet.

These attacks are symptomatic of very serious divisions of opinion on particular issues of the day. They reveal also a pervasive lack of understanding of the difficult task and vital role of our ultimate constitutional authority. At the least, they cannot but breed disrespect for law and order; at the worst, encourage resort to anarchic violence.

Although lawyers are often exhorted to heal divisions of opinion, we cannot hope to sustain in peacetime the factitious unanimity of opinion that exists in wartime. There is, however, something lawyers can do. I believe it to be the duty of the legal profession to work to remove the difficulties and doubts which beset the public, and so to reduce the impact of colliding views. The need of an informed intermediary between the Court and the purveyors of information that play so important a part in catalyzing opinion is obvious. Unlike the legislature, whose work is often not beyond the comprehension of ordinary humans, the Court operates in a framework unfamiliar and even repellent to the legendary man in the street. Judicial decisions not being self-explanatory to him, he takes his explanations where he finds them —in the press or over the air. Surely, if our profession will bestir itself, we can do something to promote enlightenment and so to displace emotion with reason.

Beyond this new role of interpreter to the public that I believe the profession should assume, there remains its traditional role of learned critic. It would be unfortunate indeed if the lawyers' reaction to the immoderate attacks of those who have no real understanding of or interest in the institutional functioning of our highest tribunal was to silence disciplined, lawyer-like criticism of the Court. It would be unfortunate if sympathetic professional criticism were wholly stilled by the fear that it might be misused by immoderates. It would be equally unfortunate if the Supreme Court, because of understandable impatience with the merits and motives of extremist attacks, were to close its ears to responsible criticism from the bar and the schools. Careful questioning of the Court's work has, I believe, played an important role in the development and growth of our system.

If, for example, in particular cases, careful and understanding examination of Supreme Court opinions reveals needlessly broad and questionable dicta; if particular decisions appear to have been reached without adequate fulfillment of the responsibility for reasoned elaborations of the law, if the Court seems to aggravate the difficult problem of keeping its work load manageable by granting certiorari in cases where "special and important reasons" for review are not readily apparent—careful and sound commentary is surely desirable.

Indeed, I have it on the best of authority that the incisive reviews of the Court's work by the late Thomas Reed Powell are sorely missed by members of the Court. It is hoped that there will emerge someone to resume these critiques.

Biographical Notes

ADOLF A. BERLE, JR.

PROFESSOR OF LAW, COLUMBIA UNIVERSITY SCHOOL OF LAW

Before joining the Columbia faculty in 1927, Professor Berle received the LL.B. degree from Harvard Law School in 1916 and practiced law in New York. From 1933 to 1938, he was Special Counsel to the Reconstruction Finance Corporation. He served as Assistant Secretary of State from 1938 to 1944, and as United States Ambassador to Brazil in 1945-46. His recent publications include *The Twentieth Century Capitalist Revolution* and *Tides of Crisis: A Primer of Foreign Relations.*

DEREK W. BOWETT

LEGAL OFFICER, UNITED NATIONS

Mr. Bowett received the M.A. and LL.B. degrees from the University of Cambridge in 1951 and the Ph.D. degree from the University of Manchester in 1955. Sometime Whewell Scholar in International Law at the University of Cambridge, he is Lecturer in Law at the University of Manchester and Barrister-at-Law of the Middle Temple and of the Northern Circuit. He joined the Legal Office of the United Nations in 1957. He is the author of *Self-Defence in International Law* and of articles in the *British Yearbook of International Law,* the *Modern Law Review,* and the *Transactions of the Grotius Society.*

CHARLES D. BREITEL
JUSTICE OF THE APPELLATE DIVISION OF THE SUPREME COURT
OF THE STATE OF NEW YORK

Justice Breitel was born in 1908 in New York City, was graduated in 1929 with an A.B. degree with high distinction from the University of Michigan, and took his degree from Columbia Law School in 1932. He was assistant in the special rackets investigation headed by Thomas E. Dewey from 1935 to 1937, and chief of the Indictment Bureau of the New York County District Attorney's Office during the period 1938-41. He served as Counsel to the Governor of the State of New York from 1943 to 1950, and was a member of many state commissions. Appointed Justice of the Supreme Court of the State of New York in 1950, he was elected to a full term in 1951 and designated to the Appellate Division in 1952.

CLIFFORD P. CASE
UNITED STATES SENATOR FROM NEW JERSEY

After receiving the LL.B. degree from Columbia in 1928, Senator Case joined the firm of Simpson, Thacher & Bartlett, where he was an associate from 1928 to 1939, and a member of the firm from 1939 to 1953. He was elected to the House of Representatives for five terms from the Sixth District of New Jersey before being elected to the Senate in 1954. He is a Trustee of Rutgers University, a member of the Council on Foreign Relations, and a Past President of The Fund for the Republic.

ELLIOTT E. CHEATHAM
CHARLES EVANS HUGHES PROFESSOR EMERITUS OF LAW
COLUMBIA UNIVERSITY SCHOOL OF LAW

When Professor Cheatham retired from Columbia in 1957, he had completed nearly thirty years on the Law Faculty. After receiving his law degree from Harvard in 1911, he practiced in Atlanta, and taught at Emory University, the University of Illinois, and Cornell University before coming to Columbia. He is Past President of the Association of American Law Schools. In 1955-56, he served as Executive Director of the Special Committee on the Federal Loyalty-Security Program of the Association of the Bar of the City of New York. His publications include *Cases and Materials on Conflicts of Laws,* 4th edition, and *Cases and Materials on the Legal Profession,* 2d edition.

KENNETH CULP DAVIS
PROFESSOR OF LAW, UNIVERSITY OF MINNESOTA LAW SCHOOL

Before joining the Minnesota faculty in 1950, Professor Davis practiced law in Cleveland and taught at West Virginia University, the University of Texas, and Harvard University. He received the LL.B. degree from Harvard Law School in 1934. He was a member of the staff of the Attorney General's Committee on Administrative Procedure, 1939-40. He is the author of *Administrative Law,* for which the Harvard Law Faculty in 1952 awarded him the Henderson Prize for a work of outstanding excellence.

LORD DENNING [ALFRED THOMPSON DENNING, P. C.]
A LORD OF APPEAL IN ORDINARY SINCE 1957

After receiving his education at Magdalen College, Oxford, Lord Denning was called to the bar in 1923, and became Queen's Counsel in 1938. He served as Judge of the High Court of Justice from 1944 to 1948 and as a Lord Justice of Appeal until 1957. He was appointed Privy Councillor in 1948. Lord Denning is President of the National Association of Parish Councils, Chairman of the Society of Comparative Legislation, and President of Birkbeck College in the University of London. He is joint editor of Smith's *Leading Cases* and of Bullen and Leak's *Precedents,* and the author of *Freedom Under the Law* (Hamlyn Lectures) and *The Changing Law.*

WILLIAM O. DOUGLAS
ASSOCIATE JUSTICE OF THE SUPREME COURT OF THE UNITED STATES

Born in Minnesota in 1898, Mr. Justice Douglas received a degree in arts from Whitman College in 1920 and his LL.B. from Columbia Law School in 1925. A member of the faculties of Columbia and Yale Law Schools from 1924 to 1928 and 1928 to 1936, respectively, he was a Commissioner of the Securities and Exchange Commission in 1936 and Chairman from 1937 to 1939. He took his seat on the Supreme Court in 1939. He is the author of *Democracy and Finance, Strange Sands and Friendly People, Beyond the High Himalayas, North from Malaya, An Almanac of Liberty, We the Judges, Russian Journey,* and *The Right of the People.*

NOEL T. DOWLING

HARLAN FISKE STONE PROFESSOR EMERITUS OF CONSTITUTIONAL LAW
COLUMBIA UNIVERSITY SCHOOL OF LAW

Following his graduation from Columbia Law School in 1912, Professor Dowling worked for some time as an assistant in the office of the newly established Legislative Drafting Research Fund, thus beginning an association which continues to this day. During the First World War, he served in the War Risk Insurance Bureau and in the Judge Advocate General's Department. He taught at the University of Minnesota before joining the Columbia faculty in 1922. For his work during and after the Second World War on the official committee and board appointed to consider the organization, procedure, and methods of naval courts, Professor Dowling received in 1948 the Navy's Distinguished Public Service Award. His *Cases on Constitutional Law*, first published in 1937, is now in its fifth edition.

WARNER W. GARDNER

SHEA, GREENMAN & GARDNER, WASHINGTON, D. C.

Born in Indiana in 1909, Mr. Gardner received his A.B. degree from Swarthmore College in 1930, and took an M.A. at Rutgers University in 1931 before entering Columbia Law School, from which he received his LL.B. in 1934. From the year after his graduation he served as Clerk to Associate Justice of the Supreme Court Harlan F. Stone, and then entered on twelve years service in the federal government. Beginning as an attorney in the Solicitor General's Office, he served successively as Solicitor of the Departments of Labor and the Interior, and was appointed Assistant Secretary of the Interior in 1946. He joined his present firm in 1947. From 1943 to 1945, he served as a Major with the Military Intelligence Service, assigned to the Sixth Army Group, for which he received the Legion of Merit and the Croix de Guerre.

WALTER GELLHORN

BETTS PROFESSOR OF LAW, COLUMBIA UNIVERSITY SCHOOL OF LAW

Professor Gellhorn received the LL.B. degree from Columbia in 1931, and has been a member of the Faculty of Law since 1933. He was Secretary to Mr. Justice Stone in 1931-32. Since 1932, he has been with various governmental agencies, including service as Director of the Attorney General's Committee on Administrative Procedure, 1939-41; Regional Attorney, Office of Price Administration, 1942-43; Special Assistant to the Secretary of the Interior, 1943-44. His publications include *Administrative Law: Cases and Comments; Federal Administrative Proceedings; Security, Loyalty, and Science; The States and Subversion; Children and Families in the Courts;* and *Individual Freedom and Governmental Restraints.*

WILLIAM T. GOSSETT

VICE PRESIDENT AND GENERAL COUNSEL, FORD MOTOR COMPANY

Mr. Gossett received his A.B. degree from the University of Utah in 1925 and his LL.B. from Columbia in 1928. Admitted to the bar in 1929 he began his legal practice in New York State. He assisted in the reorganization of Fox West Coast Theaters Corporation in 1932-35, the Wesco Corporation in 1934, and the Fox Film Corporation in 1935. In an antitrust dissolution suit from 1937 to 1941 he assisted in defense of the Aluminum Company of America and later served as General Counsel and Director of the Bendix Aviation Corporation. He practiced law as a member of Hughes, Shurman and Dwight, which became Hughes, Hubbard and Ewing, until he joined the Ford Motor Company in 1947.

RONALD H. GRAVESON

DEAN OF THE FACULTY OF LAWS, KING'S COLLEGE, UNIVERSITY OF LONDON

Professor Graveson, a member of the University of London faculty since 1938, received the LL.B. and LL.M. degrees from the University of Sheffield in 1932 and 1933, the S.J.D. from Harvard in 1936, and the Ph.D. from the University of London in 1941. He is of Gray's Inn, Barrister-at-Law. His wartime service in 1939 to 1945 includes that as Lieutenant Colonel in the Legal Division of the Control Committee for Germany. His publications include *English Legal Systems, Conflict of Laws,* and *Status in the Common Law.* For the current academic year, he is renewing his association with Harvard as Visiting Professor.

HENRY MELVIN HART, JR.

CHARLES STEBBINS FAIRCHILD PROFESSOR OF LAW, HARVARD UNIVERSITY
LAW SCHOOL

Professor Hart received the LL.B. in 1930 and the S.J.D. in 1931 from
Harvard Law School. He was Secretary to Mr. Justice Brandeis in 1931-32,
and has been a member of the Harvard faculty since 1932. He was head
attorney in the Solicitor General's Office, 1937-38; Special Assistant to the
Attorney General, 1940-41; Associate General Counsel for the Office of
Price Administration, 1942-45; General Counsel, Office of Stabilization
Administrator, and Economic Stabilization Director, 1945-46; a member
of the Attorney General's Committee on Administrative Procedure, 1939-41.
He is the author of *The Federal Courts and the Federal System* (with
Herbert Wechsler).

PAUL R. HAYS

NASH PROFESSOR OF LAW, COLUMBIA UNIVERSITY SCHOOL OF LAW

A graduate of Columbia Law School in 1933, Professor Hays has been a
member of the faculty since 1936. He has been a member, also, of the
New York State Board of Mediation and the Board of Legal Examiners
for the United States Civil Service Commission. Since 1937 he has served
as arbitrator and impartial chairman for many industries, and is at present
a member of the New York City Board of Health. He is the author of
Cases and Materials on Civil Procedure, and, with Milton Handler, of
Cases on Labor Law.

PAUL M. HERZOG

EXECUTIVE VICE PRESIDENT, AMERICAN ARBITRATION ASSOCIATION

Mr. Herzog was born in New York City in 1906, and took his arts degree
from Harvard University in 1927 and an LL.B. from Columbia Law School
in 1936. From 1937 until 1944, he served as a member and then as Chairman of the New York Labor Relations Board. He was appointed Chairman
of the National Labor Relations Board in 1945 and served until 1953. He
was Associate Dean of the Harvard University Graduate School of Public
Administration from 1953 to 1957, and has been in his present position

since January, 1958. He is presently a member of the Committee on the Applications of Conventions of the International Labor Office in Geneva.

JAMES NEVINS HYDE
NEW YORK CITY

After preparatory education at Yale and Trinity College, Cambridge, Mr. Hyde received his legal education at Columbia, where he took the LL.B. degree in 1935. He has lectured on international law at New York University Law School, and at the special summer program of the Parker School of Foreign and Comparative Law. From 1948 to 1953, he served as Adviser, Security Council and General Affairs, with the United States Mission to the United Nations.

PHILIP C. JESSUP
HAMILTON FISH PROFESSOR OF INTERNATIONAL LAW AND DIPLOMACY
COLUMBIA UNIVERSITY SCHOOL OF LAW

Born in New York City in 1897, Professor Jessup was graduated from Hamilton College with an A.B. degree in 1919, took his LL.B. from Yale University in 1924, and received the A.M. and Ph.D. degrees from Columbia in 1924 and 1927. Associated with Columbia Law School since 1925, he was appointed Hamilton Fish Professor in 1946. He served as Representative to the United Nations General Assembly from 1948 to 1952 and as Ambassador-at-Large from 1949 to 1953. His publications include *A Modern Law of Nations* and *Transnational Law*. He is a former President of the American Society of International Law, and a member of the Board of Editors of the *American Journal of International Law*.

HARRY WILLMER JONES
CARDOZO PROFESSOR OF JURISPRUDENCE
COLUMBIA UNIVERSITY SCHOOL OF LAW

Professor Jones received the A.B. and LL.B. degrees from Washington University in 1934 and 1937, and the LL.M. degree from Columbia in 1939. He attended Oriel College, Oxford, in 1934-35, as Rhodes Scholar from Missouri. He taught at Washington University and the University of California before coming to Columbia as Professor of Law in 1947. He served in the Office of Price Administration from 1941 to 1943, and as Assistant Counsel, Bureau of Aeronautics, from 1943 to 1946, while serving in the United States Naval Reserve. He has edited the second edition of Dowling, Patterson, and Powell, *Materials for Legal Method,* and is the author of *Economic Security for Americans,* and *Cases and Materials on Contracts* (fourth edition, with Patterson and Goble).

GRAYSON KIRK

PRESIDENT, COLUMBIA UNIVERSITY

Dr. Kirk became the fourteenth President of Columbia University in 1953. He received his B.A. degree from Miami University in Ohio, in 1924, his M.A. from Clark University in 1925 and his Ph.D. from the University of Wisconsin in 1930. He has taught in the fields of political science and government and became a member of the Columbia faculty in 1930. At present, he holds a professorship of international relations, which he has had since 1947.

A. DONALD MacKINNON

MILBANK, TWEED, HOPE & HADLEY, NEW YORK CITY

Born in Bushkill, Pennsylvania, in 1895, Mr. MacKinnon attended Pennsylvania State College and the University of Michigan before receiving the LL.B. degree from Columbia in 1922. He is President of the Columbia Law Alumni Association.

HAROLD R. MEDINA

UNITED STATES CIRCUIT JUDGE, RETIRED

Judge Medina received the A.B. degree from Princeton in 1909 and the LL.B. degree from Columbia in 1912. He was associated with the firm of Davies, Auerbach & Cornell from 1912 to 1918, and was senior member of Medina & Sherpick from 1918 to 1947. He taught at Columbia Law School for twenty-five years. He was appointed Judge of the United States District Court for the Southern District of New York in 1947, and became United States Circuit Judge for the Court of Appeals for the Second Circuit in 1951. He retired in March, 1958. From January to October, 1949, he presided over the trial of eleven Communists charged with conspiracy to teach and advocate overthrow of the United States government by force and violence.

FRANK C. NEWMAN
PROFESSOR OF LAW, THE UNIVERSITY OF CALIFORNIA, BERKELEY

Professor Newman received his degree in arts from Dartmouth in 1938, the LL.B. degree from the University of California in 1941, and the LL.M. and J.S.D. degrees from Columbia Law School in 1947 and 1953. He has been a member of the faculty of the University of California since 1946. He is the author of *Legislation: Cases and Materials* (with Stanley S. Surrey, '32) and his recent articles include, "The Supreme Court, Congressional Investigations and Influence Peddling," "Lobbyists' Letters," and "Money and Elections Law in Great Britain: Guide for America?"

STANLEY F. REED
ASSOCIATE JUSTICE OF THE SUPREME COURT OF THE UNITED STATES, RETIRED

Mr. Justice Reed was born in 1884 in Kentucky, and received A.B. degrees from Kentucky Wesleyan College and Yale University. He studied law at the University of Virginia and Columbia Law School. Admitted to the Kentucky bar in 1910, he was a member of Browning, Reed & Zeigler and General Counsel to the Federal Farm Board from 1929 to 1932. In 1935, he was appointed Solicitor General of the United States, in which capacity he served until his appointment to the Supreme Court in 1938. He retired from the high bench in 1957.

ARTHUR H. SCHWARTZ
SCHWARTZ & FROLICH, NEW YORK CITY

Mr. Schwartz served as Justice of the Supreme Court of the State of New York in 1952. He received the A.B. and LL.B. degrees from Columbia in 1923 and 1926. Between 1926 and 1933 he was Assistant U.S. Attorney and has been a member of the Committee on Character and Fitness, First

Judicial Department, since 1950. Formerly Chairman of the Executive Committee and Vice President of the Association of the Bar of the City of New York, he is currently serving a two-year term as President of the New York County Lawyer's Association, which is celebrating its fiftieth anniversary this year.

EUSTACE SELIGMAN

SULLIVAN & CROMWELL, NEW YORK CITY

Born in New York City in 1889, Mr. Seligman received the A.B. degree from Amherst in 1910 and the LL.B. from Columbia in 1914. He is a member of the Board of Directors of the Legal Aid Society, a Trustee of Amherst College, and President of the Foreign Policy Association.

WHITNEY NORTH SEYMOUR

SIMPSON, THACHER & BARTLETT, NEW YORK CITY

Mr. Seymour was born in Chicago in 1901, received his A.B. from the University of Wisconsin in 1920, and earned his degree in law from the Columbia Law School in 1923. He joined Simpson, Thacher & Bartlett in 1923, and was made a partner in 1929. He was President of the Legal Aid Society from 1945 to 1950 and President of the Association of the Bar of the City of New York from 1950 to 1952. He served as Special Assistant to the Attorney General during the New York water front controversy in 1954, and has been a member of the New York Temporary Commission on Courts and of the Attorney General's Committee on Anti-Trust Laws. He was chairman of the lawyers' committee for the Court of Military Appeals.

CARROL M. SHANKS

PRESIDENT, THE PRUDENTIAL INSURANCE COMPANY OF AMERICA, NEWARK

Mr. Shanks rceeived his B.B.A. degree from the University of Washington in 1921 and his LL.B. degree from Columbia in 1925. Between 1925 and 1927 he was a lecturer at Columbia Law School and taught at Yale 1929-30, before joining The Prudential Insurance Company in 1932.

ROGER J. TRAYNOR
ASSOCIATE JUSTICE, SUPREME COURT OF CALIFORNIA

Born in Utah in 1900, Justice Traynor took his arts, doctoral, and law degrees from the University of California, the last in 1927. He was an instructor in political science at the University of California until 1929 when he joined the law faculty there, remaining until his appointment as Deputy Attorney General of California in 1940. In 1939 he served as Acting Dean of the law school. Justice Traynor served as Consulting Tax Counsel to the California Board of Equalization from 1932 to 1940 and as a consultant to the United States Department of the Treasury in 1937-38. Since his appointment to California's highest tribunal in 1940, he has continued his interest in legal education by serving as a member of the California State Bar Committee on Cooperation Between Law Schools and the State Bar, and in teaching conflict of laws at the University of Chicago during the summer of 1957. He is a member of the American Law Institute Advisory Committee on the Restatement of Torts.

ROBERT B. TROUTMAN
SPALDING, SIBLEY, TROUTMAN, MEADOW & SMITH, ATLANTA

Mr. Troutman was born in Georgia in 1890 and was graduated from the University of Georgia in 1911. He studied for his law degree at Columbia Law School, where he was Editor-in-Chief of the Law Review. Upon his graduation in 1914, he returned to Georgia where he has practiced since, except for service as a Major of Infantry in the First World War. He has served as President of both the Georgia and Atlanta Bar Associations, is a member of the House of Delegates of the American Bar Association, and a Fellow of the American College of Trial Lawyers.

WILLIAM C. WARREN
DEAN OF THE FACULTY OF LAW, COLUMBIA UNIVERSITY

Before joining the Columbia faculty in 1946, Dean Warren received the LL.B. degree from Harvard Law School in 1935, and practiced law in New York and Cleveland. He has been Dean since 1952. From 1947 to 1949, he was Tax Consultant to the Secretary of the Treasury. He was a member of the Shoup Taxation Mission for Japan in 1949, and of the Van Fleet Mission to the Far East in 1954.

HERBERT WECHSLER
HARLAN FISKE STONE PROFESSOR OF CONSTITUTIONAL LAW
COLUMBIA UNIVERSITY SCHOOL OF LAW

Professor Wechsler received the LL.B. degree from Columbia in 1931, and has been a member of the New York Bar and of the Columbia law faculty since 1933. He served as Assistant Attorney General of the United States from 1944 to 1946. At present, he is Chief Reporter for the Model Code of Penal Law, American Law Institute. He is the author of *Criminal Law and Its Administration* (with Jerome Michael) and of *The Federal Courts and the Federal System* (with Henry M. Hart, Jr.).

Program: Legal Institutions Today and Tomorrow

Thursday, November 6, 1958
Association of the Bar of the City of New York, 42 West 44th Street

8:00 p.m.

I OPENING REMARKS
William C. Warren

THE COURTS AND LAWMAKING
Charles D. Breitel '32

Moderator: Harold R. Medina '12

Commentators: Henry Melvin Hart, Jr.; Roger J. Traynor

Friday, November 7, 1958
Horace Mann Auditorium, Broadway at 120th Street

9:30 a.m.

II WELCOME TO THE CONFERENCE
Grayson Kirk

THE LEGISLATIVE PROCESS
Frank C. Newman '53 JSD

Moderator: Arthur H. Schwartz '26

Commentators: Clifford P. Case '28; Paul R. Hays '33

11:00 a.m.

III   THE ADMINISTRATIVE PROCESS
Warner W. Gardner '34

Moderator: Walter Gellhorn '31

Commentators: Kenneth Culp Davis; William T. Gossett '28;
                         Paul M. Herzog '36

12:45 p.m.

Luncheon for those attending Conference
The Rotunda, Low Memorial Library

2:30 p.m.

IV   THE ROLE OF THE BAR
Whitney North Seymour '23

Moderator: A. Donald MacKinnon '22

Commentators: Harry Willmer Jones '39 LLM;
                         Robert B. Troutman '14

5:00 p.m.

Reception for those attending the Conference, and members of
   their families, given by Dean Warren and the Faculty of Law—
   Library of Kent Hall.

Saturday, November 8, 1958
Association of the Bar of the City of New York, 42 West 44th Street

10:00 a.m.

V   THE FUTURE OF INTERNATIONAL LAWMAKING
Philip C. Jessup '24

Moderator: Adolf A. Berle, Jr.

Commentators: James Nevins Hyde '35; Eustace Seligman '14

12:00 noon

Luncheon for those attending Conference, Hotel Roosevelt

2:00 p.m.

VI LEGAL INSTITUTIONS IN ENGLAND
Lord Denning

Moderator: Elliott E. Cheatham

Commentators: Derek W. Bowett; Ronald H. Graveson

(FINAL SESSION)

VII LEGAL INSTITUTIONS IN AMERICA:
OBSERVATIONS AND CONCLUSIONS

William O. Douglas '25

Moderator: Carrol M. Shanks '25

Commentators: Noel T. Dowling '12; Herbert Wechsler '31

Hotel Sheraton-East (Ambassador), Park Avenue at 51st Street

7:30 p.m.

COLUMBIA LAW SCHOOL CENTENNIAL DINNER

Presiding: A. Donald MacKinnon '22

Greetings: William C. Warren

Speakers: Stanley F. Reed '09; Lord Denning

Index

341